Media Connections between Britain and Ireland

This book examines the relationship between Britain and Ireland, specifically the central role played by print and broadcast media in communicating political, cultural, and social differences and similarities between the two islands.

The relationship between Ireland and Great Britain has a long and complex history. Given their geographical proximity and shared language one key dimension of this relationship has been the communication media – print and electronic – that have mediated this relationship. This book addresses this important, but relatively neglected, topic at a critical time in Anglo-Irish relations. Taking the long view, as well as looking in detail at specific episodes, the contributors map British-Irish interactions in print and broadcast media. This volume assesses the proprietorial and journalistic connections between various media institutions, the conditions under which media organisations operated and distribution channels employed. It considers media influences in terms of the role of media organisations in constructing national identity and promoting social change. Furthermore, this book also considers news flows between the two islands, censorship in times of conflict, cross-border influences of television, and the relationship between cinema and television.

The chapters in this book were originally published as a special issue of the journal *Media History*.

Mark O'Brien is Associate Professor of Journalism History at Dublin City University, Ireland. He is the author of *The Fourth Estate: Journalism in Twentieth-Century Ireland* (2017); *The Irish Times: A History* (2008); and *De Valera, Fianna Fáil and the Irish Press: The Truth in the News* (2001).

Media Connections between Britain and Ireland
Shared Histories

Edited by
Mark O'Brien

LONDON AND NEW YORK

First published 2023
by Routledge
4 Park Square, Milton Park, Abingdon, Oxon, OX14 4RN

and by Routledge
605 Third Avenue, New York, NY 10158

Routledge is an imprint of the Taylor & Francis Group, an informa business

© 2023 Taylor & Francis

All rights reserved. No part of this book may be reprinted or reproduced or utilised in any form or by any electronic, mechanical, or other means, now known or hereafter invented, including photocopying and recording, or in any information storage or retrieval system, without permission in writing from the publishers.

Trademark notice: Product or corporate names may be trademarks or registered trademarks, and are used only for identification and explanation without intent to infringe.

British Library Cataloguing-in-Publication Data
A catalogue record for this book is available from the British Library

ISBN13: 978-0-367-51118-0 (hbk)
ISBN13: 978-0-367-51121-0 (pbk)
ISBN13: 978-1-003-05250-0 (ebk)

DOI: 10.4324/9781003052500

Typeset in Myriad Pro
by codeMantra

Publisher's Note
The publisher accepts responsibility for any inconsistencies that may have arisen during the conversion of this book from journal articles to book chapters, namely the inclusion of journal terminology.

Disclaimer
Every effort has been made to contact copyright holders for their permission to reprint material in this book. The publishers would be grateful to hear from any copyright holder who is not here acknowledged and will undertake to rectify any errors or omissions in future editions of this book.

Contents

Citation Information	vii
Notes on Contributors	ix
Introduction *Mark O'Brien*	1
1 Oscar Wilde, Anglo-Irish networks of print and the cultural politics of needlework *Mark W. Turner*	2
2 The convict Kirwan: Viewing the nineteenth-century press through the lens of an Irish murder trial *Abigail Rieley*	16
3 Image wars: the Edwardian picture postcard and the construction of Irish identity in the early 1900s *Ann Wilson*	30
4 *Scissors and Paste*: Arthur Griffiths's use of British and other media to circumvent censorship in Ireland 1914–15 *Colum Kenny*	45
5 Fighting and writing: Journalists and the 1916 Easter Rising *Mark O'Brien*	60
6 Censorship and suppression of the Irish provincial press, 1914–1921 *Christopher Doughan*	74
7 'A bit of news which you may, or may not, care to use': The Beaverbrook-Healy friendship and British newspapers 1922–1931 *Elspeth Payne*	89
8 Tuned out? A study of RTÉ's Radio 1 programmes *Dear Frankie/Women Today* and BBC 4's *Woman's Hour* *Finola Doyle-O'Neill*	105

CONTENTS

9 Television and the decline of cinema-going in Northern Ireland, 1953–1963   118
   Sam Manning

10 Memories of television in Ireland: Separating media history from nation state   136
    Edward Brennan

11 Seamus O'Fawkes and other characters: The British tabloid cartoon
    coverage of the IRA campaign in England   150
    Roseanna Doughty

12 'More difficult from Dublin than from Dieppe': Ireland and Britain in a
    European network of communication   168
    Yann Ciarán Ryan

    Index   187

Citation Information

The chapters in this book were originally published in the journal *Media History*, volume 24, issue 3–4 (2018). When citing this material, please use the original page numbering for each article, as follows:

Introduction
Introduction: Shared Histories
Mark O'Brien
Media History, volume 24, issue 3–4 (2018) pp. 291

Chapter 1
Oscar Wilde, Anglo-Irish networks of print and the cultural politics of needlework
Mark W. Turner
Media History, volume 24, issue 3–4 (2018) pp. 292–305

Chapter 2
The convict Kirwan: viewing the nineteenth-century press through the lens of an Irish murder trial
Abigail Rieley
Media History, volume 24, issue 3–4 (2018) pp. 306–319

Chapter 3
Image wars: the Edwardian picture postcard and the construction of Irish identity in the early 1900s
Ann Wilson
Media History, volume 24, issue 3–4 (2018) pp. 320–334

Chapter 4
Scissors and Paste: Arthur Griffiths's use of British and other media to circumvent censorship in Ireland 1914–15
Colum Kenny
Media History, volume 24, issue 3–4 (2018) pp. 335–349

Chapter 5
Fighting and writing: journalists and the 1916 Easter Rising
Mark O'Brien
Media History, volume 24, issue 3–4 (2018) pp. 350–363

Chapter 6

Censorship and suppression of the Irish provincial press, 1914–1921
Christopher Doughan
Media History, volume 24, issue 3–4 (2018) pp. 364–378

Chapter 7

'A bit of news which you may, or may not, care to use': the Beaverbrook-Healy friendship and British newspapers 1922–1931
Elspeth Payne
Media History, volume 24, issue 3–4 (2018) pp. 379–394

Chapter 8

Tuned out? A study of RTÉ's Radio 1's programmes Dear Frankie/Women Today *and BBC 4's* Woman's Hour
Finola Doyle-O'Neill
Media History, volume 24, issue 3–4 (2018) pp. 395–407

Chapter 9

Television and the decline of cinema-going in Northern Ireland, 1953–1963
Sam Manning
Media History, volume 24, issue 3–4 (2018) pp. 408–425

Chapter 10

Memories of television in Ireland: separating media history from nation state
Edward Brennan
Media History, volume 24, issue 3–4 (2018) pp. 426–439

Chapter 11

Seamus O'Fawkes and other characters: the British tabloid cartoon coverage of the IRA campaign in England
Roseanna Doughty
Media History, volume 24, issue 3–4 (2018) pp. 440–457

Chapter 12

'More difficult from Dublin than from Dieppe': Ireland and Britain in a European network of communication
Yann Ciarán Ryan
Media History, volume 24, issue 3–4 (2018) pp. 458–476

For any permission-related enquiries please visit:
http://www.tandfonline.com/page/help/permissions

Notes on Contributors

Edward Brennan, School of Media, Technological University Dublin, Ireland.

Christopher Doughan, Independent Scholar.

Roseanna Doughty, School of History, Classics and Archaeology, University of Edinburgh, UK.

Finola Doyle-O'Neill, School of History, University College Cork, Ireland.

Colum Kenny, Emeritus Professor of Journalism, Dublin City University, Ireland.

Sam Manning, School of History, Anthropology, Philosophy and Politics, Queen's University Belfast, Northern Ireland, UK.

Mark O'Brien, School of Communications, Dublin City University, Ireland.

Elspeth Payne, Department of History, Trinity College Dublin, Ireland.

Abigail Rieley, School of History, Art History and Philosophy, University of Sussex, Brighton, UK.

Yann Ciarán Ryan, School of English and Drama, Queen Mary University of London, UK.

Mark W. Turner, Department of English, King's College London, UK.

Ann Wilson, Department of Media Communications, Cork Institute of Technology, Cork, Ireland.

INTRODUCTION

Mark O'Brien

The relationship between the two islands of Great Britain and Ireland has a long, complex and compelling history. Given their geographical proximity and shared language one key dimension of this relationship and its complex history has been the connections and interactions between the various media of communication—print and electronic—that have, over the centuries, mediated this connection through times of union, separation, harmony and conflict.

The articles in this double special issue stem from the 'Shared Histories: Media Connections Between Britain and Ireland' conference held in 2016. The conference, hosted by the National Library of Ireland, was organised by the School of Communications Dublin City University, the Centre for Media History Aberystwyth University, the Newspaper & Periodical History Forum of Ireland, and this journal, *Media History*.

At a timely moment in the history of Ireland, England, Scotland and Wales, over two days a multitude of panels discussed the different kinds of media that have informed the relationship between the two islands and considered under what conditions various media operated and to what, if any, effect. Taking the long view as well as looking in detail at particular inflection points, the conference examined how the development of relationships between the peoples of the two islands have been influenced by shared histories of media exchange and interaction.

This double special issue draws together a considerable number of papers from the conference and examines the role that media played in the formation of identity and the impact that, at different times, various forms of media—newsbooks, the telegraph, radio, television, cinema—have had on mediating, reflecting and challenging the relationship between both islands. In a similar vein, it examines how media organisations and media professionals operated at times of conflict and contestation as well as at times of friendship and professional co-operation.

It remains only for the conference organisers, Mark O'Brien, Tom O'Malley and Siân Nicholas, to thank those who participated in the conference and this special edition.

Disclosure statement

No potential conflict of interest was reported by the author.

OSCAR WILDE, ANGLO-IRISH NETWORKS OF PRINT AND THE CULTURAL POLITICS OF NEEDLEWORK

Mark W. Turner

This article focuses on the journalism of Oscar Wilde, and in particular a single review of a history of needlework, to explore the connections between British and Irish print media in the 1880s. By understanding the significance of the review, we can begin to see the overlapping networks of print in Ireland and Britain in the late-19th century. We also learn something about Wilde's approach to writing about Ireland. While he may not have written directly about Ireland across his oeuvre, he does in this review demonstrate his interests in Irish cultural politics which were being discussed in Anglo-Irish print media at the time. It is through connections in print–the way Wilde's review is part of broader, topical discourses about contemporary Ireland–that we come to understand Wilde's subtle intervention in some of the most significant cultural and political questions of his day.

For most of the 1880s, before finding his real literary fame as a playwright in the 1890s, Oscar Wilde was a jobbing journalist in London. He reviewed extensively–books, drama and art–for the London evening newspaper, the *Pall Mall Gazette*, most of which was published anonymously. But he also wrote for a diverse range of other titles, including the *Dublin Literary Magazine*, the *Dramatic Review*, and the *Court and Society Review*. In addition to his regular reviewing, in November 1887 he became editor of a woman's magazine, *Woman's World*, which he hoped to transform from a conventional women's monthly into a more modern hybrid combining elevated and aesthetic discussions of fashion and dress alongside serious opinion. Apart from his journalistic writing, much of his other writing appeared in periodicals–his poems, fiction and essays mostly appeared first in titles such as the *Fortnightly Review*, *Blackwood's Magazine*, *Lippincott's* and the *Irish Monthly*. In short, Wilde was closely enmeshed in the press, whether writing anonymously or under his own signature.

Wilde wrote for the press, but as a keen-witted and strikingly turned out Aesthete who lectured widely in Britain and the USA in the 1880s, he was also a subject much discussed by the press, in the increasingly personality-interested world of late-nineteenth century New Journalism. As the daily paper the *World* reported of his American tour in 1882: 'A young Irishman in knee-breeches exhibits himself to New Englanders for a stipulated number of dollars per evening and his cackle is telegraphed to us at the rate of sixpence a word' (*World*, 8 March 1882, 9). We get a sense of the swiftness of the media networks of which Wilde was a part, as the telegraph brings news of the lecturing Dandy from America to London where it appears in a daily Society paper. Though Wilde was clearly immersed in the press as a subject and a writer, and despite the extent of Wilde's work as a reviewer, this body of writing in his oeuvre tends to be understudied, by Wilde scholars and others. However, it was often through the topical nature of his journalistic writing–speaking to and of the present–that we see Wilde at his most politically engaged.[1]

Wilde left Ireland, never to return on a permanent basis, to attend Oxford in 1874. His relationship to Ireland, at least as we find it expressed by him in print, can sometimes appear ambiguous and distant.[2] Wilde came from a proud, Protestant nationalist family and his mother especially was an important voice for Irish nationalism; she frequently published prose and poetry in the press, and Wilde's brother, Willie, worked for various London publications. However, despite the staunchly nationalist background, Wilde himself infrequently wrote directly about the contemporary Ireland, this a time when Fenianism was on the rise, when Home Rule was high on the political agenda and the general 'Irish Question' was a politically sensitive topic. During his 1882 tour of America, he was more vocal than usual about support for the Irish nationalist cause, and in speeches and interviews, often in front of an Irish-American audience, he openly spoke of this support. But that was in America and infrequent generally.[3] While there is evidence that Wilde took a more direct interest in Ireland elsewhere, his most overt interventions were cultural and appeared in his journalism.[4]

Wilde's first pieces of journalism were published in Irish newspapers and periodicals–a lengthy review of London's Aesthetic Grosvenor Gallery in the *Dublin University Magazine*, an account of the 'Tomb of Keats' in the *Irish Monthly* and a discussion of the Irish antiquarian and artist Henry O'Neill in *Saunders's News-Letter*. Wilde's mother had written for the *Dublin University Magazine* and, likely, family connections helped him secure these early commissions. Later, when a regular reviewer for the *Pall Mall Gazette*, he frequently drew attention to Irish culture and history, and in the reviews and extensive 'literary notes', he wrote for *Woman's World*, he reviewed writers as diverse as his own mother, the emerging poet W.B. Yeats and the gritty realist novelist May Hartley, who wrote about working-class Dublin. His engagement with Ireland in print, then, tended to be in the sphere of culture rather than contemporary politics.

When Wilde became editor of the *Woman's* Magazine, he sought to develop a hybrid periodical which combined some elements of the conventional, popular woman's monthly –fashion news, for example–with serious discussion of women's writing and culture and articles of opinion of the kind found in periodicals such as the *Nineteenth Century*. The 'Literary Notes' section of *Woman's World*–twelve of which Wilde wrote, usually signed 'by the editor'–stand out in his journalism for their length. These extended pieces were usually upwards of 4000 words, far longer than the reviews published elsewhere, and covered up to ten or twelve different volumes in each 'note', combining short reviews of several books along with brief discussions of literary and other cultural matters, especially connected to women. He 'noted' new fiction, biography, poetry and criticism by and about women, commented on contemporary women's events, and generally promoted an elevated discussion of women's cultural issues. These notes, or 'paragraphs' as he called them, were in tune with the wider mission of the magazine, and helped set the tone. On one occasion, Wilde made the striking decision to devote his entire 'Literary Notes' section to a favourable review of a single work, a history of needlework: Alan S. Cole's translation of Ernest Lefébure's *Embroidery and Lace: Their Manufacture and History from Remotest Antiquity to the Present Day*. This review appeared in November 1888, under the title, 'A Fascinating Book,' and my argument here is two-fold: firstly, that by understanding the significance of this review and the ways it connects to the Anglo-Irish press, we can begin to see the overlapping networks of print in Ireland and Britain in the late nineteenth century; secondly we learn something about Wilde's approach to writing about Ireland by understanding how the wider print media context worked. While he may not have written directly about Ireland across his oeuvre, a review such as 'A Fascinating Book' points to Wilde's interests in the cultural politics of Ireland which were being discussed and disseminated in Anglo-Irish print media at the time, and which were clearly part of his thinking since he was a young man. It is through connections in print–the way Wilde's review is part of broader, topical discourses about contemporary Ireland–that we come to understand Wilde's subtle intervention in some of the most significant cultural and political questions of his day.

Wilde and 'A Fascinating Book'

Wilde writes warmly and approvingly of 'Mr. Alan Cole's carefully-edited translation,' calling it 'one of the most fascinating books that has appeared on this delightful subject.' If we know this review today, it is probably because it features so strikingly, often verbatim, in *The Picture of Dorian Gray*. As Joseph Bristow has documented well,[5] Wilde takes extensive material from the 1888 review and integrates it into chapter eleven of the book form of the novel (chapter nine of the magazine publication), in which Dorian, having been riveted by a 'yellow book without a plot,' learns to worship the senses and explore the 'New Hedonism.' Comparing Wilde's review of Cole's translation with his novel, we find many of the exact same phrases and sentences that Wilde borrows or paraphrases from Cole. This review is almost always read by scholars as an example of Wilde's textual recycling, the way the novel includes material from previously published contexts, or sometimes for the way it speaks to Wilde's materialist understanding of Aestheticism, of beautiful things. However, the review speaks to the one of the chief concerns and ongoing discourses of *Woman's World*, the links between women's work and women's artistic production that is seen not only in this particular review, but across a range of the magazine's contents.

Like Lefébure and Cole, Wilde particularly supports the suggestion that needlework, in which 'woman is sovereign,' be championed for its artistic merits and beauty ('A Fascinating Book,' *Woman's World*, November 1888, 108).[6] Needlework was a common topic in women's magazines in the period, usually in the form of gendered discussions often linked to the reproduction of patterns for readers to follow in their own needlework at home. There is some of this in *Woman's World*, but not much. Shunning the reliance on providing cutting patterns which appear in popular women's magazine rivals, Wilde preferred a more elevated discussion of needlework, emphasizing this form of creative activity in relation to art, history and female labour, all of which were important topics in his magazine in other ways. In this way, 'A Fascinating Book' takes its place alongside an ongoing discussion of these topics, presented, for example, through non-fiction articles about women artists and in Wilde's attention to women's work and history in his reviews. Women's needlework had been an important form of labour in Ireland since the devastating famine of the 1840s, and it continued to be significant in more recent times, in the wake of the 1880-3 famine in Donegal.[7] It was continually being discussed across Anglo-Irish print outlets. For Wilde, the subject of needlework provides an opportunity to articulate (or, at least suggest) the confluence of the history of beautiful things and women's work. He writes that 'M. Lefébure's book suggests the question of whether it is not rather by the needle and the bobbin, than by the brush, the graver or the chisel, that the influence of woman should assert itself in the arts.'[8] Wilde, Cole and Lefébure all agree that women's needlework should be taken as seriously as the fine arts of painting and sculpture, that is, as seriously as male art history. If we look more widely at the discourse of needlework at the time, what emerges is a complex and layered set of meanings, which speaks to women's history, contemporary women's philanthropy, women's labour, and Aestheticism.

The translator Alan Summerly Cole (1846–1934) was the son of Henry Cole, an important civil servant and the key figure in founding and organizing the complex of institutions at South Kensington.[9] Alan spent his entire working life at South Kensington, in the Department of Science and Art, and gradually ascended the institution's hierarchy, at one point being considered for the position of director. A textile historian, Cole was a noted specialist in embroidery and lace, and in addition to writing short books and catalogues on the history of needlework, he lectured frequently on the subject in London and beyond. Wilde knew Cole (they met at the painter James McNeill Whistler's home) and he writes about one of his lectures and his efforts to support lacemaking in Ireland, in a literary note in *Woman's World* in 1889.[10] Regular readers of the magazine would have already been familiar with Cole, from his own article 'Tapestry-weaving' (September 1888) and from H.E. Keane's 'Lace-making in Ireland' (March 1888) which outlines the ongoing rejuvenation of lace-making in Ireland and credits Cole for his important work:

> In the Cork Exhibition of 1883 Lady Colthurst and Mrs. Ludlow Beamish had, amongst other women's industries, an exhibition of local lace. All who understood the matter looked and shuddered to see so much clever, dexterous handiwork so wasted. The Committee did more than shudder; they prevailed upon the South Kensington authorities to send over Mr. Alan Cole to lecture, and show good specimens of ancient lace. Through this means, and the very great patience, kindness, and perseverance of Mr. Cole and Mr. Brennan, RHA, head of the Cork School of Art, a peaceful revolution has taken place. ('Lace-making in Ireland', *Woman's World*, 196)

One needn't over-emphasize Keane's use of the word 'revolution,' particularly since, when alluding to the political difficulties of contemporary Ireland earlier in the article, she passes over what she calls this 'delicate subject,' preferring to focus on women's labour and art. Nevertheless there was a 'peaceful revolution' taking place in Ireland–a cultural revolution founded on revivalism, on the rediscovery and promotion of a vision of Ireland's history. Within revivalist aesthetics, Keane warns against the use of staid nationalist symbols in contemporary lacemaking:

> Unfortunately, in this country [Ireland] the traditions regarding design have been more inspired by sentiment than knowledge of art. A distorted harp, a few caricatured

shamrocks, occasionally an Irish deerhound, with a round tower placed beside him, as though it were his kennel–these oddly sorted emblems furnished the stock-in trade of many of designer. (Keane, 'Lace-Making in Ireland', 196)[11]

Interestingly, the argument is against a stereotyped revival of the Irish past, in favour of artful design combined with great skill. It is within the context of this ongoing discussion of aesthetics, cultural politics and national identity that Wilde's review can usefully be read.

Irish Needlework and the Anglo-Irish Press

Throughout the 1880s, Cole made repeated visits to Ireland, delivering a series of lectures encouraging designers and lace-workers to join forces to help revive and energize Irish lacemaking, visiting arts schools and convents in Cork, Dublin, Belfast, Limerick and elsewhere and his movements as a go-between linking Ireland and London were well known. Beginning in 1884, the popular daily and weekly press in England and Ireland, not just women's magazines, reported on Cole's visits. A report from July 1883, published in the *Times*, is typical:

> IRISH LACEMAKING.—In compliance with the wishes expressed by the authorities of the schools of art and the art industrial exhibitions now being held at Cork and at Limerick, the Lords of the Committee of Council on Education recently deputed Mr. Alan Cole, of the Science and Art Department, to deliver lectures upon the art of lacemaking at both these towns. These lectures fully reported by the local press were given in the course of last week, and the early part of the present week, and attracted considerable audiences, and a marked desire has been manifested to improve Irish lace work, by providing lace makers with new patterns, and giving them opportunities of consulting specimens of old lace … ('Irish Lacemaking,' 26 July 1883, 10)

A few months later, in January 1884 when Cole was in Cork, Limerick and Belfast, the *Times*, with a hint of arrogance, again reports his visit, 'delegated by the Education Committee to render such help as might be asked':

> The form of artistic training for which encouragement is now being solicited commands peculiar sympathy. For Irishwomen of the poorer classes the conditions of life are especially hard. They have to eke out a meager livelihood with constant care, and with little of the passionate pleasure of political and social warfare which sweetens the lot of Irish masculine existence. The horizon of a potato patch, with no further prospect than the occasional relaxation of the confessional, is confined and melancholy. Artistic cultivation in its more ordinary aspects is not within their reach … .Yet there is a kind of art she can practice with success, and for the initiated it comprises almost all artistic possibilities. With the needle or its equivalent she is able to invade and occupy the inmost domains of fancy, and to realize images of artistic beauty. ('Irish Lace-Making,' *The Times*, 23 January 1884, 7)

The Belfast News-Letter both advertised and published reports on the lectures:

> By offering this assistance, the Lords of the Committee of the Council on Education hope that it will lead to the development in local schools of art in Ireland of classes of designers,

MEDIA CONNECTIONS BETWEEN BRITAIN AND IRELAND

which will benefit the community in general. This country has already gained distinction in this beautiful manufacture, and any additional light that can be shed upon the subject will be received with satisfaction. ('The Art of Lacemaking,' 12 January 1884, 5)

Ten days later, a detailed three columns worth of reporting on Cole's lecture indicates the significance of these visits for Irish readers. (see *Belfast News-Letter*, 22 January 1884, 7) As these reports suggest, a number of topics are brought together in the reporting of the visits: encouragement of female work; an aestheticizing of the needleworkers' experience through artistic labour; the promotion of Irish industry. Discussions extended beyond the ephemeral press into pamphlet culture, widening the circuit of print discussion further still.[12] Some of the reports cite other Irish papers and some are reprints of the London press (for example, the usually very pro-Ireland *Pall Mall Gazette*); furthermore, lectures were sometimes published as pamphlets, ensuring another form of print circulation, so that there was an ongoing flow and circuit of print moving across and between Ireland and Britain tracing and discussing Cole's endeavours.

Coverage of this kind, tracking Cole's movements back and forth, announcing his arrival, publicizing and reporting on his events, continued throughout the 1880s, in titles including the *Irish Examiner*, the *Nation*, the *Kerry Sentinel*, the *Kerry Evening Post*, and the *Tuam Herald. Freeman's Journal*, Ireland's oldest paper and in the 1880s a supporter of Charles Parnell and the Irish Parliamentary Party, was particularly attentive to Cole's visits and to the larger context of the work to revive lace. In December 1886, *Freeman's Journal* writes of the demise of the lacemaking in Ireland, 'that half a century ago promised to provide a thriving' industry, but:

> has now all but died out, and has only been dragging on a spasmodic existence for the last 15 years in spite of very many well meant and charitable efforts to encourage it. In 1840 there were over 50 lace centres in Ireland, in 1886 the number has dwindled to barely twelve. ([No title], *Freeman's Journal*, 6 December 1886, 5, col 1.)

In 1888, in their Parliamentary News section, the paper followed discussions about whether the project with Cole would continue. Throughout the spring and summer of that year, uncertainty about whether funding would be forthcoming from Westminster to enable further visits prompted questions in Parliament, in particular from the important Home Ruler advocate and Irish nationalist MP Justin McCarthy and subsequent coverage in *Freeman's* (and elsewhere).[13] Going by the amount and tenor of Anglo-Irish press reports, the scheme was clearly a popular one. An article in 1889 on the Department of Science and Art's annual report informs us that the scheme was officially discontinued in 1887, but was renewed due to pressure from a range of people, leading to renewed visits in 1889 to Limerick, Clonnel, Cork and Youghal. (*Freeman's Journal*, 27 June 1889)

By 1888 and the time of Wilde's review of Cole's translation, the project had reached maturity and was well known. What is clear is that Cole's visits to Ireland were part of an ongoing, cooperative effort enabled by the Government in Westminster, managed via a network of arts institutions, convents and schools in London and Irish cities, to initiate new forms of industry in Ireland. It was 'official', in that it was condoned and funded by the Department of Education in Westminster, but it relied on more informal and even casual forms of contact to keep it going. Indeed, it was through close personal relationships that the links were maintained and consolidated, particularly between James Brennan, head master at the Cork School of Art from 1860-89, and Cole. Brenan knew Cole from his frequent trips to London, and according to the curator Vera Ryan, Brenan 'moved easily and urbanely between Ireland and England.' Furthermore, as Ryan notes, it was at the 1883 Cork Exhibition that Cole and Brennan seemed to hatch their plans for cooperation:

> Alan Cole ... was perhaps the most influential of the 10,000 visitors to the 1883 Exhibition in Cork. His auspicious visit was recalled by James Brenan in a lecture delivered to the ACSI [Arts and Crafts Society of Ireland] in 1897. The two men, who had met in London, famously walked through the exhibition, noting the poor design of exhibits and contrasting this with the high standards of execution.[14]

Thereafter, they quickly firmed up plans to engage convents and others with a view to inspecting women's needlework and offering lectures over an extended period. The key to reviving needlework, in their view, was to raise the standard of artistry to that of the already impressive skill and artisanship evident in women's needlework.

Women, Philanthropy and Revivalism

The Government and the art institutions were not alone in seeking to intervene in the domestic political and cultural economy of Ireland. Middle class and aristocratic female philanthropy was crucial to these efforts, creating a particularly potent alliance of official and unofficial reformers with varying interests and reasons for addressing poverty in contemporary Ireland. These philanthropic efforts also were widely discussed and disseminated in the press. For example, a brief article by Cole, 'The Revival of Irish Lace,' published in the *Pall Mall Gazette* in March 1887, acknowledges the role of philanthropy in taking on the Irish cause:

> Besides what the convents are doing—and this with the aid of Government grants, through the Science and Art Department—a committee of ladies and gentlemen has for the last two years offered prizes for lace patterns ....Then, as to getting lace made from these new patterns, this difficulty has been largely met by the gracious patronage of her Majesty the Queen, who has for the last two years selected certain of the prize-winning patterns and given commissions for laces to be made from them. ('The Revival of Irish Lace,' *Pall Mall Gazette*, 11)

Similar reports in the Irish press discuss the role of prominent titled ladies–the *Tuam Herald* notes the efforts of the Countess of Aberdeen, 'an Irishwoman by sympathies,' ('Irish Industries in Belgravia,' 22 August 1891) and *Freeman's Journal* credits Countess Spencer with supporting Cole's lectures (20 February 1884). But these are just two passing examples among the many Anglo-Irish press reports in which women feature regularly.

Philanthropic women–middle and upper class women in Dublin or in London, and women who moved between Dublin and London–were central to the needlework revival as patrons who oversaw various organizations focused on what were called the 'home arts and industries.' Such cottage industries–textiles, needlework, etc. –have tended to be overlooked in conventional cultural histories of the period, in particular those histories which foreground 'arts and crafts' rather than 'home arts and industries.' As Janice Helland writes, in an excellent corrective to this history, it is important to understand the distinctions that have come to define these different movements in the overall revivalist movements of the 1880s-90s:

> The gap that existed between home arts and industries and the Arts and Crafts movement can be located in this space between urban and rural and, most significantly, between professional and amateur; home arts are consistently categorized as amateur. Nineteenth-century debates tended to suggest that professionals had been publicly trained while amateurs had been educated privately and that professionals earned their living from their craft. However, in the instance of cottage workers, the overriding designator was undoubtedly class and gender (peasant and poor, female with no status).[15]

In other words, class and gender have become the faultlines which demarcate how we have tended to understand this significance of 'arts and crafts', on the one hand, and 'home arts and industries' on the other. However, the press reports tend not to make such distinctions, and the point of Cole's whole project is to combine artistry with skill, and to make products for markets.

One of the most prominent of the London-based 'home arts and industries' organizations was the Donegal Industrial Fund (DIF), located in Wigmore Street, with patronage from the upper middle-class Englishwoman Mrs. Earnest (Alice) Hart, who had carried out philanthropic work with London's East End poor, and aristocratic Lady Londonderry. The DIF aimed to encourage women's labour in cottage industries in Ireland, with a view to marketing and selling these Irish goods in the metropolis. According to Helland, Hart

> organized teaching centres and outreach programmes to bring the product in line with what the urban consumer desired, she ascertained how to move the goods from remote areas to the city, and she resolved to secure wholesale buyers in London.[16]

The DIF was not alone, however, and their work coincided and overlapped with the work of other similar philanthropic organizations founded and led by women (notably, the Irish Industries Association and the Highland Home Industries), that similarly focused on the rejuvenation of cottage arts and industries as a means of combating poverty and reinvigorating local economies in impoverished parts of Ireland, Scotland and Wales.

The press reporting of the work of middle-class philanthropists like Hart and, even more so, aristocratic women such as Lady Londonderry, reveal the colonialist framework in which the work was undertaken. In 1887, *The Lady's World* (the predecessor to Wilde's magazine, in fact) remarked that the embroidery recently produced by the DIF:

> was another striking proof of how much might be done in these islands to assist the cottage industries among the Irish peasantry. Mrs. Ernest Hart, who has taken such great interest in the Donegal Industrial Fund, assured us that the wool is the produce of Irish sheep, is carded and spun by the cottagers, and finally dyed and woven by them, to be in turn embroidered by hand chiefly with national Irish designs. ('Society Gossip,' *The Lady's World*, 75)

The authenticity of the works produced was an important part of the marketing of these goods in the metropolis: these were textiles woven or embroidered by *real* Irishwomen, who were using *real* indigenous methods, with *real* Irish materials, in *really poor* surroundings. Among the range of products branded by the DIF were the 'Kells designs'–taken from the medieval Book of Kells (dragons, arrows, beasts) and other manuscripts and ancient monuments which provided 'authentic' national symbols of Ireland, or 'patriotic objects' in the service of national rejuvenation.[17] The fetishization of authenticity and the display of the native and the fruits of her labour reached a highpoint in the Irish Exhibition in London in 1888, during which Hart oversaw the building of a mock-Irish village, complete with facsimile buildings, streets, cottages and with Irish women needleworkers brought over and displayed for visitors, to add further authenticity to the well-intended simulacra.[18] As Helland notes, the exhibition was just one of many similar events in which the arts and industries of colonized peoples were put on display in the imperial centre, in the manner of the Great Exhibition of 1851. Such attempts to 'authenticate the exotic others,'[19] or, perhaps more accurately given the discourse of the Irish, the 'primitive other,' were not uncommon, but they do point to the complexity of philanthropic interventions like those of the DIF. As Diana Maltz suggests in her study of women's philanthropy and British aesthetic movements at the end of the nineteenth century, 'these female philanthropists sought to civilize the poor through art':

> Rather than promoting spectatorship of the fine arts in gallery settings, they introduced the poor to craftsmanship firsthand by teaching lace-making, spinning, and embroidery. As employers promising decent wages and a better livelihood in return for artistic work, many female aesthetes advocated a visionary economics in which poor people could achieve economic stability through aesthetic cottage industries. Yet, at the same time, within the greater context of late Victorian capitalism, such programs were doomed to failure without the long-term auxiliary support and marketing *savoir-faire* of their mother-founders. Programs like the Donegal Industrial Fund and Highland Home Industries were inspired by the popular back-to-the-land ethos, as well as specific Irish and Scottish nationalisms.[20]

However, as Maltz goes on to note, there is clearly some ambiguity about the way female emancipatory philanthropic movements were themselves implicated in complicated colonialist ideologies linked to an essentially conservative paternalism.[21] Wilde was ambivalent about the merits of philanthropy –'charity creates a multitude of sins,' he writes in 'The Soul of Man Under Socialism'–and while his wife Constance was deeply involved in charitable bazaar culture, Wilde was far less convinced by the paternalist forms charity work could often take.

The different kinds of press reports around Cole's visits to Ireland suggest at least two ways that the Irish needlework industry was reported. In many reports, we see a story about 'official', Government-funded attempts to address Irish poverty through forms of cultural production. The emphasis here is on political economy, in contexts of decades of poverty, and on the ongoing political realities around the 'Irish Question' and self-determination. In other reports, the revival of Irish needlework is about the link between female philanthropy, female labour, and art. Frequently, these two discourses intersect, as they likely would have done for readers of Wilde's review of Cole's translation. His readers would have been particularly familiar with people like Cole and Alice Hart, and they would have read articles by and about them in women's magazines including Wilde's, but also in the daily press, on both sides of the Irish Sea.

Conclusion

Wilde's unusually lengthy review of Cole/ Lefébure, a book little noticed by the usual literary outlets,[22] tells us more about his relationship to contemporary Irish politics than at first appears. What he admires in the book is a history of beautiful art–embroidery and lace–an art form in which Ireland has a particular stake, past and present. Cole was known to Wilde's readers, from references in his own magazine, but also more widely for his ongoing Irish visits, themselves part of a much wider set of cultural and political interventions at a number of levels. Firstly, the revival of lacemaking in the early and mid-1880s was part of the burgeoning and broader, nationalist revivalist movement in Ireland, which encouraged a return to the art, images, stories, histories and language from Ireland's pre-colonial past at a time when the future of Ireland–whether as part of Britain or as a sovereign nation–was deeply contested. Secondly, the discourse around needlework was part of cultural and political attempts by politicians and others, in England and Ireland, to encourage cottage industries, as a way of boosting the economic strength of Ireland, in the wake of a century of famine and widespread poverty. Thirdly, the emphasis on encouraging economic vitality was imagined through the educating and empowering of female labour, through Cole's ongoing lectures and visits to convents and art schools. All of this, I suggest, should be brought to bear on how we understand Wilde's positive review of Cole–the lace revivalist–and Lefébure–the needlework historian. These various strands can be seen in networks of print in the Anglo-Irish media, in women's monthly magazines, in the daily and weekly newspapers, in pamphlets and in books. In other words, print culture mediated the cultural and political meanings at work in the discourses of needlework. In his four thousand-word review, Wilde's engagement with the politics of Irish colonization isn't overt, but his understanding of the cultural politics of the day, and the networks of print of which he was a part, is certainly there between his lines.

In part, this is simply the way journalism works. A review is meant to be topical, so in reading 'A Fascinating Book' in the context of related discourses is not an especially challenging intellectual move. That it hasn't been done to date with Wilde may say more about how we view literary and other journalism than it does about the material itself. 'A Fascinating Book' was not his last, and it was by no means his most direct, journalistic intervention into Irish politics. That was still to come, in 1889, when Wilde's review of an Irish historical romance by J.A. Froude made clear his political engagement with contemporary Ireland. The review of this 'dull' novel opens by telling us that:

> Blue-books are generally dull reading, but Blue-books on Ireland have always been interesting. They form the record of one of the great tragedies of modern Europe. In them England has written down her indictment against herself and has given to the world the history of her shame. If in the last century she tried to govern Ireland with an insolence that was intensified by race hatred and religious prejudice, she has sought to rule her in this century with a stupidity that is aggravated by good intentions.

And he concludes the review by saying:

> There are some who will welcome with delight the idea of solving the Irish questions by doing away with the Irish people. There are others who will remember that Ireland has extended her boundaries, and that we have now to reckon with her not merely in the Old World but in the New. (Wilde, 'Mr. Froude's Blue-Book,')

Here, Wilde is unambiguous in his view of recent Irish history and of his understanding of the importance of the Irish diaspora, and why and how the necessity for those extended boundaries came about. Hitherto, Wilde's public discussions of Ireland tended to be folded into other discourses, as we see in 'A Fascinating Book.' Reviewing Froude, he is more direct and politically sharp, but the political landscape in Ireland had changed by 1889, under the ruthless governing of the Tory Chief Secretary of Ireland, Arthur Balfour. Following the introduction of Balfour's suppressive Irish Coercion Act, which led to the imprisonment of hundreds of people and the removal of basic rights like trial by jury, Wilde seems to have taken the opportunity to make his politics known. In a review of Wilfrid Blunt's poems, in January 1889, he admires the sonnets, 'composed in a bleak cell of Galway Gaol' and suggests that they:

> are full of things nobly conceived and nobly uttered, and show that though Mr. Balfour may enforce "plain living" by his prison regulations, he cannot prevent "high thinking," or in any way limit or constrain the freedom of man's soul. (Wilde, 'Poetry and Prison,')

Art wins out in the context of oppression. In these two reviews which come late in Wilde's career as a journalist, he explicitly uses 'culture' (the review of books) as a means through which to address 'politics,' more overt than his strategy in 'A Fascinating Book,' but perhaps not so different in understanding the cultural realm as also a political one. In fact, from the very start of his writing career, his journalism pays great tribute to Irish culture, demonstrating that through an engagement with art, Wilde is able to express and recover something of Ireland's historical dignity and a time of Irish oppression. For Wilde, it is through material culture and art, through a book about the beautiful history of lace, for example, that his nationalistic consciousness shows itself most fully.

Disclosure Statement

No potential conflict of interest was reported by the author.

Notes

1. For a full discussion of Wilde the journalist, see Stokes and Turner, *Complete Works of Oscar Wilde*. See also Turner, 'Journalism'.
2. For important discussions of Wilde and Ireland, see: Clayworth, "Revising a Recalcitrant Patriot"; Coakley, *Oscar Wilde*; Kibberd, *Inventing Ireland*; McCormack, *Wilde the Irishman*; McCormack, "Wilde's Dublin"; Pine, *The Thief of Reason*.
3. For a full discussion of Wilde's public discussion of Ireland during his American tour, see Wright and Kinsella, "Oscar Wilde, A Parnellite Home Ruler and Gladstonian Liberal".
4. On Wilde's journalism and Ireland, see Stokes and Turner, *The Complete Works of Oscar Wilde*, xxvi ff.

5. See Bristow, *The Complete Works of Oscar Wilde,* 406–408.
6. Reprinted in Stokes and Turner, *The Complete Works of Oscar Wilde*, 88.
7. For a discussion of the tensions between women's paid labour and unpaid labour in the needlework industry, especially the convents, see O'Toole, "Exquisite Lace".
8. Stokes and Turner, *The Complete Works of Oscar Wilde*, 88.
9. On the history of the South Kensington museums (later, the Victoria and Albert Museum), see Burton, *Vision & Accident*, esp. chapters 1–5.
10. See Stokes and Turner, *The Complete Works of Oscar Wilde*, 212–13.
11. For an excellent discussion which situates Keane's article in relation to Wilde's Irish interests as editor of *Woman's World*, see: Strachan and Nally, *Advertising, Literature*, 167–69.
12. For example, two lectures by Cole delivered at the Royal Dublin Society, at the invitation of the Metropolitan School of Art in Dublin, were published as pamphlets. See: Cole, *Two Lectures*.
13. See the *Freeman's Journal* for the following dates: 15 May 1888; 27 July 1888; 17 November 1888. Interestingly, *Freeman's Journal* was one of the small number of papers that reviewed Cole's translation of Lefébure, linking the history explicitly to the revival of lace in Ireland; see 9 November 1888.
14. Ryan, *Made in Cork*, 19.
15. Helland, *British and Irish Home Arts and Industries 1880–1914,* 2.
16. Ibid., 5. See also Helland, chapter 2 for an excellent and full discussion of the Donegal Industrial Fund.
17. Helland, 31. On the use of Celtic designs in the Celtic Revival, see Edelstein, *Imagining An Irish Past*. Wilde was keenly aware of Celtic iconography and symbolism, as he demonstrates in a number of his reviews. See, for example, 'Early Christian Art in Ireland,' *Pall Mall Gazette*, 17 December 1887, 3, (reprinted in Stokes and Turner, *The Complete Works of Oscar Wilde*, 38–9) or his review of Yeats in 'Three New Poets,' *Pall Mall Gazette*, 12 July 1889, 3 (reprinted in Stokes and Turner, *The Complete Works of Oscar Wilde*, 234–7).
18. See Helland, *British and Irish Home Arts and Industries 1880–1914,* 50–1.
19. Ibid., 56.
20. Maltz, *British Aestheticism*, 33.
21. Ibid., 215–16.
22. Given the scarcity of reviews of Cole's translation, it's interesting to note that an anonymous review appeared in the pro-Irish *Pall Mall Gazette*, 26 September 1888, likely not by Wilde; see Stokes and Turner, *The Complete Works of Oscar Wilde*, 408.

Bibliography

[Anon]. "Irish Industries in Belgravia." *Tuam Herald*, August 22, 1891.
[Anon.]. "Irish Lacemaking." *The Times*, July Thursday 26, 1883, 10.
[Anon.]. "Irish Lace-Making." *The Times*, January 23, 1884, 7.
[Anon.]. "Lace-Making in Ireland." *Freeman's Journal*, June 27, 1889, 5.
[Anon.]. [No title]. *Freeman's Journal*, December 6, 1886, 5, col. 1.
[Anon.]. "Society Gossip." *The Lady's World*, January, 1887, 75.
[Anon.]. "The Art of Lacemaking." *Belfast News-Letter*, January 12, 1884, 5.
[Anon.]. "The Art of Lacemaking." *Belfast News-Letter*, January 22, 1884, 7.

[Anon]. "Lectures on Lace." *Freeman's Journal*, February 20, 1884.

Bristow, Joseph, ed. *The Complete Works of Oscar Wilde*, Vol. 3. *The Picture of Dorian Gray*: The 1890 and 1891 Texts. Oxford: Oxford University Press, 2005.

Burton, Anthony. *Vision & Accident: The Story of the Victoria and Albert Museum*. London: V&A Publications, 1999.

Clayworth, Anya. "Revising a Recalcitrant Patriot: Oscar Wilde's Irish Reviews Reconsidered." *Forum for Modern Language Studies 2002* 38, no. 3 (2002): 252–60.

Coakley, David. *Oscar Wilde: The Importance of Being Irish*. Dublin: Town House, 1994.

Cole, Alan S. "Tapestry-weaving." *Woman's World*. September, 1888. 485–490.

Cole, Alan S. "The Revival of Lace." *Pall Mall Gazette*, March 10, 1887. 11.

Cole, Alan S. *Two Lectures on the Art of Lace Making*. Dublin: Metropolitan School of Art, 1884.

Edelstein, T.J. *Imagining An Irish Past: The Celtic Revival, 1840–1940*. Chicago: The David and Alfred Smart Museum of Art, The University of Chicago, 1992.

Helland, Janice. *British and Irish Home Arts and Industries 1880–1914: Marketing Craft, Making Fashion*. Dublin and Portland, OR: Irish Academic Press, 2007.

Keane, H.E. "Lace-making in Ireland." *Woman's World*. March, 1888. 195–199.

Kibberd, Declan. *Inventing Ireland*. London: Jonathan Cape, 1995.

Lefébure, Ernest. *Embroidery and Lace: Their Manufacture and History from Remotest Antiquity to the Present Day*. Translated by Alan S. Cole. London: H. Grevel and Co., 1888.

Maltz, Diana. *British Aestheticism and the Urban Working Classes, 1870–1900: Beauty for the People*. Basingstoke: Palgrave, 2006.

McCormack, Jerusha, ed. *Wilde the Irishman*. New Haven and London: Yale University Press, 1998.

McCormack, Jerusha. "Wilde's Dublin; Dublin's Wilde." In *Oscar Wilde in Context*, edited by Kerry Powell, and Peter Raby, 17–27. Cambridge: Cambridge University Press, 2013.

O'Toole, Fintan. "Exquisite Lace and Dirty Linen: The Taming of Girl Power." In *The Arts and Crafts Movement: Making It Irish*, edited by Kreilkamp Vera, 179–93. Boston: McMullen Museum of Art, Boston College, 2016.

Pine, Richard. *The Thief of Reason: Oscar Wilde and Modern Ireland*. Dublin: Gill and Macmillan, 1995.

Ryan, Vera. *Made in Cork: the Arts and Crafts movement from the 1880s to the 1920s*. Cork: The Crawford Art Gallery, 2017.

Stokes, John, and Mark W. Turner, eds. *The Complete Works of Oscar Wilde*, vols. 6 and 7, *Journalism: Parts I and II*. (Oxford: Oxford University Press, 2013).

Strachan, John, and Claire Nally. *Advertising, Literature and Print Culture in Ireland, 1891–1922*. Basingstoke: Palgrave, 2012.

Turner, Mark W. "Journalism." In *Oscar Wilde in Context*, edited by Kerry Powell, and Peter Raby, 270–77. Cambridge: Cambridge University Press, 2013.

Wilde, Oscar. "Mr. Froude's Blue-Book." *Pall Mall Gazette*, April 13, 1889, 3. Reprinted in John Stokes and Mark W. Turner, eds. *The Complete Works of Oscar Wilde*, vols 7, *Journalism II*. (Oxford: Oxford University Press, 2013). 203–206.

Wilde, Oscar. "Poetry and Prison." *Pall Mall Gazette*, January 3, 1889, 3. Reprinted in John Stokes and Mark W. Turner, eds. *The Complete Works of Oscar Wilde*, vols 7, *Journalism II*. (Oxford: Oxford University Press, 2013). 149–152.

Wright, Thomas, and Paul Kinsella. "Oscar Wilde, A Parnellite Home Ruler and Gladstonian Liberal: Wilde's Career at the Eighty Club (1887–1895)." *May I Say Nothing?* (The Oscholars, August, 2015). accessed July 31, 2018. https://oscholars-oscholars.com/may-i-say/.

THE CONVICT KIRWAN
Viewing the nineteenth-century press through the lens of an Irish murder trial

Abigail Rieley

The murder of Maria Kirwan by her husband William Kirwan is one of the most significant Irish homicide trials of the nineteenth century. An important case in both British and Irish legal history, it helped to bring about a criminal court of appeal. An extraordinary amount of original trial and legal documents have also survived giving a unique insight into the background of the case. As such, an analysis of the media coverage is particularly revealing. With this context, it is possible to look at the factors driving the news as well as the underlying ideologies of the newspapers that covered the trial and its aftermath. Using 1052 pages of coverage gathered from a keyword search of the British Newspaper Archive, this article looks at three main areas of reporting—the autonomy of the Irish press, the state of the Irish justice system and attitudes towards domestic violence.

Introduction

In the winter of 1852/1853, the Kirwan murder was on everybody's lips. The case had such notoriety that editors from John O'Groats to the Shires knew that their readers wanted the latest on 'the convict Kirwan'. This was a story that reached to the heart of the establishment as the Courvoisier case[1] had 12 years before, although the two cases were very different. While Courvoisier's execution had stirred the debate over public executions the Kirwan case had the potential to usher in both fundamental change and a full court of criminal appeal. This was one of the most notorious murder trials of the decade and Kirwan became one of that select group of criminals known by surname alone. On 31 December 1852, a letter writer on the Kirwan case to the *Morning Post* used Courvoisier as a cautionary example of why accused men's protestations of innocence should not be taken at face value.[2] Eleven years later it was Kirwan who was name checked, along with more recent poisoners Smethurst and Palmer by the *London Evening Standard* in an editorial on the unpredictability of the death penalty.[3]

But the appeal of the Kirwan case was not simply sensation—this was a genuine piece of legal history in the making. On foot of the case, Kirwan's barrister, Irish Nationalist MP Isaac Butt, brought forward the *New Trials (Criminal Cases)* Bill in 1853, which reached its second reading in Westminster in June of that year. The right already existed to appeal in a civil case but Butt argued. 'But let him be tried for his life before the very same judge and the very same jury, and he has no redress whatever against the error of the judge in point of law or the mistake of the jury in fact.'[4] While Butt's bill was defeated it is still recognised today, in both British and Irish law, as an important point in the journey towards a full court of criminal appeal.

The Kirwan case, so controversial in its time, provides us with a unique lens through which to view the era. A major news story, widely covered and in depth, by newspapers across the political spectrum, big and small, daily or weekly, becomes much more than the sum of its parts. Crime news of its nature can reveal the underlying assumptions and prejudices of a society. As media scholar, Chris Chibnall explained in the introduction of his seminal work *Law-and-Order News* (1977)

> There is perhaps, no other domain of news interest in which latent press ideology becomes more explicit than in what we may term 'law-and-order news'. Nowhere else is it made quite so clear what it is that newspapers value as healthy and praiseworthy or deplore as evil and degenerate in society.[5]

As his notoriety grew Kirwan became a cypher for many of the issues being debated by the press. In his name, writers of editorials or letters had a shorthand that could provide a reader familiar with the case context for any number of issues regardless of whether they were reflected in the facts of the case. Kirwan could be used to argue not just the use of circumstantial evidence, death penalties and coroner's courts but also victim blaming, sectarianism or Anglo Irish politics—the last two topics having very little to do with the case itself but more with the subsequent coverage. Kirwan became a shorthand for many of the problems of his day and, as his story unfolded, an eager press pored over every development.

At its heart, the Kirwan case is a standard example of spousal murder equally recognisable by audiences in England, Wales, Scotland or Ireland. In the (miraculously surviving) prosecution brief prepared for chief counsel John George Smyly, a familiar story is told.[6] William and Maria Kirwan had been married for 12 years. When they married, William already had a secret second family[7] with a woman called Theresa Kenny. In the summer of 1852, Maria and William were staying in the picturesque fishing village of Howth in County Dublin, while their house in the city was being painted. Their landlady in Howth Margaret Campbell described raised voices and sounds of a scuffle coming from their room.[8] Margaret Doyle, who kept a small shop in the village, said Maria Kirwan once told her she had heard rumours her husband was having an affair and would leave him if she found evidence.[9] Howth woman Catherine Kelly said Maria had severe bruises she had attributed to a beating from her husband.[10] Kelly said Maria had been delighted to hear that her husband's second family were planning to move to Australia.

Washerwoman Margaret Gillas had done laundry for the couple. Her statement describes an incident 2 weeks before the murder when Maria Kirwan arrived at her house before dawn. Her hair was loose and she was not wearing her stays. She told the witness that her husband was after her and that the marriage had always been violent. Gillas later washed the sheet Maria Kirwan's body had been wrapped in and pointedly noted in her evidence 'a considerable quantity of black blood under where her seat was. It was congealed and like what would be after a woman's confinement'.[11] These details were not public as none of these women, with the exception of Margaret Campbell, were called to give evidence at the trial[12] but it is possible, even probable, that Dublin journalists, would have become aware of these claims in the course of their coverage of the story.

On 6 September 1852, Maria Kirwan and her husband went out to Ireland's Eye, a small island not far from the harbour. Artist William painted while his wife read and swam. When the boat came to collect them that evening, William was alone. The two boatmen helped him to search and, just as darkness fell, they made the grim discovery. Maria Kirwan was half lying in the water at a spot called the Long Hole. She was dead.

Nineteenth-century Ireland had a reputation as a violent country but statistics paint a more complex picture. In his valuable comparative study of homicide rates in mid- and early nineteenth-century Ireland, Richard McMahon argues that rates of adult homicides were broadly comparable with those in England and Wales. While the Irish rate was higher than England, 1.97 per 100,000 compared to 1.28 per 100,000,[13] spousal murders were rare. Between 1847 and 1849 there were 14 in Ireland, a rate of just 0.16 per 100,000. In her study of violence in post-Famine Ireland, historian Carolyn A. Conley notes that both press and judges in Ireland claimed wife killing was a rare occurrence.[14] But the Kirwan case would have stood out as a news story whatever the rate had been. The middle-class backgrounds of both victim and accused, the existence of a second family and an ambiguous prosecution was a combination that would not have occurred very often in a journalist's career. That alone would have guaranteed a high degree of press interest.

The popularity and importance of crime news in British newspapers have been well covered by the previous scholarship. By comparing the cases listed for trial in the Old Bailey in the eighteenth century with those that appeared in the newspapers, Peter King has given a valuable insight into what made trials 'newsworthy'[15] while Rosalind Crone has examined the popularity of crime news in both broadsheets and the popular Sunday press in the early nineteenth century.[16] However, there have been no similar studies examining Irish audiences or publication. While court news was a significant feature in the majority of daily Dublin papers an Irish audience would not necessarily have viewed it the same as an English audience. Conley has shown Irish attitudes to crime tended to be more sympathetic towards the perpetrator than in England, Scotland or Wales.[17] The coverage of the Kirwan case demonstrates those differences and the 'latent ideology' beneath them. Using the British Library's British Newspaper Archive (www. britishnewspaperarchive.co.uk) I searched for the keywords 'Kirwan' and 'murder' between September 1852 and January 1853. What follows is an analysis of over 1050 articles across 272 publications across Ireland, England and Scotland. This broad approach has ensured that, while some individual articles might have been missed, thanks to the common practise of 'scissors-and-paste' journalism, any major story will be within the sample even if the original is missing.

The Autonomy of the Irish Press

For a seasoned reporter, it would have been clear from the inquest this was to be a complex case. Convened at the guesthouse where the Kirwan's had stayed, the inquest took place the day after the body had been found and after it had been washed. Kirwan actively interviewed witnesses and, at the request of the jury, took the stand himself.

While inquests varied from case to case, under the Coroners Act (Ireland) 1846, one had to be organised close to where the body was discovered once a sudden death had occurred[18] with a local coroner and jury. As W.E. Vaughan notes in *Murder Trials in Ireland 1836–1914* 'The coroner's court was relatively informal, allowing the jurors and bystanders to intervene in a way that would have been unthinkable at the assizes.'[19]

At Kirwan's trial the coroner, Henry Davis, was asked if he had asked the accused man to question witnesses. He replied, 'I did; my reason for so doing was because there was more or less suspicion attached to him at the time.'[20] The first story appeared in the *Freeman's Journal*[21] on 8 September. Reports also appeared in *The Advocate, or Irish Industrial Journal*[22] and the *Dublin Evening Mail*. The following morning, the *London Evening Standard*[23] reprinted Freeman's report and the story was picked up by several more Dublin papers, notably the *Dublin Evening Post* and the *Dublin Evening Packet and Correspondent*. Between 8 September and 21 September, the inquest was covered by 24 different papers across Ireland, England and Scotland, including the main London dailies—a decent spread for a picturesque tragedy.

There is a key figure behind the scenes before the case comes to trial who may have stirred up the press interest. Several of the statements in the brief mention a Mrs Byrne or 'lady in black'[24]. It appears that Major Henry John Brownrigg, the deputy inspector general of the constabulary, was concerned that she was interfering with the investigation. It is possible that she also contacted the Dublin newspapers based on stories that subsequently appeared. It is likely Maria Byrne's allegations were behind an unusual move by the deputy inspector general. The *Evening Packet* explained:

> Reporters attended but were informed by Major Brownrigg that it was deemed necessary that the inquiry should be private, as well as for the furtherance of the ends of justice, as to avoid publication of ex parte statements prejudicial to the accused gentleman.[25]

Despite being barred the Dublin press had attended the hearing and possibly met Maria Byrne on her way in or out. They would have had an inkling of how sensational the case could be. The evidence that she gave that day, recorded in the brief, would certainly have whetted their appetites. She said she knew the dead woman for many years, having been a neighbour. Her husband had been a fellow artist. She had accused Kirwan of attempting to poison his wife with tincture of henbane, on a prior occasion. And possibly also killing her husband.[26]

There was also a principal to fight. Gaining press access to official events had been an ongoing struggle for more than a decade.[27] When the press was barred from the second hearing, the *Freeman's Journal* did not mince their words in an editorial on 16 October.

> There may be many cogent reasons shown for carrying on an investigation privately through even several adjournments, but we can admit none for the conclusion of a secret examination, and the committal of a prisoner for trial without publication of the grounds on which he had been committed.—Were such a course tolerated by the public or slurred over by the press, it would lead us back to the dark days of the Star Chamber, the black dungeon, and the torturer.[28]

Several London papers picked up on the story. On Monday, 11 October, the *Morning Post*, *Morning Advertiser* and *London Daily News* all ran with the fact that the Dublin press had been excluded from the first committal hearing. The *Daily News* made the distinction that 'a government inquiry and not a magisterial investigation as it was expected' had begun.

The *Freeman's* editorial was widely reprinted, with *The Examiner*[29] and the *Morning Post*[30] among those concerned at the exclusion of the press. At the same time, a rather more salacious angle was being circulated. Credited to the *Morning Herald*, the story referred to an Arklow fisherman who had heard screams coming from Ireland's Eye and the news that Kirwan had married another woman days after burying his wife. The story was widely reprinted reaching the northern tip of Scotland in the *John O'Groats Journal*[31] and Cornwall in the south in the *Cornish Telegraph*.[32] It is likely the story had been leaked by Maria Byrne as these details are based on the evidence of a Howth fisherman, Thomas Larkin. Larkin was asked directly if he knew a Mrs Byrne.[33] It is clear from the brief that this was not asked of every witness so it is reasonable to assume Brownrigg had his suspicions. Even before the trial had started there was huge public interest. By the end of October, with the case still, to come to trial, the Kirwan case had appeared in 136 stories across Ireland and England.

Irish Justice on Trial

The trial began on 8 December, at the Commission for Oyer and Terminer, the assize court used to prosecute crimes of a serious nature. All the Dublin press were in attendance but The *Dublin Evening Mail* set the scene. The court was 'densely thronged in every part' and Kirwan, when he appeared, was 'about 45 years of age; was dressed with scrupulous neatness, and composed himself during the day with the utmost firmness and self-possession'.[34] In England, the *London Daily News*, *Morning Chronicle* and *Morning Post* had all flagged the start of the trial.[35] The *Evening Standard* flagged the case as the second story in their Ireland column under the headline Charge of Murder Against Mr Kirwan.[36]

The trial ran for 3 days and the prosecution did not build as strong a case as they could have. The only evidence of domestic abuse came from Margaret Campbell, the landlady, who said she had heard Kirwan 'miscall' his wife. 'I heard him call her a strumpet; I heard him say, "I'll finish you".'[37] Under cross-examination, she admitted inconsistencies with earlier statements. On the second day, Theresa Kenny, the other woman, did not appear when called to the stand.[38] Under cross-examination from Isaac Butt, the Crown's pathologist Dr George Hatchell was unable to determine the cause of death[39] and could not rule out simple drowning.

The prosecution case was that Maria Kirwan had died from suffocation, by being 'burked'.[40] The defence argued that she had gone swimming too soon after eating and suffered an epileptic fit.[41] After two days of evidence, the jury retired at 7 pm on 10 December. They had been gone for 40 minutes when Judge Philip Crampton called them back to ask if they had a verdict.[42] When they still did not have a verdict at 11 pm, the judge told them they could remain in the jury room for the night, with no refreshments as these were not allowed by law. He told them 'I hope you have your great coats.'[43] They arrived at a verdict within 10 minutes and found Kirwan guilty. After the judge sentenced him to hang Kirwan addressed the court:

> I consider myself to be a doomed person, from the trial that has taken place, and the sentence about to be passed; and I state these matters as well out of regard for my own

memory as for the sake of those friends who have been with me, who know my character from childhood, who know my innocence, and who feel it yet as I do.[44]

For the Dublin press, this was a satisfactory conclusion. The *Freeman's Journal* and *Dublin Evening Mail* had dominated the coverage, both papers who habitually carried heavy court coverage. Rather more unusual in their comprehensive coverage were the *Evening Packet and Correspondent* who were usually more concerned with the bankruptcy hearings as was the conservative *Saunders Newsletter*.

We have no way of knowing precisely why editorial decisions were made but it is worth noting that there was pressure for space that week. A critical budget meant that the future of Lord Derby's minority Conservative government was hanging in the balance. As the *Galway Mercury and Connaught Weekly Advertiser* noted on the 11th 'If there be any of the Liberal Irish members absent from London they should forthwith return to their Parliamentary duties, for an opportunity is near at hand of striking a fatal blow at the existence of the present Government.'[45] So for many papers space was tight. The *Brechin Advertiser* devoted a total of 4 columns to parliamentary proceedings, including the Irish Tenants Bill and the financial statement as well as a leader column on the proposed introduction of a House Tax. Their coverage of Kirwan was reduced to five lines although their London correspondent noted 'The papers today contain a long account of the trial at Dublin of Mr Kirwan for the murder of his wife. The unhappy man has been sentenced to death. It is painfully evident, however, that the jury was starved into a unanimous verdict.'[46]

The London Evening Standard, which had shown a keen interest in the trial from the beginning, had cut the final days content although they used Kirwan's speech from the dock in full.[47] They also ran an editorial arguing the faults of the case. 'A careful perusal of the report of the trial, however, has we own left upon our minds a doubt we cannot refrain from making known to the extent of our opportunity.' They did not, they said, come to this conclusion from any prejudices.

> Let us not be supposed partizans. For Mr Justice Crampton we have the most sincere respect, and even admiration. We believe there to be no better judge ever adorned the bench of either country, and of the religion and politics of Mr Kirwan we know absolutely nothing—he may be, and from his name probably is, a Roman Catholic, and therefore a disaffected person; or he may be a Protestant and a loyal man, but we know nothing of him beyond what the reported trial tells.[48]

The controversy began to build as letters in Kirwan's defence began to appear in the press. Kirwan was sentenced to hang on 18 January but on 24 December Judge Crampton, wrote to the undersecretary, recommending the sentence be commuted for transportation for life.

> My recommendation to commute the sentence to transportation for life was not founded on my own doubts as to the propriety of the verdict or of the prisoner's guilt but on my doubts as to what the verdict would have been had the matters put forward since the trial been in the [first] instance laid before the jury and credited by them.[49]

Of course, Judge Crampton's words were not public, but the newspapers passed their own judgement. The *Dublin Evening Packet and Correspondent* wrote;

> If innocent of the crime it is contended that monstrous injustice is still inflicted upon Mr Kirwan in subjecting him to any punishment whatever; and if guilty, it is affirmed that the extreme sentence of the law should be carried out.[50]

The *Liverpool Mail* declared Kirwan's reprieve 'The Power of Public Opinion and the Press'[51] while the *Leicester Mercury* warned of the dangers of convicting on unsafe circumstantial evidence and called for appeals in criminal cases.[52] The criticism of the circumstantial evidence grew so loud that the foreman of the trial jury, John Dennis, took the highly unusual move to write into the papers to justify the jury's decision.

> We felt that this defence was due to ourselves as honest, and we believe not mistaken men; that it was due to public opinion, so industriously abused, to the ends of the truth and to the sacred character of trial by jury in this country.[53]

Dennis was not the only member of the trial personnel who felt the need to justify proceedings in the face of public pressure. William Kemmis, the recently retired Crown Solicitor[54] also wrote in insisting that everything had been properly conducted.

> As Crown solicitor, and therefore responsible to the public, I challenge the most searching scrutiny into the entire course of proceeding in this case, in which I am not yet conscious of any neglect or violation of public duty.[55]

The Undersecretary himself, John Wynne, also wrote to papers to say the Lord Lieutenant of Ireland, Lord Eglington had not bowed to public pressure or any other kind of pressure and had purely gone on the advice of the trial judges when commuting Kirwan's sentence.[56] The same day Wynne's letter appeared so too did a letter from the coroner who had overseen the inquest. Davis had taken personally some of the criticism of Irish coroners' courts that had appeared the Irish and British press since the verdict.[57]

Opinion was sharply divided. The *Dublin Weekly Nation* on 15 January saw special treatment being offered to a man of Kirwan's privileged position. When moved to Spike Island Convict Depot in preparation for his transportation, they claimed that, rather than wearing the usual prison clothes, Kirwan was dressed in a 'fashionable black suit' and overcoat. 'Kirwan's antecedents, and the particularly un-Irish characteristic characteristics of his crime continue to secure him a considerable amount of sympathy from the English press.'[58] The story was picked up by other papers and two days later a letter from Richard Grace, the governor of Spike Island, confirmed Kirwan was an ordinary prisoner and received no special treatment.[59] Letters soon appeared from the prisons inspector and the governor of Kilmainham to set the record straight concerning Kirwan's travelling attire.[60] The idea of one law for the rich and another for the poor had caught on with the Irish press, especially the more liberal, Catholic publications.

Violence Against Women

But for all the political fallout and press posturing, this was a simple case of spousal murder. Even though the strongest evidence of domestic abuse had not been heard in the trial, that Kirwan had treated his wife badly was recognised by most. Summarising the evidence after the trial the *Times* remarked 'the case of Mrs Kirwan will retain a painful notoriety even in the dismal annals of Irish crime'.[61] Sympathy was often in short supply from those who wrote letters about the case. Many took an almost lascivious delight in the idea of a woman in mortal peril, like JEHU whose letter appeared in both the *Standard* and the *Morning Advertiser* on 22 December. Taking delight in the intellectual challenge of a who-dunit he suggested:

> might it not have been that some person in the dusk of the evening, either passing accidentally, or coming purposely, in a boat near the spot, and seeing a comely woman undressed, and quite alone and unprotected, assaulted her, and having committed violence to her person, aggravated the foul atrocity to murder.[62]

Many papers were unhappy with the tone of the coverage and some of the letters that were appearing from readers. The *Cambridge Chronicle and Journal* noted on 15 January:

> there is a strange and morbid sympathy with murderers just now: let a man be convicted of having taken the life of a fellow-being, especially if the victim be a woman, and straightaway a host of sympathisers start up and move heaven and earth to avert the penalty he has earned.[63]

But it was another letter examining the Kirwan evidence that really crossed the line with its imagery. Evoking the 1781 painting by Henry Fuseli, the writer who signed themselves TG speculated;

> Yes he killed her; but how? The doctors say in somehow that's not very clear, as by pressure, as Hercules killed Antaeus—not a very likely story; rather impossible to be done now-a-days by living men, or, if done, most unquestionably the pressure might squeeze out one scream but would certainly prevent two. Or perhaps Mr Kirwan sat on Mrs Kirwan like a night-mare, and killed her so— ...

Radical weekend paper *The Examiner* commented:

> There is the hideous zest of a Thug in these imaginings; and in most of the letters on the convicts behalf, it is remarkable that no touch of pity ever appears for the victim, who is sometimes treated almost despitefully, as if it were her fault that her precious husband's life were brought into jeopardy.[64]

The *Examiner*'s comment was widely reprinted and quoted by the Irish press with coverage across political and sectarian lines. The *Dublin Evening Mail*, *Saunders Newsletter* and *The Ulsterman*, all conservative in nature, also gave the story prominence. The story appeared in more than 20 publications overall. Many papers added their own comment, like the *Waterford Chronicle* who wrote 'and we may add, that in Ireland, generally speaking, no second opinion exists as to the strict justice of that result'.[65] There may also have been more sympathy for the victim but the newspaper coverage is too focused on a good story to show that.

Conclusion

The case of William Burke Kirwan is almost unique in that there is not only detailed newspaper coverage and comment but also a full transcript of the trial itself and the original prosecution brief containing all witness statements. This full chronology of investigation, trial and coverage would be rare across the British Isles but is even more so for an Irish case. Few briefs prepared for the Crown in Irish cases have survived and most that do are not as detailed or comprehensive as the Kirwan brief.[66] The sheer volume of material written about the Kirwan case, triggered by its controversial nature and a volatile time, makes it a unique lens through which to view its context. A high profile and emotive case like this will throw up not only the usual prejudices and biases but also matters peculiar to itself.

In the Kirwan case, for example, the quickness of the authorities to write into the papers was unusual but this was a volatile time. In January 1853, the first trials were being listed for the soldiers involved in the Sixmilebridge election affray, an incident in July 1852 where six people were killed after soldiers opened fire on a group of voters and protestors at a local election. The coroners' inquest returned a verdict of murder but this had been overturned by the Attorney General.[67] The *Anglo-Celt*, a nationalist Cavan publication, had written an article in August 1852 calling the killings 'wilful and deliberate murder' and at the time of the Kirwan case, the trial of the editor for libel was hotly anticipated.[68] Against this setting, it is easier to understand why the Crown would have felt it so important to stress that Irish courts were run properly or that prisoners with any privilege would not receive any special treatment. Against this backdrop, it is also perhaps easier to see why Major Brownrigg would have been quite so nervous about gossip and leaks in his investigation. The quickness to act, the nervousness of reaction would not necessarily show when dealing with the Sixmilebridge affair itself, but an administration acutely aware of how it is viewed and judged might be quicker to act to stop a second fire breaking out.

The Kirwan case also demonstrates the nascent solidarity among the Irish press. Despite differences in political outlook of the papers they worked for Dublin journalists were a close knit group. Charles Gavan Duffy, one of the founders of the *Nation* and future Young Irelander, wrote of the journalists he knew starting out in the 1830s:

> The editors of the three peculiarly Catholic papers at that time were all Protestants, and the co-editors of a pre-eminently Protestant organ had been born and bred Catholics. To the reporters, for the most part, public life was a stage play, where a man gesticulated and perorated according as his role was cast by his stage manager.[69]

But for all his complaints of cynicism, Duffy knew that solidarity well. He had been part of a mass walkout of journalists in protest to Daniel O'Connell's strong criticism of the press during an after dinner speech in 1839.[70] The first representative association for journalists had been established the year before, although it did not last.[71] This sense of solidarity seems to have been intrinsic to the Irish press throughout the nineteenth century. In his memoir, *Irish Times* journalist Andrew Dunlop describes multiple instances of newspapers withholding coverage of speeches or events when they were not given access or felt they had been insulted as a professional body.[72]

The response of the Dublin press to being excluded from the government inquiry of the Kirwan case fits very well with this sense of solidarity. The editorial comment from the *Freeman* in reaction to this was part of an ongoing conversation with the Crown that was part of Irish journalism's affirmation of its professional identity.

As is so often the case with spousal murder Maria Kirwan, as the victim, is almost invisible. The letters tend to see her as part of an enjoyable problem to solve, while the newspapers themselves are more interested in the more flamboyant character of a murderer than the sad story of his victim. There are some instances of headlines referencing Mrs Kirwan's case rather than referring to her killer. The *Times* synopsis of the case, for example, does this when putting a heavy emphasis on the domestic violence. But the *Times* coverage is unusual. While this was not a factor of this research, it has been noticeable that the coverage of the case has divided roughly along liberal and conservative lines. On the liberal side, they are more likely to worry about the tone of the press coverage or that the fate of the victim is being ignored. They are also more likely to side with the Irish press when more sectarian motives are discussed. Conservative and unionist titles were more likely to campaign for Kirwan's release. This was particularly true in Ireland with staunchly unionist titles like the *Waterford Mail* and the *Dublin Morning Herald* bucking the trend and supporting Kirwan. This is simply an observational note but a fuller statistical examination of the data would be an interesting area of further study.

Because of the Kirwan case's almost unique attributes, the amount of surviving material, the political fallout and the huge public interest, it becomes a particularly revealing way of looking at the press who cover it. This is not Chibnall's standard 'law-and-order' news, it is a special category of murder, the type that Orwell was referencing in his tongue and cheek description of the perfect English murder.[73] Perhaps it is because this such a 'non-Irish' crime as the *Nation* called it, that the British press covered it as they did. The Kirwan case is not only a very specific mirror to hold up but also a uniquely revealing one. Such rarities act as a dark mirror on a developing medium.

Disclosure statement

No potential conflict of interest was reported by the author.

Notes

1. Swiss born François Benjamin Courvoisier (August 1816–6 July 1840) was a valet convicted of murdering his employer Lord William Russell. Around 40,000 people attended his execution including both Dickens and Thackeray. FRANCOIS BENJAMIN COURVOISIER, Killing > murder, 15 June 1840.
2. 'Declarations of Innocence by Convicts'.
3. *London Evening Standard*, 31 December 1863.
4. Hansard, *Hansard's Parliamentary Debates*, 127:963.
5. Chibnall, *Law-and-Order News*, x–xi.
6. Anon, 'Murder of Maria Kirwan on Irelands Eye'
7. Evidence of Theresa Kenny confirming her relationship with and children by Kirwan, Anon., 'Prosecution Brief', 113.
8. Evidence of Margaret Campbell, ibid., 27.
9. Evidence of Margaret Doyle, ibid., 72.
10. Evidence of Catherine Kelly, ibid., 33.
11. Evidence of Margaret Gillas, ibid., 70.

12. Armstrong, *Report of the Trial*.
13. McMahon, *Homicide in Pre Famine and Famine Ireland*, 13–15.
14. Conley, *Melancholy Accidents*, 61. Conley has produced several valuable studies on the nineteenth-century courts, including her examination of the treatment of women by the courts *No Pedestals: Women and Violence in Late 19th Century Ireland* (1995) and *Certain Other Countries: Homicide, Gender and National Identity in Late Nineteenth Century Ireland, Scotland and Wales,* in which she also examines how homicide trials can throw a spotlight on underlying societal issues.
15. King, 'Making Crime News'.
16. Crone, 'Publishing Courtroom Drama for the Masses, 1820–1855'.
17. See particularly *Certain Other Countries* for a comparative study.
18. Vaughan, *Murder Trials in Ireland, 1836–1914*, 42.
19. Ibid., 14.
20. Evidence of Henry Davis *Report of the Trial*, 41.
21. 'Melancholy Accident'.
22. 'Melancholy Occurrence at Ireland's Eye', *The Advocate: Or, Irish Industrial Journal*, 8 September 1852.
23. 'Melancholy Occurrence at Ireland's Eye', *London Evening Standard*, 9 September 1852.
24. Evidence of Michael Nangle, Anon., 'Prosecution Brief', 17.
25. 'The Late Case of Drowning At Irelands Eye', *Evening Packet and Correspondent*, 9 October 1852.
26. Evidence of Maria Byrne, ibid., 30.
27. O'Brien, 'Journalism in Ireland', 16.
28. 'The Late Mysterious Case of Drowning At Ireland's Eye', *Freeman's Journal*, 16 October 1852.
29. 'The Tale of Mystery', *The Examiner*, 23 October 1852.
30. 'The Late Mysterious Case of Drowning on Ireland's Eye'.
31. 'Charge of Murder'.
32. 'The Charge of Murder Against an Artist'.
33. Evidence of Thomas Larkin, Anon., 'Prosecution Brief', 29.
34. 'Commission of Oyer and Terminer'.
35. All three papers ran a short paragraph explaining that the case was ready to start but carried their main trial reports over the next day or so.
36. 'Ireland', *London Evening Standard*, 8 December 1852.
37. Evidence of Margaret Campbell, Armstrong, *Report of the Trial*, 14.
38. Ibid., 32.
39. Ibid., 34.
40. Ibid., 60.
41. Ibid., 58–64.
42. Ibid., 81.
43. Ibid., 82.
44. Ibid., 91.
45. 'The Tenant Right Bill'.
46. 'From Our London Correspondent'.
47. 'Extraordinary Trial for Murder'.
48. Ibid.

MEDIA CONNECTIONS BETWEEN BRITAIN AND IRELAND

49. Vaughan., *Murder Trials in Ireland, 1836–1914*, 297. The 'matters put forward' that Crampton was referring to are affidavits gathered by solicitor John Boswell in support of Kirwan. The affidavits were published widely in various newspapers and Boswell also published them in pamphlet form as *The Defence of William Bourke Kirwan condemned for the alleged murder of his wife, and now a convict at Spike Island.*
50. 'The Case of the Convict Kirwan'.
51. 'Reprieve of Mr Kirwan: The Power of Public Opinion and the Press'.
52. The Case of Mr. Kirwan'.
53. Dennis, 'Kirwan's Case'.
54. *Saunders's News-Letter*, 1 January 1853.
55. 'The Convict Kirwan'.
56. 'Ireland', *The Morning Chronicle*, 27 January 1853.
57. Ibid.
58. 'Kirwan the Murderer'.
59. Grace. 'The Convict Kirwan'.
60. Hitchens and Allison, 'To the Editor of Saunder's News-Letter'.
61. 'The Trial of Mr. KIRWAN, at Dublin'.
62. 'The Case of Mr. Kirwan'.
63. The Convict Kirwan'.
64. 'The Kirwan Case', *The Examiner*, 1 January 1853.
65. 'The Murderer Kirwan'.
66. Vaughan., *Murder Trials in Ireland, 1836–1914*, 97.
67. 'CORONER'S INQUEST (SIX-MILE BRIDGE). (Hansard, 16 November 1852)'.
68. 'Law Intelligence'.
69. Gavan Duffy, *My Life in Two Hemispheres*, 1:27.
70. Inglis, *The Freedom of the Press in Ireland, 1784–1841*, 221. O'Connell had used his speech to blame the press for failing to support his new repeal society. They responded by refusing to cover the speech. Duffy's then editor, Michael Staunton, who ran the *Morning Register* tried to respond but was shouted down.
71. O'Brien, 'Journalism in Ireland', 15.
72. There are several accounts of Dublin journalists acting together as a group dating back to the 1820s, see O'Brien 'Journalism in Ireland' for more detail. For later examples see Dunlop, *Fifty Years of Irish Journalism*, 72–3. Fellow journalist Matthias McDonnell Bodkin was also enthusiastic about that camaraderie in both his autobiography *Recollections of an Irish Judge – Press, Bar and Parliament* and his novel, *White Magic.*
73. Orwell, 'Decline of the English Murder'.

ORCID

Abigail Rieley ⓘ http://orcid.org/0000-0002-2478-9777

Bibliography

Armstrong, John Simpson. *Report of the Trial of William Burke Kirwan: For the Murder of Maria Louisa Kirwan, His Wife, at the Island of Ireland's Eye, in the County of Dublin, on the 6th*

September, 1852, before the Hon. Judge Crampton and the Rt. Hon. Baron Green, at the Commission Court, Green-Street, on 8th and 9th December, 1852. Dublin: Printed by Alexander Thom 87 Abbey-street for Her Majesty's stationary office, 1853.

Bodkin, Matthias MacDonnell. *White Magic. A Novel*. Chapman & Hall, 1897.

Bodkin, Matthias MacDonnell. 1914. *Recollections of an Irish Judge*. London: Hurst and Blackett.

"Charge of Murder." *John O' Groat Journal*, 22 October 1952, sec. Accidents and Offences.

Chibnall, Steve. 1977. *Law-and-Order News: An Analysis of Crime Reporting in the British Press*. London: Tavistock Publications.

"Commission of Oyer and Terminer." *Dublin Evening Mail*, 8 December 1852.

Conley, Carolyn. *Melancholy Accidents: The Meaning of Violence in Post-Famine Ireland*. Lanham, MD: Lexington Books, 1999.

Conley, Assistant Professor of History Carolyn A. *Certain Other Countries: Homicide, Gender, and National Identity in Late Nineteenth-Century England, Ireland, Scotland, and Wales*. Columbus: Ohio State University Press, 2007.

1852. "CORONER'S INQUEST (SIX-MILE BRIDGE)." Hansard, 16 November 1852. https://api. parliament.uk/historic-hansard/commons/ Accessed 13 October 2017

Crone, Rosalind. 2012. "Publishing Courtroom Drama for the Masses, 1820–1855." In *Crime, Courtrooms, and the Public Sphere in Britain, 1700–1850*, edited by David Lemmings, 193–216. London, United Kingdom: Routledge.

"Declarations of Innocence by Convicts." *Morning Post*, 31 December 1852.

Dennis, John A. "Kirwan's Case." *Saunder's News-Letter*, 10 January 1853.

Dunlop, Andrew. *Fifty Years of Irish Journalism*. Dublin: Hanna & Neale, 1911.

"Extraordinary Trial for Murder." *London Evening Standard*, 11 December 1852.

"From Our London Correspondent." *Brechin Advertiser*, 14 December 1852.

Gavan Duffy, Charles. 1898. *My Life in Two Hemispheres*. 1969. Dublin: Irish University Press. Vol.1;2 vols.

"General News Section." *Saunders's News-Letter*, 1 January 1853.

Grace, Richard. "The Convict Kirwan." *Cork Examiner*, 17 January 1853.

Hansard, Thomas Carson. "Hansard's Parliamentary Debates." Vol. 127. Great Britain. Parliament, 1853.

Hitchens, H., and Robert Allison. "To the Editor of Saunder's News-Letter." *Saunder's News-Letter*, 13 January 1853.

Inglis, Brian. 1954. *The Freedom of the Press in Ireland, 1784–1841*. London: Faber.

"Ireland." *London Evening Standard*, 8 December 1852.

"Ireland." *Morning Chronicle*, 8 December 1852.

"Ireland." *The Morning Chronicle*, 27 January 1853.

Kemmis, William. "The Convict Kirwan." *Cork Constitution*, 8 January 1853.

King, Peter. "Making Crime News: Newspapers, Violent Crime and the Selective Reporting of Old Bailey Trials in the Late Eighteenth Century." *Crime, Histoire & Sociétés/Crime, History & Societies* 13, no. 1 (2009): 91–116.

"Kirwan the Murderer—Removal of the Prisoner." *Dublin Weekly Nation*, 15 January 1853.

"Law Intelligence—Crown Prosecution for Libel—the Sixmilebridge Affair.' *The Evening Freeman*, 28 December 1852.

McMahon, Richard. 2013. *Homicide in Pre Famine and Famine Ireland*. Liverpool: Liverpool University Press.

"Melancholy Accident—Death of a Lady by Drowning." *Freeman's Journal*, 8 September 1852.

"Murder of Maria Kirwan on Irelands Eye, the Queen against Wm. Burke Kirwan : Brief on Behalf of the Crown on the Prosecution of the Prisoner. October and December Commission." Dublin, Ireland, 1852. National Archive of Ireland.

O'Brien, Mark. 2011. "Journalism in Ireland: Evolution of a Discipline." In *Irish Journalism before Independence: More a Disease than a Profession*, edited by Kevin Rafter, 9–21. Manchester: Manchester University Press.

Old Bailey Proceedings Online (www.oldbaileyonline.org, version 7.2, 14 October 2017), June 1840, trial of FRANCOIS BENJAMIN COURVOISIER (t18400615-1629).

Orwell, George. "Decline of the English Murder." *Tribune*, 1946.

"Reprieve of Mr Kirwan: The Power of Public Opinion and the Press." *The Liverpool Mail*, 1 January 1853.

"The Case of Mr. Kirwan." *Leicestershire Mercury*, 1 January 1853.

"The Case of Mr. Kirwan." *London Evening Standard*, 22 December 1852.

"The Case of the Convict Kirwan." *Dublin Evening Packet and Correspondent*, 1 January 1853.

"The Charge of Murder Against an Artist." *The Cornish Telegraph*, 20 October 1852, sec. General News.

"The Convict Kirwan." *Cambridge Chronicle and Journal*, 15 January 1853.

"The Late Mysterious Case of Drowning on Ireland's Eye." *Morning Post*, 18 October 1852.

"The Murderer Kirwan." *Waterford Chronicle*, 8 January 1853.

"The Tenant Right Bill." *Galway Mercury, and Connaught Weekly Advertiser*, 11 December 1852.

1852. "The Trial of Mr. Kirwan, at Dublin." *The Times*, 11 December 1852. The Times Digital Archive

Vaughan, W. E. *Murder Trials in Ireland, 1836–1914*. Dublin: Four Courts Press in association with the Irish Legal History Society, 2009.

IMAGE WARS: THE EDWARDIAN PICTURE POSTCARD AND THE CONSTRUCTION OF IRISH IDENTITY IN THE EARLY 1900S

Ann Wilson

Picture postcards became immensely popular in the first decade of the twentieth century, in Ireland as elsewhere, and billions of them passed through post offices worldwide. Their imagery was largely dictated by market forces, and they penetrated all sectors of society, communicating values and concepts even to those who were unwilling or unable to engage with other media such as books and periodicals. During this period the concept of Irish identity was very fluid, and several nationalist groups had emerged whose aim was to develop a distinct Irish culture worthy of the respect of both Irish and non-Irish people. Picture postcards became seen as a means towards achieving this aim, but also of seriously undermining it. This paper examines reports from Irish newspapers from 1900 to 1910 on the postcard phenomenon, and the social anxieties and fears they reveal.

Introduction/historical Context

The picture postcard is not usually considered in histories of the media, perhaps because of its status as an item of lowly and ephemeral popular culture. However, during the first decade of the twentieth century, because of its worldwide penetration and popularity, it became a powerful means of spreading concepts and values. It was cheap to buy and send and it allowed individuals to quickly manipulate and communicate ready-made, varied and constantly updated imagery and text to an extent that has only recently become again possible with the advent of the internet and social media.

This paper examines the picture postcard phenomenon of the early twentieth century as it related to Ireland, where millions of them circulated during the Edwardian period. It looks at the various developments which led to their widespread use and popularity, and as a result to an enormous and complex worldwide industry churning out an ever-changing variety of products for a voracious market. People used the picture postcard in many ways, as a personal memento, greeting card, gift, collectable and for keeping in touch. However, it is its role as a medium of mass communication that will primarily be examined in some detail in the last section of this paper, which will focus on the anxieties and controversies engendered by two types of cards, those featuring Irish stereotypes and those judged to be obscene or indecent. Such issues have been discussed in relation to other popular media during this period, such as newspapers and early cinema, but this paper adds to our understanding by examining a similar and substantial but heretofore neglected area of contestation – picture postcards.[1]

The Picture Postcard Industry

The picture postcard phenomenon was made possible partly because of developments in postal organization and regulations. During the nineteenth century, as Ferguson has recounted, the speed and frequency of mail delivery increased considerably due to improvements in transport technology, and cheap postal rates were introduced based on weight.[2] The first plain postcards, without imagery, are widely agreed to have been issued by the Austrian Postal Administration in 1869.[3] They were thin, buff-coloured pieces of card of a standard size and format, designed to be easily and cheaply sorted and transported, with space for an address and stamp on one side and a short message on the other. Other countries quickly followed, including Britain (and Ireland) in 1870, where the postage price was fixed at a halfpenny. Postcards soon became widely adopted worldwide because they were so quick and easy to write and cheap to send. In the decades that followed they became an important communication tool for businesses and governments, and for individuals who wished to connect with others without the elaborate and often tedious formalities that had become conventionally associated with letter writing. Concerns were expressed by some about a perceived resulting decline in literacy and about loss of privacy, but, as with the anxieties expressed about social media today, economics and convenience mostly overrode these.

Developments in printing and photography facilitated and encouraged the addition of imagery to postcards, although initially this was mainly used for advertising. Greeting cards, tourist views and pictures of hotels and restaurants in postcard form began to appear in Germany, Austria and Switzerland in the 1870s and 1880s.[4] Postcards featuring the newly completed Eiffel Tower (which could be bought and postmarked from the top of the structure itself) were printed for the Paris Exhibition of 1889, and by the early 1890s a wide variety of picture postcards was available in many European countries. The industry began to grow in Britain and Ireland after 1894, when the Government relinquished its postcard monopoly and allowed production by private manufacturers. The USA's first official colour postcards were sold at The Worlds Columbian Exposition in Chicago in 1893, and most restrictions against the private printing of picture postcards were lifted there in 1898.[5]

The addition of imagery to cards further reduced the possible size of any added message, as nothing other than the stamp, name and address was allowed on the non-picture side. Individualized communication therefore needed to be squeezed into the available space around the image. Postal authorities in different jurisdictions cooperated in enforcing the rules related to postcards, and insisted on standardized sizes, weights and formats to facilitate speedy and efficient handling and processing. In 1902, however, the British Post Office allowed the sending of postcards with divided backs, one half for the user to write a message and the other for the address and stamp, allowing the image to dominate the front without the necessity of writing over or around it. These cards could only be sent within Britain and Ireland until other countries followed suit, which France did in 1904, Germany in 1905 and the United States and Japan in 1907.[6] The result was an enormous boom in the production, purchasing, sending and collecting of picture postcards, so much so that in 1903 the *Glasgow Evening News* gloomily forecasted that within the next decade Europe would be 'buried beneath picture postcards'.[7] Bjarne

Rogan has calculated that in the first two decades of the twentieth century between 200 and 300 billion postcards were produced and sold worldwide.[8]

The production of picture postcards was mainly commercial, but they were also sponsored by groups with political and other specific interests to promote. They were bought because of their visual appeal and/or message. They featured an exhaustive variety of images, both black-and-white and coloured, and usually accompanied by some sort of text title or caption. These included land-, town- and seascapes; notable buildings; modern forms of transport; newsworthy events, especially disasters; political and sporting figures; attractive females and celebrities; cute children and animals; 'interesting' foreign people; rural workers and comic and satirical cartoons. However, any subject was possible, although some of the more risqué ones, deemed sexually or politically offensive or socially dangerous, were censored. Despite the cheap price of picture postcards, the massive numbers sold meant that their production, distribution and sale generated huge profit, and their subject matter tended to be market driven. Postcard publishers focussed mostly on subjects (and messages) that they saw as broadly popular, or that had at least a profitable niche attraction, and imagery was frequently hand-coloured, embossed, partly cut-out or highlighted with glitter, lace, hair or fur in order to maximize its visual and tactile appeal. It could also be combined with other imagery and with text, including poetry, to produce complex montages or convincingly 'realistic' scenes. Constant innovation was important to keep people buying, so that card producers, in order to stay in business, had to keep a fine balance between popular, tried-and-tested products and novelties which could prove to be either widely successful or a waste of company resources.

Picture postcards could also be 'real' photographs, personal photographs printed as a postcard either by using a new type of Kodak camera or by a commercial company that provided such a service.[9] Postcards could be bought from shops, street traders and/or vending machines in every town and village in Ireland, as well as from railway stations, on ships and at even the most remote tourist spots. Purchasers gave postcards as gifts to others, sent them through the post, or kept them themselves, often collecting them in specially designed albums. Collectors made contact with each other through specialist magazines and the mainstream press, so that they could share and exchange cards. They were also, of course, used or posted as holiday souvenirs, but this was not as dominant a function of postcards as it became later. As the telegraph and telephone were not yet accessible to many people, they were particularly popular as a means of quick, informal communication, similar to texting in the early twenty-first century, and this was facilitated by the frequent daily postal deliveries of the era. They were also used to maintain contact with distant friends and relatives, filling in gaps between letter writing, and to send greetings on special occasions, such as birthdays, Christmas, Easter and Valentine's Day, taking a sizeable share of the market from conventional greeting cards. Postcards sent on Saint Patrick's day often had attached a small packet of shamrock seeds.[10] Wang, Tucker and Haines have described modern social networking technologies as phatic (rather than information-delivering) technologies, because they mainly function 'to establish, develop and maintain personal and social relationships,' especially when those relationships 'have been stretched across time-space'.[11] By this definition, picture postcards were arguably the most significant phatic technology of the early twentieth century.

The picture postcard phenomenon was an international one, and big postcard firms in particular, such as the London-based Raphael Tuck & Sons, described by the *Freeman's Journal* in 1904 as 'the principal manufacturers of postcards', advertised and sold their products in many countries.[12] They also outsourced many aspects of their production, and most early postcard printing, for instance, was centralized in Germany. Postcards featuring images of distant places and people, both imported and locally produced, were sold in Ireland, and images of Ireland, often produced by non-Irish companies, were sold abroad.[13] Irish people, therefore, including those who had no ability or desire to read the books, magazines and newspapers of the period, were exposed via postcards to a large variety of new images, along with the ideas and values they communicated.

Picture Postcards in Edwardian Ireland

After 1894, publishers in both Britain and Ireland were quick to see the commercial potential of picture postcards, and many existing photography, stationary and greeting card companies now diversified to include postcards. Two important examples of such companies were the large British firms Raphael Tuck & Sons and Valentine's (originally established in Dundee, Scotland), both of which had international markets and offices in many countries. New companies were also established to supply (and encourage) the demand. Dublin-based firms such as Lawrence, Eason's and Hely's were prominent on the Irish market, although they had competition from a myriad of local producers throughout the country as well as from foreign firms. It is difficult to establish the proportion of Irish to non-Irish cards circulating in Ireland during this period, but postcard collections which have survived from the time, as well as commentaries in newspapers, suggest that there were far more of the latter than the former.[14] Often there is little obvious difference between Irish and foreign cards, as companies such as Valentines, for instance, bought photographic imagery from Lawrence, and Irish companies also reused pictures, motifs and formats from elsewhere.

As was the case in other countries, the Irish media frequently commented on the new 'craze'. The *Cork Examiner* reported 'an enormous increase in the use of pictorial postcards' in 1904.[15] The following year it cited the opinion of the Postmaster General that a measurable decrease in letter delivery could be attributable to the increase in postcards, of which 734,500,000 had been delivered in the United Kingdom the previous year, an increase of nearly 20%.[16] According to the *Irish Independent* in 1906 the number of postcards passing through the Irish post alone was estimated at 32,800,000, although by May the following year it was predicting that the craze was dying out.[17] However, the numbers sent through the post continued to increase, albeit at a decreasing rate. During the first decade of the twentieth century in Ireland picture postcards became ubiquitous, almost impossible to avoid, so that for instance a visitor to Killaloe in County Clare in 1907 saw one area of the town so dominated by shops selling them that he thought it could be called 'Pictorial Avenue ... all the doors and windows decorated with comic life, Irish life, country life, town life, high life, low life, and no life ... '.[18]

Commentators worried that Irish entrepreneurs were not fully exploiting the business potential of this new phenomenon. According to the *Derry People* in 1904:

It is quite certain that not one-hundredth of the picture pasteboards bought with money earned in Ireland are produced in this country. Our stationers' shops are full of cards with views of Irish scenery and notable buildings and works of art. Nearly all are placed on the market by English firms. English photographers, English lithographers, and English printers reap the benefit, as well as the astute English capitalists who study the public taste and cater for it.[19]

In response, Irish newspapers often went out of their way to praise and promote postcards published in Ireland. The *Anglo-Celt* reported in 1904 on postcards produced by J.A. Coleman of Bailieborough:

It always gives us pleasure to record the enterprise of a resident in our towns, go-ahead being unfortunately so rare in Ireland ... It is no exaggeration to say that the fifteen (in packet) ... for a shilling are far superior to many of the Continental cards we have seen ... . The man or woman who purchases an imported card while one of Coleman's is to be had is a poor sort of patriot.[20]

McGinly and Mackey's postcards produced (in Dublin) from peat also received a considerable amount of newspaper coverage, with the *Freemans Journal* assuring readers that 'The postcards were designed and printed in Ireland, and the paper was manufactured in Ireland, whilst the fact that it is made from Irish peat, "each card a bit of the old sod", is a unique souvenir to friends abroad.'[21] The Celbridge Peat Paper Mills in Kildare also produced postcards 'made from Bog of Allen peat'.[22] Companies such as these saw a marketing advantage in their products being identified as distinctively Irish, especially if they focussed on Irish or Irish emigrant markets. Sometimes non-Irish companies used misleading names or trademarks to suggest that their products were Irish or made in Ireland, and the Irish Industrial Development Association (IDA) took measures against these, successfully bringing a case for instance against a London-based picture postcard company which wanted to call itself 'Shamrock and Co'.[23] The IDA also took the General Manager of the Great Northern Railway of Ireland to task about his company's use of foreign-printed picture postcards, despite the fact that they were purchased from a Dublin firm. He said he hadn't known they were printed abroad and it wouldn't happen again.[24]

Nevertheless Irish newspapers ran numerous advertisements and editorial promotions for non-Irish postcard producers, particularly for Raphael Tuck.[25] This company's cards were described as 'exquisite', 'unique' and 'humorous ... [but] free from the slightest trace of vulgarity'.[26] The *Killarney Echo* conceded that 'The firm's productions are all works of Art, and if Irishmen and women must send to England for their postcards, etc., Messrs Tuck and Sons give the best value we know of.'[27] Irish newspaper commentators were impressed by any attractive Irish-themed postcards, regardless of where they were produced, pointing out their potential for promoting tourism to the country. Examples were the various bestselling Irish 'views' published by the London and North-Western Railway. 'The sale of the cards have been phenomenal', enthused the *Freeman's Journal*,

with over five and a quarter million having been purchased up to date ... The new sets, which are specially devoted to Ireland, will, no doubt play a large part in directing tourist traffic to Ireland, whose scenic beauty they depict with artistic skill.[28]

As a writer in the *Kerry Weekly Reporter* stated in relation to the issuing of a new set of Kerry views by the Pictorial Stationary company in London: 'Really artistic view postcards constitute a splendid recommendation to health and holiday resorts, and as they are circulated without cost to the authorities should prove a valuable form of advertisement.'[29]

The picture postcards that circulated in Ireland in the first decade of the twentieth century showed the same breadth and variety of subject matter as elsewhere. They could be seen as entertaining, amusing, emotive, educative, propagandistic, titillating, irritating or offensive, depending on the viewer. They constructed fabulous, seductive and convincing fantasies, pictured Ireland to Irish people and to others, and brought the spectacle of the wider world to even the most determined stay-at-homes. They forged and maintained connections between geographically widely separated people and places. Often the exact same cards circulated in North America, Australia and Europe as in Britain and Ireland, as was the case with images of female music-hall stars who toured internationally, such as Marie Studholme, Maude Fealy, Marie Corelli, Zena and Phyllis Dare and Gertie Millar.[30] These images, many published by the Rotary Photographic Company in Middlesex, became enormously popular with young Irish women, and Hely's of Dublin regularly advertised 'assorted actresses' in various newspapers. The influence of postcard imagery on Irish women was commented on in the *Evening Herald* in 1904, in which a writer noted the 'abnormally large' number of 'imitation "Gibson girls" in Dublin', a fad attributed to the popularity of postcards and other printed material based on the fashionable and idealized 'Gibson girl' image popularized by the American illustrator Charles Dana Gibson (1867–1944).[31] Gibson girl images, like the photographic postcards of carefree, glamorously dressed and bejewelled stars from musical theatre, must have presented a very seductive model of femininity to many young Irish women, especially compared to more conventional Irish Catholic female role models such as the Virgin Mary. Throughout the twentieth and early twenty-first centuries such celebrity constructs have increasingly been perceived as enormously socially powerful, and are now the focus of a vast (and growing) literature on beauty ideals, gender norms and what Driessens calls the 'celebritization' of society and culture.[32]

There were other anxieties about the possible social effects of postcard use. The fact that the message was open and could be viewed by anyone caused concerns similar to those expressed today about internet privacy settings and data accessibility. Postcard senders sometimes used code, shorthand or mirror writing to counteract this, although, as is the case now, many seem to have been unconcerned about who saw what they wrote. Indeed, some writers took advantage of the semi-public nature of postcard communication by using it to insult and defame those against whom they had a grudge, and several cases of libel via postcard were reported in newspapers of the period.[33] Decreasing literacy was another worry, as postcards encouraged a reliance on visual imagery as a means of expression, as well as word abbreviations and modified grammar and punctuation, as is common in social media communication today. In 1904 an *Evening Herald* article blamed the postcard for a 'the decay of epistolary style', commenting rather drily 'the habit of writing two or three words on the edge of, say, the "Colosseum by Moonlight" or "Tea Planting in Ceylon" will accentuate the brevity of the modern letter-writer, whose geography, however, it will presumably improve.'[34]

Anxieties About Picture Postcard Imagery

As early as 1903 some commentators were expressing strong reservations about the messages communicated by postcard imagery. The *Ulster Herald*, for instance complained about the large number of 'silly objectionable cards ... sent through the post by young persons.' The writer went on to quote an opinion piece from the periodical the *Irish Rosary*, which railed against the increasing numbers of cards which were

> calculated to appeal to the idle, the silly, the vacuous, and the fabulous mind. They are comic, pseudo-comic, epicene, suggestive, smutty, silly, crude, coarse, and oftentimes outright vulgar. A study of these things make one amazed at the shallow-wittedness, or even the lack-wittedness, that the purchasers of them will consent to be amused by.[35]

Examples of objectionable subjects were given in a related article in the *Fermanagh Herald*:

> Seaside scenes; bulgy females – elderly and irate – clad in burstingly tight bathing dresses; skinny, frightened-looking men, being tyrannically ill–used by the plump, elderly amazons aforesaid, younger men and women performing dear knows what idiotic pranks, and convulsed with laughter at their own drollery.[36]

Two types of card, however, were perceived as particularly problematic, and both were used by commentators to make claims about Irishness and Irish identity, what it was and what it was not (or should not be). The first featured reproductions of long-popular caricatures of Irish people, and the second imagery judged to be obscene.

Irish Caricatures

The establishment of a distinct, separate Irish identity – distinct particularly from that of Britain – was seen as important by many groups in the early twentieth century. Cultural Irishness was regarded by them as an essential prerequisite for any kind of national self-respect, let alone the political independence which many felt would shortly be granted to the country in the form of Home Rule. To this end, groups such as the Gaelic Athletic Association (1884), the Gaelic League (1893) and the Irish Literary Theatre (1899) were formed. The Gaelic League, founded partly in response to Douglas Hyde's famous speech 'The Necessity for De-Anglicising Ireland' (1892), was primarily a language revival association.[37] However, it also had a much broader cultural nationalist agenda, which included a resistance to the influx, mainly from Britain, of popular modern mass-cultural forms, such as musical theatre, cheap periodicals and picture postcards. The group aimed to replace these with specifically Irish cultural products: Irish dance, games and literature and imagery that would appeal to popular taste while still being distinctively Irish. The Gaelic League thus promoted picture postcards that were Irish-made and reproduced positive images of the country and its people.[38]

It soon became apparent however that an image war was being waged both nationally and internationally, and that many people, both Irish and non-Irish, were still happy to buy, and profit from, what the League and others saw as offensively negative, 'stage-Irish' postcard caricatures of Ireland and the Irish, featuring imagery such as a wild-looking, drunken and foolish 'Paddy', accompanied by a pig. Such caricatures had a long history, originating during the twelfth-century Norman conquest of Ireland when Gerald of Wales characterized Irish people in his writings as violent, savage and uncivilized, and had hardened through subsequent centuries of strife between Britain and Ireland.[39] De Nie argues that this 'wild Irish' image was combined in the seventeenth and eighteenth centuries with depictions of the Irishman as 'a bumbling drunkard or fool', and in the nineteenth century both of these were 'blended with popular theories about race and character' that scientifically 'proved' the Irish people's natural inferiority and inability to rule themselves.[40] The concept of the Irish as racially 'different' was regularly reinforced during the nineteenth and early twentieth centuries by British politicians, writers and comic artists as a means of explaining repeated Irish acts of resistance to anglicization. As L. Perry Curtis has shown, such ideas inspired the images of violent, ape-like Irishman, dark and heavy-jawed, that became a staple of popular British periodicals such as *Punch*.[41] De Nie argues that attitudes towards Catholicism and class also fed into Irish stereotypes, in that the Irish were seen as religiously subservient peasants, ignorant and economically backward, and content to live in abject poverty and muck.[42] Hence the frequent depiction of 'Paddy' with a pig. Colonialism and empire building transmitted these stereotypes throughout the world, and they were expressed in a range of popular media.

In 1903 the Inchicore Workingmen's Club branch of the League in Dublin appointed subcommittees to pressurize local shopkeepers to remove from their windows 'pictorial postcards ridiculing the Irish character'.[43] In 1905 the *Kerryman* reported that in Killarney 'degrading and insulting' postcards were exhibited in many shop windows, showing 'a gross and disgusting caricature of the Irishman'.[44] A year later, these images were still in evidence, and a writer in the 'Sinn Fein notes' section of the paper criticized 'the universal scattering by Irish traders of these English made scurrilities', while also attributing them to a deliberate plan by the English to defame the Irish, a not unusual conclusion at the time: 'it is time that this buffoonery should cease and Irishmen realize that these man monkey monstrosities are the false creations of the foul English mind expressly made to belittle the Irish in the world's eye'.[45] Such cards were certainly not only produced by English companies, however, and the Dublin-based Lawrence company, for instance, was responsible for many of them.

The problem was also reported in other Irish towns, to the extent that a letter of complaint, signed 'An American Citizen', was sent to the *Irish Independent* in 1908, referring to

> the picture postcard type, which wants to show us what an Irish courtship looks like: the colleen is invariably represented in her bare feet. I have seen others, representing a half drunken Irishman embracing a pig, and still a crowd surrounded the window and smiled at the glaring affront.[46]

In America itself, to which millions of Irish people had emigrated during the nineteenth century, determined measures were taken to combat these images, which were especially publicly visible around Saint Patrick's Day when parades were held in various cities. The protest campaigns seem to have been primarily spearheaded by the Irish Catholic organization, the Ancient Order of Hibernians (AOH), which was concerned to perpetuate an image of Irish-American Catholics that was sober and respectable. An address by John T. Keating to a meeting of the AOH in Chicago, reportedly attended by 500 people, particularly objected to popular representations which gave Irish people ape-like features, stating that they were 'a libel on the Irish physiognomy'. He added that his ancestors 'were as comely as any race of people under the sun, and the Irish women of today are noted for their facial charms.'[47] According to the *Limerick Leader,* resolutions asking for government action against these postcards were sent to President Roosevelt, 'who expressed sympathy with the members of the Celtic race', with the result that a law was passed banning them from travelling through the American mail.[48] Another Irish-American group, the United Irish League, organized a boycott of offending shops, and 'With one exception all the merchants in the main business streets heeded the boycott warning of the league and removed the caricatures from their show windows.'[49]

Despite these actions, however, the problem resurfaced in 1908, when the Irish-American Union in Chicago called for further boycotting and police action. The *Cork Examiner* quoted from 'the leading Catholic paper, published under the official sanction of Archbishop Quigley':

> One of the insulting caricatures ... represents St Patrick astride of a pig, a mitre upon his head, a clay pipe in his mouth. Other insults represent monkey-faced Irishmen astride of fat porkers, of course with clay pipe accompaniment ... Fancy the shameless audacity of men who could put out a picture postal card portraying St. Patrick doing the Salome dance![50]

The 'Salome dance' presumably refers to both Oscar Wilde's notorious banned play, first published in French in 1891, as well as to the salacious 'Dance of the Seven Veils' regularly performed by the entertainer Maud Allan since its premiere in 1906 as part of her show *Vision of Salomé* in Vienna. The connection of either to Saint Patrick would have been seen as deeply offensive to Irish Catholics. The newspaper again called for a boycott, citing the consumer power of the 1,150,000 'upright, influential' Irish-American Catholics living in Chicago. Clearly, however, boycotting and banning could only have a limited effect, as the 'Paddy and his Pig' imagery was too appealing to consumers. In Ireland it could be combated to an extent by denouncing the selling and buying of such postcards as flagrant 'shoneenism', an increasingly powerful insult as the popular mood became more nationalist.[51] To this was added the determination announced in the *Kerryman* in 1906, to replace the offensive caricatures with 'healthy, clean, Irish-made cards', an approach very much in line with that of the Gaelic League.[52]

Considering the level of newspaper outrage at these images, it is worth noting as a postscript that the Irish media could be surprisingly unsympathetic when it reported on the perpetuation of negative postcard stereotypes of other groups, as the *Cork Examiner* did in 1906:

> In Milwaukee, which is the centre of the German population of the Republic, there is a fierce indignation over certain picture postcards which represent Hans as unusually fat and prodigiously bibulous. Still, small voices have been heard declaring that the offending representations are true to fact, but the Milwaukee Germans are convinced that they are being libelled.[53]

The media debates in the early twentieth century about 'Stage Irish' postcard imagery reflect the sensitivity felt by many Irish people at the time to the way Irishness was perceived, and the complete indifference of many others. That this war of images was fought at the level of the humble postcard suggests that it was recognized during this period as a potentially powerful and convincing medium, its very cheapness and ephemerality broadening its reach to people who were not necessarily receptive to other media messages.

Obscene Postcards

Attempts to replace long-held negative Irish stereotypes with more positive ones were arguably mainly of concern to Irish people, but worries about obscene imagery on postcards surfaced wherever postcards were available, although attitudes to obscenity, and concepts of it, varied in different cultures. In Ireland, commentators were coy about defining it, even as they vigorously denounced it. A report in the *Cork Examiner* in 1906 of a case brought before the local magistrates illustrates this well. The defendant, Ernest Rosehill, was brought before the court to explain why cards seized from his shop at 10, Grand Parade in Cork should not be destroyed, and during the proceedings his defence solicitor attempted to define the term 'obscenity' using Nutall's dictionary. He was however immediately silenced by the presiding magistrate, who declared: 'There is no need of defining indecency for us, or obscenity either'.[54] Yet Rosehill was tried, and convicted, on the grounds that he exhibited obscene postcards for sale.

Whether a particular postcard was regarded as obscene, indecent or immoral seems to have been decided based mainly on common-sense judgments passed by local magistrates who examined and discussed each card brought to their attention, usually by concerned citizens or groups such as the Ancient Order of Hibernians or the Young Men's Catholic Society. An official announcement by the Postmaster General in 1904 did not clarify matters, merely stating that

> by the provisions of the Post Office Protection Act 1884, any person who sends by post a postal packet (which term includes a postcard), having thereon any words, marks, or designs of an indecent, obscene, or grossly offensive character, is guilty of a misdemeanour, and is liable to be fined or imprisoned for twelve months.[55]

Decisions at local level were influenced by pressure groups, by social norms in relation to what was usually seen as acceptable, as well as by concepts of art. The Rosehill case in 1906 was partly defended on the grounds that the defendant was a 'stranger', not long settled in Cork, and

> In other countries people were not so particular as here in regards to pictures and postcards, and his client judged by the standard of other places and not by the standard of Cork. In other countries he had seen cards flaunted in the shop windows as bad as, if not worse than, those that were now sought to be condemned.[56]

Rosehill was also prosecuted for the same offence in 1908, and this trial generated discussions among the magistrates and solicitors on 'mixed bathing', which was represented on some of the cards, whether this was acceptable behaviour in Ireland (it was, in Youghal, apparently), and the appropriate attire for it in places where it was acceptable. The defending solicitor also drew a comparison with art images, asking the Head Constable, who had seized the cards in question, what he 'would think if he went to the National Gallery and saw the Velasquez for which the State paid £7,000 or £8,000.'[57] The Velasquez painting referred to was probably the *Rokeby Venus*, a mid-seventeenth-century nude purchased in 1906 for the National Gallery in London. The magistrates were not convinced that there was a valid comparison to be made, and Rosehill was again convicted. The reporting of such cases allowed public declarations of, but also challenges to, Irish mores and values. However, the vagueness of the language used in many of these discussions and judgments must have hampered rational decision-making, and is well illustrated by the statement of one prosecutor when faced with three problematic cards: 'The first two cards are corrupting and disgusting, but the third is mere filth.'[58]

The Drogheda branch of the Gaelic League was warned about 'indecent' postcards in 1903, when an address by a Fr. Finnegan informed them of the presence in local shop windows of cards 'that should bring the blush of shame to the face of any Irish maiden'.[59] The priest attributed the display of these cards to 'shoneenism', as he and many other commentators saw them as a potentially contaminating force coming from outside Ireland, often described as from 'strangers', England or, also frequently, France or 'the Continent'. This fear of external contamination of a native Irish purity is a constant theme in denunciations of offensive postcards, as in 1906 when a magistrate announced that he fined a shopkeeper for displaying them because he was 'determined to keep the windows of Dublin clean'.[60] The *Irish Independent,* reporting on the case, fully approved, adding that

> Numerous prosecutions for offences of this sort have in recent years taken place in England, and it is apparently from that country that the objectionable cards have found their way into Ireland. On this point we are strictly Protectionist, and would gladly see an absolutely prohibitive tariff put on such imports.[61]

The main concern expressed was that such images would corrupt the youth of Ireland, particularly girls. As stated in the *Anglo Celt* 'The circulation or interchange of such postcards does incalculable damage, especially when they get into the hands of callow youth and girls ignorant of the world's ways.'[62] A *Cork Examiner* editorial on the 1906 Rosehill case stated that the police involved deserved 'the commendation of every decent and clean-minded citizen' as 'we do not know of anything more calculated to deprave the youth of any community than that indecent or obscene pictures could be procured or purchased'. Referring to the images as evidence of a 'moral cancer', the writer finishes, somewhat smugly, with a claim that 'the code of proprieties which exists on the Continent is, happily, not applicable in this country.'[63] Magistrates at the Queenstown Petty Sessions in 1908 were told of the circulation of indecent postcards in Queenstown which were 'imported from other lands' and that, as a result, 'there was grave danger that the purity of our young people's lives may become tarnished, and that which we prized as a great treasure might be lost.'[64] Fr Philip O'Doherty, addressing a large Gaelic League meeting in County Donegal in 1907, communicated essentially the same message, framing it dramatically within a historical metanarrative:

> [the Irish] had withstood the Confiscations, they had defeated the sword of Cromwell, they had survived the perfidy of William. Every page of their history was a page of blood, but at the same time a page of glory, for they had kept the pearl of purity. It was in his opinion the duty of the Gaelic League and of Irishmen as a whole ... to use their every endeavour to stem that horrible traffic [in picture postcards] ... Was that purity that they so dearly cherished to go down before the foul, filthy things of England?[65]

There must have been a demand for such postcards, or they would not have been stocked and displayed in defiance of such campaigns, and many of those that caused so much worry seem to have generated mostly amusement among the wider population. At Athlone petty sessions in 1909

> Sergeant Wilson, who prosecuted, said his attention was attracted to the display window of the defendant's shop by a number of young factory girls laughing around it. He examined the postcards on view, which he considered very indecent, and purchased the one produced, which was abominable, and which was exposed for sale in the window. The defendant laughed at it, and said it was not at all indecent.[66]

Similar anxieties were expressed during the period about other imported media. The Irish Catholic Truth Society was established in 1899 to counteract cheap foreign reading material by producing competitive pamphlets and booklets designed as suitable for Irish Catholics. A number of vigilance associations were formed countrywide, and The Dublin Catholic Vigilance Association was established in 1911. Its stated aim was the safeguarding of people 'against the three chief sources of contamination in modern society, viz.: the corrupt Press, the obscene picture, and the indecent stage performance'.[67] Also in 1911, in Limerick, a Catholic sodality group managed to pressurize a number of local newsagents not to sell popular British Sunday titles, and a few days later gathered a crowd to successfully intercept them at the train station, publicly burning them 'amidst a scene of great enthusiasm, the band playing hymns while the obnoxious journals burned, and then the Dead March (Saul) over their ashy remains.'[68] The members of the Dublin Catholic Vigilance Association engaged with civic authorities to achieve such ends as having the plots and staging of plays changed so that no 'objectionable features' remained, preventing the introduction of 'indecent dancing' in music halls, limiting the Sunday opening hours of cinemas, and enforcing regulations about minimal light levels in them. In conjunction with Dublin Corporation, they also appointed and consulted with film censors, who were directed to ban or cut films which included nudity, sexual innuendo, various forms of 'impropriety' and the irreverent treatment of religious subjects.[69]

Conclusion

Discussions about picture postcards in Ireland in the first decade of the twentieth century bring us right to the heart of some of the many tensions and anxieties of that period in relation to nationalism, internationalism and modernity. As a medium, and despite its low status, the postcard was clearly taken seriously as a transmitter of values and concepts, so much so that various influential groups as well as newspaper commentators had no reservations about advocating and resorting to censorship, boycotting and criminal prosecution in order to limit and control what it communicated. Newspaper coverage of the postcard phenomenon reveals clearly some of the divisions in Irish society at the time, between those who worked hard to construct a culturally protected, Catholic and respectable Irish identity, and those who really didn't care about such concepts; between focused, idealistic nationalists, pragmatic capitalist entrepreneurs, and consumers who had their own particular aims and preferences, often unrecognized or dismissed. Reports and discussions on picture postcards reveal a major fear of many of those who were focused on a particular ideal vision of Ireland, the fear of the popular and its power to fuel resistance. This was frequently expressed as a worry about the tide of popular culture coming in to Ireland from abroad, as in Hyde's 'De-Anglicisation' speech of 1892, but really it seems to have been at least as much a fear of popular opinion and taste within Ireland. Left to themselves, callow Irish youths and shop girls were in danger of cheerfully welcoming the seductive tide of foreign culture, and indeed were already doing so. Yeats was not the only one to recognize that Ireland was 'like soft wax' during these years, and picture postcards came to be seen by many as one of those forces which could significantly determine the form into which it would harden.[70]

Disclosure Statement

No potential conflict of interest was reported by the author.

Notes

1. O'Brien, *The Fourth Estate;* Condon, *Early Irish Cinema*
2. Ferguson, "A Murmur of Small Voices," 169.
3. Staff, *The Picture Postcard & its Origins,* 46.
4. Ibid, 50–54.
5. Ibid, 62.
6. Carline, *Pictures in the Post,* 54.
7. Ibid, 9.
8. Rogan, "An Entangled Object," 31.
9. *Cork Examiner,* September 19, 1905; "Portraits on Postcards," *The Derry People,* September 12, 1908.
10. "They Say That," *Kerry Evening Star,* March 10, 1910.
11. Wang, Tucker and Haines, "Phatic technologies in modern society," 84–85.
12. *Freemans Journal,* October 28, 1904.
13. "New Postcards," *Cork Examiner,* October 19, 1905.
14. Wilson, "Constructions of Irishness," 92–117.
15. *Cork Examiner,* August 18 1904.
16. *Cork Examiner,* August 11 1905.
17. *Irish Independent,* August 9, 1906; "A change of Taste", *Irish Independent,* May 10 1907.
18. "Killaloe Notes," *Nenagh Guardian,* August 31, 1907.
19. "Picture Post Cards," *Derry People,* December 3, 1904.
20. *Anglo-Celt,* December 17, 1904.
21. "By the Way," *Freemans Journal,* December 19, 1905.
22. *Connaught Telegraph,* December 31, 1904.
23. "The Irish Trade Mark. More Misleading Titles," *Cork Examiner,* February 14, 1908.
24. *Freemans Journal,* July 20, 1908.
25. "Picture Postcards," *Cork Examiner,* July 14, 1900; "Raphael Tuck's Postcards," *Freemans Journal,* September 3, 1904.
26. *Cork Examiner,* June 15, 1906; "Messrs. Raphael Tuck & Sons," *Drogheda Argus and Leinster Journal,* November 19, 1904.
27. *KIllarney Echo,* June 1, 1907.

28. "London and North-Western Railway Picture Postcards," *Freemans Journal*, December 22, 1906.
29. "View Post Cards," *Kerry Weekly Reporter*, June 30, 1906.
30. Kelly, "Beauty and the Market," 99–116.
31. "Reform in Paris," *Evening Herald*, November 2, 1904.
32. Driessens, "The Celebritization of Society and Culture", 2013.
33. *Kerry Sentinel*, January 6, 1892, 2; *Kerry News*, September 20, 1907, 3; *Leitrim Observer*, April 13, 1912, 6.
34. *Evening Herald*, July 23, 1904.
35. "Picture Postcards," *Ulster Herald*, October 3, 1903.
36. "Picture Postcards," *Fermanagh Herald,* October 3, 1903.
37. Hyde, "The Necessity for De-Anglicising Ireland," http://www.thefuture.ie. Accessed April 19, 2014.
38. "The Gaelic League," *Irish Examiner*, August 31, 1898; "Irish Language Week," *Freemans Journal* March 6, 1906.
39. De Nie, *The Eternal Paddy,* 136.
40. Ibid, 175.
41. Curtis, *Apes and Angels*
42. De Nie, *The Eternal Paddy,* 414.
43. "The Gaelic League," *Evening Herald*, October 17, 1903.
44. "'Clear Air" notes," *Kerryman,* September 2, 1905.
45. "Sinn Fein notes. Killarney," *Kerryman*, October 13, 1906.
46. "Insulting Postcards," *Irish Independent*, April 9, 1908.
47. "A.O.H. and Postcard Caricatures," *Anglo-Celt*, April 6, 1907.
48. "'Irish" Postcards," *Limerick Leader*, April 24, 1907.
49. Ibid.
50. *Cork Examiner*, April 7, 1909.
51. *Connacht Tribune*, July 31, 1909.
52. "Sinn Fein notes. Killarney," *Kerryman*, October 13, 1906.
53. "Notes and Comments," *Irish Examiner*, April 2, 1906.
54. *Cork Examiner*, December 12, 1906.
55. *Fermanagh Herald*, December 1904.
56. *Cork Examiner*, December 12, 1906.
57. "Indecent Postcards," *Cork Examiner,* June 20, 1908.
58. "More Indecent Postcards," *Freemans Journal*, April 16, 1908. There was a lack of legal clarity throughout Britain as well as Ireland in relation to terms such as 'obscenity' and 'indecency' in the early twentieth century, as shown in Cox, Stevenson, Harris and Rowbotham, *Public Indecency in England 1857–1960,* Chapter 3, 44–64.
59. "Gaelic League in Drogheda," *Drogheda Argus and Leinster Journal*, October 10, 1903.
60. "Indecent Pictures. Mr Drury's Strong Comments," *Freemans Journal*, January 25, 1906.
61. "Clean Windows," *Irish Independent*, January 25, 1906.
62. "Latton Notes," *Anglo-Celt*, June 16, 1906.
63. *Cork Examiner*, December 12, 1906.
64. "Indecent Postcards in Queenstown," *Cork Examiner*, June 19, 1908.
65. "A Hosting of the Gael," *Donegal News,* August 3, 1907.
66. "Indecent Postcards," *Freemans Journal*, October 13, 1909.
67. Paul, The Catholic Vigilance Association, its Aims and Results, 54.

68. quoted in O'Brien, *The Fourth Estate*, 9.
69. Paul, The Catholic Vigilance Association, its Aims and Results, 57–8.
70. Yeats, *Autobiographies*, 199.

Bibliography

Carline, Richard. *Pictures in the Post. The Story of the Picture Postcard and its Place in the History of Popular Art*. London: Gordon Frazer, 1971.

Cox, David J, Kim Stevenson, Candida Harris, and Judith Rowbotham. *Public Indecency in England 1857–1960 'A Serious and Growing Evil'*. London: Routledge, 2015.

Curtis, L. Perry Jr. *Apes and Angels: The Irishman in Victorian Caricature*. Washington, D.C: Smithsonian Institution, 1971.

De Nie, Michael. *The Eternal Paddy: Irish Identity and the British Press, 1798–1882*. Madison: University of Wisconsin Press, 2004.

Dixon, F. E. "Pioneer Publishers of Dublin Picture Postcards." *Dublin Historical Record* 32 (September 1979): 146–147.

Driessens, Olivier. 2013. "The Celebritization of Society and Culture: Understanding the Structural Dynamics of Celebrity Culture." *International Journal of Cultural Studies* 16 (6): 641–657.

Ferguson, Sandra. "'A Murmur of Small Voices': On the Picture Postcard in Academic Research." *Archivaria*, North America, 60 (September 2006) 167–184. Accessed September 19, 2014. http://journals.sfu.ca/archivar/index.php/archivaria/article/view/12520/13654.

Hyde, Douglas. 'The Necessity for De-Anglicising Ireland'. 1892. Accessed April 19, 2014. http://www.thefuture.ie.

Mathews, P.J. *Revival. The Abbey Theatre, Sinn Féin, the Gaelic League and the Co-Operative Movement*. Field Day Monographs, Cork: Cork University Press, 2003.

McMahon, Timothy. *Grand Opportunity. The Gaelic Revival and Irish Society, 1893–1910*. Syracuse: Syracuse University Press, 2008.

O'Brien, Mark. 2017. *The Fourth Estate: Journalism in Twentieth-Century Ireland*. Manchester: Manchester University Press.

PAUL, Rev. "The Catholic Vigilance Association, its Aims and Results." The Torch, Catholic Truth Annual and Conference Record, Dublin, Catholic Truth Society, 54–63, 1919.

Rogan, Bjarne. "An Entangled Object: The Picture Postcard as Souvenir and Collectible, Exchange and Ritual Communication." *Cultural Analysis* 4, no. 1 (2005): 31–57.

Staff, Frank. *The Picture Postcard & Its Origins*. London: Lutterworth Press, 1966.

Wang, Victoria, John V. Tucker, and Kevin Haines. "Phatic Technologies in Modern Society." *Technology in Society* 34 (2012): 84–93.

Wilson, Ann. "Constructions of Irishness in a Collection of Early Twentieth-Century Picture Postcards." *The Canadian Journal of Irish Studies* 39, no. 1 (2015): 92–117.

Yeats, W.B. *Autobiographies*. London: Macmillan, 1966.

SCISSORS AND PASTE
Arthur Griffith's use of British and other media to circumvent censorship in Ireland 1914–15

Colum Kenny

This article examines how Arthur Griffith, arguably the most significant political journalist in Ireland during the first two decades of the twentieth century, tried to circumvent United Kingdom government censorship at the outset of World War I. It recalls that Griffith, 'father' or founder of Sinn Féin, edited and substantially wrote a succession of publications that frequently annoyed the authorities, which had already suppressed two of his titles. The author describes how, in an effort to tell stories that would otherwise be censored, Griffith twice weekly from late 1914 to early 1915 published a newspaper entitled Scissors and Paste in which he reproduced certain reports from other newspapers that were not banned, relying especially upon British titles. The author examines Griffith's selective methodology, identifies sources of news and their frequency of citation in Scissors and Paste and charts the fate of this test of press freedom during war.

Scissors and Paste is an example of how news agendas are set partly by the editorial selection of both particular stories and particular angles or aspects of those stories. Almost all of its news stories were written by journalists who had no relationship, even a distant one, with its editor. Many had first appeared in newspapers that espoused different editorial positions from that of the editor of *Scissors and Paste*.

Yet, by reprinting those stories in his paper for 'advanced' or radical nationalists, Arthur Griffith as editor provided a distinctive perspective on current events. A striking aspect of *Scissors and Paste* is that its editor relied centrally on reports published first in leading *British* newspapers, reprinting them without seeking permission from their editors. When Griffith republished these reports in Ireland, alongside stories from sources less well-known but also freely available from abroad, his Irish paper attracted the ire of the authorities. The latter closed *Scissors and Paste* and broke up the press on which it was printed.

Griffith was a prolific editor and journalist,[1] and *Scissors and Paste* was not Griffith's only paper to be suppressed. His first Irish title, the *United Irishman* (1899–1906) was periodically seized and threatened by officials. However, a successful defamation action by a Catholic priest finally closed it.[2] The authorities suppressed his next title. This was *Sinn Féin* (1906–1914), named after the political organisation that he founded.[3] For its part *Éire Ireland* lasted just a few months in 1914, closing upon the suppression of

James Larkin's and James Connolly's *Irish Worker* also.[4] Griffith protested that, to the best of his knowledge, *Éire Ireland* 'complied with British military orders' in respect to what journalists were free to write about during the war' that had begun that year. But machinery used to print the *Irish Worker* had been seized by the authorities and Mahon's, who printed Griffith *Éire Ireland*, were unwilling to run the risk of its printing press being likewise seized or smashed.[5]

Censorship in general in Ireland during World War I merits further study. Ó Drisceoil suggests that, although it was an irritant and an obstacle, radicals believed that censorship could ultimately be overcome.[6] Indeed Griffith barely paused to draw breath before he was back in print.

Scissors and Paste Launched

Eight days after the final issue of *Éire Ireland* appeared, the first issue of *Scissors and Paste* was on sale. Seán T. O'Kelly, a former colleague of Griffith and president of Ireland from 1945 to 1959, later recalled its foundation:

> After the cessation of *Sinn Féin*, *Éire*, the *Irish Volunteer* and the *Irish Worker* newspapers it looked as if we were not going to have any newspaper that could voice the opinions of the anti-British and the pro-Irish element in the country. I remember attending a meeting which was held, I think, in the Irish Freedom Office, No. 12 D'Olier Street, at which Tom Clarke, Seán MacDermott, Arthur Griffith and myself were present to discuss the situation about a newspaper. As a result of this discussion it was decided on the suggestion of Griffith that perhaps we could get away with the publication of a weekly paper which would not publish any editorial while it would be made up of news and statements extracted from British newspapers. Griffith thought he could arrange the news in such a way as would to some extent, at any rate, effectually expose British propaganda and would in reality give the public an idea of the anti-British viewpoint. He thought this was worthy of trial. It would be necessary, he said to put headings of his own to the news but he would try to do this in a way that, in the, beginning at any rate, would not too greatly anger the British so that we might be able to continue to publish the paper. We all agreed this was a very good idea and that it should be tried. The I.R.B. agreed to provide money for this experiment. Griffith hit on the name *Scissors and Paste* for this weekly journal.[7]

Scissors and Paste was printed by that very same printer who had felt constrained by fear to cease printing *Éire Ireland*. Mahon's was evidently persuaded that Griffith's decision to republish news reports already published in papers available in Ireland could not pose a threat to its own printing operation. And, indeed, a total of twenty-two issues of *Scissors and Paste* were published, on Wednesdays and Saturdays: the first on Saturday 12 December 1914 and the last on Saturday 27 February 1915. Each issue was four pages long and cost one halfpenny.

Within the pages of *Scissors and Paste* fifteen titles are identified more than five times each as the sources of its republished news reports. The three leading sources were English: the *Times*, the *Morning Post* and the *Daily Mail*, with 71, 56 and 51 citations respectively. These totals do not include a weekly feature entitled 'From the German wireless' that was largely constituted by further reports from the same three papers, filling between one and two columns of each issue.

The only other titles cited more than five times each were the *Daily News* (46), *New York American* (30), *Daily Chronicle* (20), *Evening Herald* (17), *Irish Times* (17), *Evening Mail* (16), *Labour Leader* (16), 'Daily Independent'—as Griffith in *Scissors and Paste* referred to the paper entitled since 1905 the *Irish Independent* (13), *Forward* (13), *Freeman's Journal* (11),[8] *Sunday Chronicle* (8) and *Daily Citizen* (6). A full list of the 82 sources used by Griffith for his news stories, showing how often they were cited, is appended below. Calculated by citation, it is evident that three leading English newspapers accounted for more than two-fifths of the news in *Scissors and Paste*. The fourth biggest source of stories was also English, the *Daily News*. Even a cursory inspection of *Scissors and Paste* shows that were one to calculate column inches rather than the incidence of citation as given here, the same British newspapers would still be dominant. All copies of *Scissors and Paste* (as well as Griffith's earlier *Éire Ireland*) are available to read online at the website of the South Dublin County Libraries.[9]

William Randolph Hearst's *New York American* lies in fifth place as a source. It provided a trans-Atlantic perspective on, for example, the question of American neutrality and the flying of national flags by passenger vessels. While there was in the stories taken by Griffith from the *New York American* no particular Irish angle, or sympathy for Irish nationalists, it is perhaps worth noting that fourteen years later during the first visit to America by a head of government of the Irish Free State William T. Cosgrave would say that, 'Ireland will never forget William Randolph Hearst, who has always been one of her best and truest friends.'[10]

For its part the *New York Times* features on just three occasions in *Scissors and Paste*. The pieces were 'An American war correspondent on the German army in France,' 'Atrocity mongering' and 'American war correspondent: replies to Conan Doyle.' Each was written by James O'Donnell Bennett (1870–1940), who worked mainly for the *Chicago Tribune* and became known as the 'dean of journalists' in that city. In 1914, he and some other US correspondents visited Belgium and there tracked the German army with its consent, later becoming embroiled in print in a dispute with Sir Arthur Conan Doyle about the extent of German war atrocities. The author of *Sherlock Holmes* had written for the *Daily Chronicle* in London that 'Prussia' was degrading the standard of modern warfare. O'Donnell Bennett would later write a memorable series on Chicago's gangland but also special pieces on the Eucharistic Congress in Chicago and on W.T. Cosgrave's American visit of 1928.[11] Later, after the USA entered World War I, the *New York Times* itself would be described in another of Griffith's papers as 'rabidly anti-Irish' and 'more anti-Irish than the London or the *Irish Times*.'[12]

In quite a few cases Griffith's sources themselves frankly relied on other media, print and broadcast, that I do not identify in the list. For example, on 27 January 1915 Griffith reproduced from the *Irish Times* (of the previous day) its report taken from the *Fatherland*, which the editor of the *Irish Times* described as a newspaper 'conducted by Germany's agents in New York.'[13] Headed 'Germany's friends', the report listed races and nations 'praying for the success of Germany.' It included 'Ireland … the Boers, the Jews … besides the great mass of the American people'. The 'Ireland' found in *Fatherland*'s list of friends was evidently not one represented in respect of its view on the war by most Irish members of parliament or by the editor of the *Irish Times*.

Relevant News for Advanced Nationalists

Arthur Griffith consolidated in one place for advanced Irish nationalists relevant news that had already been deemed fit to print. Where W.T. Stead's *Review of Reviews* described in general terms what had recently appeared in various journals, and the popular British *Tit Bits* was a random collection of secondary reports and miscellanea, *Scissors and Paste* almost entirely consisted of verbatim extracts from other papers. Griffith was, it may be said and not entirely facetiously, an early news aggregator. However, it should be added that it was quite common for newspapers generally then to base some of their reports substantially on reports read in foreign newspapers. Indeed, in the very first issue of his *United Irishman* Griffith had derided 'the proverbial scissors-and-paste policy of the *Irish Times*' in relying on reports reprinted from abroad to support its editorial line on foreign affairs.[14] More pointedly, for years the Irish Unionist Alliance had been reprinting reports from British and Irish publications, some nationalist, to bolster the editorial objective of its regular *Notes from Ireland*. During 1913, for example, these included extracts from the *Freeman's Journal*, *Daily Express*, *Northern Whig*, *Daily Citizen* and *Daily Herald* amongst other newspapers. Now Griffith turned the table politically and went the whole way as an aggregator when constrained from writing as he wished.

Some years after Griffith died his acquaintance and doctor Oliver St John Gogarty recollected that *Scissors and Paste* had been

> composed of extracts from the daily press but extracts so skillfully juxtaposed that the paper was almost as effective as that suppressed. I remember one item. It was an extract from an English paper printing the humane orders for the preservation of aigrets and underneath was a copy of the orders to machine gun thousands of Indians at Amritsar, known afterwards as the Amritsar massacre.[15]

Gogarty's memory was faulty, as the Amritsar or Jallianwahla Bagh massacre did not take place until April 1919, but his comment captured Griffith's methodology and that methodology ensured the paper's demise.

The full list of eighty-two titles from which Griffith pulled news pieces for *Scissors and Paste* included papers published as far afield as Belfast, Buenos Aires, San Francisco and Sydney. The breadth of his editorial interest impressed those who worked with him during his twenty years as an editor, as did his appetite for reading in general. The range of his sources suggests that he was not just one of the most productive journalists in Ireland but also one of the best-informed public figures in terms of international affairs.

Constraints of Censorship

Griffith at the outset cheekily highlighted the constraints of censorship. His very first number of *Scissors and Paste* contained a short editorial headed 'Ourselves,' this word being a translation of the Gaelic 'Sinn Féin.' In it Griffith wrote that

> It is high treason for an Irishman to argue with the sword the right of his small nationality [sic] to equal political freedom with Belgium, or Serbia, or Hungary. It is destruction to the property of his printer now when he argues with the pen. Hence while England is fighting the battle of Small Nationalities **Ireland** [the use here of bold typeface presumably a reference to the title of Griffith's preceding publication] is reduced to **Scissors and Paste**. Up to the present the sale and use of these instruments have not been prohibited by the British Government in Ireland.

This editorial incidentally demonstrates that it is not true to say that *Scissors and Paste* consisted *entirely* of reprinted material. However, apart from an original report on the Aonach Irish fair in this same issue, Griffith generally depended for news reports and analysis on pieces first printed by other titles. Some titles were Irish, including for example Dublin's *Daily Express* for a report that two leading Irish-American papers (the *Irish World* and the *Gaelic American*) were now prohibited in Ireland. Another story concerned the arrest of a Sinn Féin member with a large family (from the *Clonmel Nationalist*), another the seizure by police in Cork of copies of *Scissors and Paste* (from the '*Daily*' [*Irish*] *Independent*) and another some hissing at Dublin's Theatre Royal during a rendition of 'God Save the King' (from the *Evening Herald*).

Griffith surely found it ironic to have to quote reports from British newspapers on the suppression of an Irish publication such as the *Irish Worker*. On 2 January 1915 he quoted London's *Daily Citizen*: 'The *Irish Worker*, the organ of the Irish Transport Workers' Union [sic], which was suppressed three weeks ago, has reappeared, having been printed by the press of the Socialist Labour Party at Glasgow. Mr James Connolly is acting as editor in the absence of Mr J. Larkin in America.' A few weeks later, on 10 February, the London *Times* served as his source for this:

> On the arrival at the North Wall, Dublin, on Saturday afternoon, of a steamer from Glasgow, a police inspector and a number of constables went on board and seized some bundles of a weekly paper named the *Worker*. The *Worker*, which is printed in Glasgow, is believed to be a successor to the *Irish Worker*, one whole issue of which was seized some time ago by the military authorities, under the Defence of the Realm Act.[16]

The next issue of *Scissors and Paste* carried another London *Times* report, on the secret seizure of Irish-American papers shipped to Europe.

Indeed, not even the London *Times* itself was free from interference, as highlighted by Griffith on 13 February 1915 when he reprinted a report by it that dispatches of its Washington correspondent were reaching London 'with sentences cut in half and rendered unintelligible' by the English Press Bureau.[17] It was one of a number of pieces he reproduced referencing wartime censorship of English newspapers. Just how extensive was the British government's effective control of media there and beyond, including in respect to Reuters, has been debated.[18] David Monger argues that 'recent interpretations show that the [British] press could act with considerable autonomy despite censorship' during World War I.[19]

Griffith took full advantage of any latitude by reprinting British press pieces least pleasing to the government. For example, he highlighted the plight of Jews in Russia, one of England's allies.[20] These reports in *Scissors and Paste* may be contrasted with unpleasant pieces published by Griffith earlier in his editorial career that were hostile to Jews who supported English policy or who engaged in moneylending. The pieces about Russia reflected a maturing perspective on Jews, whose aspiration for a Zionist homeland he supported, but they were also a means of embarrassing the English. Some of Griffith's critics have overlooked both these and his other articles favourable to Jews, as I have discussed elsewhere.[21] Also overlooked until recently was his support for the election of the Jewish Albert Altman to Dublin Corporation in 1903.[22] Scapegoating Griffith for Irish anti-Semitism involves ignoring both the full content and broader context of what he published.[23]

Mutt and Jeff

Griffith sometimes used ridicule to embarrass England, quoting for example the text of an early 'Mutt and Jeff' cartoon that was syndicated throughout the United States. This text suggested that Germany was prepared to fight to the last German—while England was merely ready to fight to the last Frenchman.[24]

The very 'Mutt and Jeff' routine that Griffith reprinted was highlighted in a 1972 study of newspapers and US neutrality as a prime example of the way in which unfavourable press commentary on the British war effort had developed in the United States by the winter of 1914–15. One particular source of tension between London and Washington was disagreement about the use of a freighter named the *Dacia*, and Griffith ensured that his readers were kept informed of its fate.[25]

Scissors and Paste published no pictures. But the reports that it reprinted referred to alarming aspects of the new warfare of 1914 to 1918, including to submarines in the Irish Sea and aerial attacks on England, as well as to the British bombardment of towns such as Freiburg which was 'not situated within the range of operations' according to German official sources quoted in a London *Daily Mail* report that Griffith promptly reproduced. Also of continuing interest today are reports repeated in *Scissors and Paste* concerning the *Lusitania* both flying the US flag and being listed as a Royal Navy reserve merchant vessel. On 24 February 1915, Griffith reprinted a London *Morning Post* report that Sir Edward Grey had stoutly denied that the United Kingdom intended to sink a US ship and blame the Germans. It did not have to. On 7 May that year a U-boat sank the *Lusitania*, and there is still a debate about that vessel's function and behaviour at the time.

Griffith scored points by selecting news from British sources that could be read as reflecting poorly on England. He used pieces from Hearst's *New York American* and elsewhere to underline differences between the neutral USA and a belligerent Britain. He also quoted old items from the *Freeman's Journal* against that paper, highlighting ostensibly contradictory or embarrassing positions taken by it on national issues down the years.[26] He had a long-standing antipathy to it.[27]

Literary and Historical Items

The editor of *Scissors and Paste* also supplemented its news reports with items extracted from literary and historical works, all deployed by Griffith without further comment to make a relevant point about contemporary circumstances. Thus, in the very first issue Griffith republished part of a fine speech that in 1797 the Irish lawyer John Philpot Curran had made when defending Peter Finnerty, printer of the radical *Press* newspaper. Finnerty was jailed then and again in 1811 for criminal libel of the powerful. Percy Bysshe Shelley is believed to have been in 1810–11 the anonymous author of a poem supporting Finnerty that until 2006 was thought to have been lost.[28] Irish authors subsequently quoted included Jonathan Swift, Henry Grattan, Edmund Burke, Thomas Davis, Samuel Ferguson, the Marquis of Dufferin and George Bernard Shaw. Verses that he published included translations of European poets by 'Fr Prout' (Rev. Francis O'Mahony) and James Clarence Mangan.

Griffith published too the views of British, American and other foreign writers where these coincided with his own, especially on the English or on England and the war. Writers cited included H.G. Wells, Peter Kropotkin, John Stuart Mill, Sir Henry Jones, Rev. A.C. Hill, Cardinal Mercier of Belgium and Homer Lea, an American soldier of fortune and author. From Victor Hugo's *The Man who Laughs*, a book that includes some phrases in Irish, Griffith extracted a reference to one Barkilphedro who was 'an Irishman who had denied Ireland— a bad species,' according to Hugo.

Advertising

There was one part of *Scissors and Paste* that was original. This consisted of a small but steady stream of advertising on the back page, some of it pointedly political and no doubt a further irritant to Dublin Castle.

Scissors and Paste was published at 67 Middle Abbey St., two doors up from where my grandfather had his advertising agency. But while Kevin Kenny had helped Griffith by managing the business side of Sinn Féin's *Leabhar na hÉireann: The Irish Year Book* in both 1910 and 1911,[29] I have been unable to determine if he sought any advertisements for Griffith's *Scissors and Paste*.

Five businesses advertised in every edition of *Scissors and Paste*. These were (in descending order of space purchased) Whelan's shop at 17 Ormond Quay, Lawler's of Fownes Street (inviting readers to purchase rifles, bayonets, Volunteer whistles and blankets, etc.), Corrigan the undertaker and Philip Meagher 'tea and wine merchant' (equal space purchased), and Cahill's cod-liver oil.

Gleeson's 'tailors and drapers' placed the only double-column advertisement, each week from the third issue onwards. Dolphin Pharmacy persisted for the first twelve weeks. Lucania bicycles of Maynooth, the business of a future governor-general Domhnall Ó Buachalla, advertised most weeks. The outfitters T.J. Loughlin's, under its slogan 'practical patriotism,' also supported *Scissors and Paste*. However, when it came to paying for space, the bounds of Loughlin's practical patriotism went no further than week seven. The only other commercial advertisers in *Scissors and Paste* were the Irish Book Company, Dublin; Felix McGlennon, London, for *The marching songs of the Irish volunteers*; 'Xmas cards' by Seaghan Ua Peatain at Muinntear na laimhe deirge, Belfast; 'Artistic Christmas cards' by Sinéad Nic Annsaoi, Blackrock, Co. Dublin.

Whelan's, the biggest advertiser, boasted a wide range of goods from jewellery, pipes and cutlery to GAA outfits and books. The books included a new edition of Michael Doheny's *The Felon's Track* to which Griffith had contributed a foreword. Whelan's advertising was decorated by the only illustration ever to appear in *Scissors and Paste*. This consisted, (from week 7 to week 21) of a drawing of a baby and ball under the slogan 'You score for Ireland a nation every time you buy from Whelan & Son'.

A very small number of personal notices appeared in *Scissors and Paste*—for rooms to let, thanksgiving to the Little Flower of Jesus, a male teacher of Irish sought, a house wanted, a couple of deaths (Tomás MacConglinne and Una Ní Dhúbhlaoich) and two 'in memoriam' (Séamus Ó Cionnaith of Bray, 1890, and Edward Hugh Cassidy). However, *Scissors and Paste* also carried notices for concerts, fairs and meetings of some interest to the authorities. In the first issue the 'Aonach' fair was promoted as 'the place to defend Ireland'. Held at the Abbey Theatre it boasted forty Irish exhibits. Small notices were placed by local companies of the Irish Volunteers, Cumann na mBan, Óglaigh na hÉireann, Connradh na Gaedhilge (sic), Sinn Féin and the Irish Citizen Army. The Independent Labour Party of Ireland advertised a lecture series including one by R.S.T. Saye, described as 'the well-known Indian Nationalist:' readers were advised that 'If you wish to know what British misgovernment has done for India, come.' Its other lectures were by Miss M.E. Duggan ('Legal Reforms from the Feminine and Labour Standpoint'), Francis Sheehy-Skeffington ('Three Phases of War'), Walter Carpenter ('The War that Matters') and Countess de [sic] Markievicz, ('Russia As It Is'—'being her personal experiences in that country during a long sojourn there'). All were in the Trades Hall (later the Torch Theatre) in Capel Street, Dublin.

Rifle, Revolver and Suppression

Quite strikingly, a Cumann na mBan raffle for a Lee-Enfield rifle was advertised,[30] while Company E of the Irish Volunteers informed readers that its planned raffle of a revolver was postponed.[31]

The *Spark*, a small but lively nationalist publication, was advertised too. Griffith himself is said to have written for the *Spark*, which in February 1915 conducted a poll of its readers based on the question, 'Who is the Irish nationalist whom Dublin wishes most to honour?' Griffith reportedly headed that poll, such as it was, followed by Eoin MacNeill and then Alderman Tom Kelly of Sinn Féin. By the time that the result was announced in March, *Scissors and Paste* had been suppressed: 'The name of Arthur Griffith has been chosen by a majority of readers of the *Spark* .... What Ireland owes to Griffith, to his patriotism, to his self-sacrifice, and to his ability and earnestness will one day be told. The man's modesty prevents it being known to his contemporaries.'[32]

The third from last issue of *Scissors and Paste* (20 Feb. 1915) carried two small but distinctive notices. The first was for a meeting to be held outside Mountjoy Prison to protest against the imprisonment of one 'Mr Bannister, Secretary of the Irish Anti-Vaccination League.' It advised that, 'Every conscientious objector should attend.' The second notice advertised a forthcoming 'picture show and demonstration' at Croydon Park, a property in the Marino district of Dublin used by the Irish Transport and General Workers' Union for recreational purposes and for drilling by the Irish Citizen Army. The planned event included the presentation to Countess Markieviecz of a 'splendidly-illuminated address from the Committee of the above Union in recognition of her services during the great Lock-out' in Dublin two years earlier. At a time of war, such advertisements no doubt irked some in power.

The last four issues of *Scissors and Paste* carried a notice from the Wolfe Tone Memorial Committee promoting a Robert Emmet Anniversary Celebration in the Rotunda, on 4 March 1915. It noted that, 'The commemoration address will be delivered by Mr. Arthur Griffith.' The manager of this event, J.T. Jameson, was an early newsreel cameraman and exhibitor whose Irish Animated Picture Company is said to have operated three of the nine cinemas in Dublin in 1913. That year too he filmed Patrick Pearse addressing a Wolfe Tone Commemoration at Bodenstown, his well-known newsreel of Pearse being repeatedly screened in Dublin—'to tremendous applause' as Thomas Clarke wrote.[33] From such advertisements alone it is evident that *Scissors and Paste* was not simply a collection of random press cuttings. It had a clear editorial slant.

The final issue of *Scissors and Paste* appeared on 27 February 1915. It included an item from Dublin's *Evening Herald* headed, 'The Bombardment of the Dardanelles.' This reported the opening shots in what was to become a disastrous assault during which, over the coming months, very many members of Irish families died at Gallipoli, among them one of my grand-uncles, Jack Murphy of Tralee. Messages from his group at Sulva Bay appealed urgently for reinforcements. Murphy added, 'The wire must be cut ... firing is very near'.[34] At Gallipoli and elsewhere on the front line people soon learned the harsh realities of modern warfare. It was a time for critical journalism, but the government that was about to send so many soldiers to their deaths in the Dardanelles ensured that Arthur Griffith could not make points about the war by recycling second-hand stories in his latest paper.

The authorities suppressed *Scissors and Paste*, as they also closed around that time some other pesky titles of what was occasionally termed 'the mosquito press' in Ireland.[35] Entering Mahon's printing works the police dismantled machinery employed to produce Scissors and Paste, doing so in such a manner as to prevent the machinery's further use.[36] This was but one of the ways in which attempts were made to manipulate Irish public opinion during World War I.[37] Seán T. O'Kelly was there during the police raid:

> It happened that I was the only person present when they called. The Inspector read out for me a proclamation issued by order of, I think, the Chief Secretary, suppressing the newspaper *Scissors and Paste*. I remember trying to start an argument with Inspector Campbell as to the reason for the suppression. I pointed out to him the fact that there were no editorial views of any kind expressed in the paper, therefore it could not be said that editorially we were hostile to the British. I pointed out also the fact that all the news published in our paper had already been published in some newspaper or weekly journal in Great Britain, but of course all this had no effect. Campbell was very good-humoured. He said he was just an official carrying out his orders and that I could disobey the order at my own risk. That was the end of *Scissors and. Paste*.[38]

On 10 March Laurence Ginnell MP raised at Westminster the use of the Defence of the Realm Act in respect to suppressing Irish newspapers. Under-Secretary of State for War Harold Tennant MP thereupon described *Scissors and Paste* as 'a sheet consisting of cuttings from papers selected for their derogatory references to the cause or military operations of the Allies and for their praise of the methods and successes of the enemy.' He noted that, 'All the copies of the paper, as well as the printing plant, were seized on the 2nd instant.'[39]

Indefatigable, Arthur Griffith would be back in print in June 1915, with the first number of his next title, *Nationality*.[40] *Nationality* continued to appear even when he was later interned in Britain following the rebellion in Dublin in 1916. During that time, when Griffith was imprisoned, the acting editor of *Nationality* back in Ireland recalled that

> Mr Arthur Griffith used to say that England had surrounded Ireland with a paper wall. On the inside of the wall the British Government wrote whatever it wished Ireland to believe about the outside world. On the outside of the wall it wrote whatever it wished the outside world to believe about Ireland. It was possible for the British government to do this because of its control of the Press and the great Press Agencies.[41]

But Griffith's internment then (and again later on the pretext that he and others had plotted with Germany), and his election first in 1918 as a member of parliament and subsequently in 1922 as president of the Irish Dáil (rebel assembly) that had endorsed the Anglo-Irish Treaty and was planning the creation of the new Irish Free State,—as well as his tragic death a few months later,—were events that lay in the future when *Scissors and Paste* was suppressed.

Disclosure Statement

No potential conflict of interest was reported by the author.

Notes

1. Kenny, "'An Extraordinarily Clever Journalist'."
2. *United Irishman*, 17 March 1906; *Freeman's Journal*, 12 Mar. 1906; *Irish Times*, 12 Mar. & 22 Feb. 1906 (includes offending text), 13 and 20 July 1907; *Sunday Independent*, 11 Mar. 1906; Lyons, *Recollections*, 69.
3. Meehan, "The Prose of Logic and of Scorn'."
4. Newsinger, "'A Lamp to Guide Your Feet'," 90; Curry, "*The Worker*," 75.
5. Griffith and Seaghan T. O'Ceallaig to readers of *Éire Ireland* 1914. Printed letter. A copy at the end of the microfilm run of *Éire Ireland* in the National Library of Ireland.
6. Ó Drisceoil, "Keeping Disloyalty within Bounds?"; Pennell, "Presenting the War in Ireland"; There is a file of confidential official censorship orders of 1915–1918 among Kevin J Kenny's papers in the DCU Media Archive (Kenny, *Irish Patriot, Publisher and Advertising Agent*, 106).
7. Seán T. O'Kelly Witness Statement (Bureau of Military History WS1,765, part 2 [1951–2]).
8. This total is for news stories. It excludes items quoting only the nineteenth-century *Freeman's Journal*.
9. http://source.southdublinlibraries.ie/handle/10599/11384/browse?type=title.
10. *Chicago Herald and Examiner*, 23 Jan.1928.
11. *Scissors and Paste*, 3 and 6 Feb. 1915; *New York Times* 7, 11 and 17 Sept. 1914, 17 and 24 Jan. 1915—and on 6 Feb. 1915 a riposte by Conan Doyle that Griffith did not republish (https://www.arthur-conan-doyle.com/index.php?title=Germany%27s_Policy_of_Murder); Klekowski, *Americans in Occupied Belgium*, 61–6; Kenny, *Irish-American Odyssey*, 193–5.'
12. *Nationality*, 8 June 1918.

13. Keller, *States of Belonging*, 141–8.
14. *United Irishman*, 1 April 1899.
15. Gogarty, 'A talk on Arthur Griffith' (undated), W.T. Cosgrave Papers 285/345, Royal Irish Academy.
16. For this title see Curry, "*The Worker.*"
17. For this body see Cook, *The Press in War-Time.*
18. For references see Putnis and McCallum, "Reuters, Propaganda-inspired News."
19. Monger, "Press/Journalism."
20. *Scissors and Paste*, 23 and 27 Jan. and 20 Feb. 1915.
21. Kenny, "Arthur Griffith."
22. Davison and Altman O'Connor, "'Altman the Saltman'."
23. Kenny, "Sinn Féin, Socialists and 'McSheenys'."
24. *New York American*, 8 Dec. 1914; *Scissors and Paste*, 13 Jan. 1915 citing the *San Francisco Examiner*.
25. O'Keeffe, *A Thousand Deadlines*, 52; *Scissors and Paste*, 13 and 16 and 27 Jan. 1915, 3 Feb. 1915.
26. See *Scissors and Paste* nos 4 (re Parnell), 16 (re Fitzgerald, Grattan, Tone, Stephens, O'Leary, Kickham, Parnell), 18 (re Parnell) and 20 (re Parnell). These items are separate from the eleven where Griffith used the *Freeman's Journal* as a source of news reporting or analysis.
27. Larkin, "Arthur Griffith and the *Freeman's Journal.*"
28. Curran, *Life of John Philpot Curran*, i, 362–2.
29. Kenny, *Irish Patriot, Publisher and Advertising Agent*, 22–4, 30.
30. *Scissors and Paste*, 30 Dec. 1914, 9 Jan. and 17 Feb. 1915.
31. *Scissors and Paste*, 9 and 13 Jan. 1915.
32. The *Spark*, 7 March 1915, cited at Maye, *Arthur Griffith*, 63,
33. Kelly, *The Fenian Ideal*, 223; Rockett et al., *Cinema and Ireland*, 33.
34. Kenny Papers (DCU Media Archive); Kenny, *Irish Patriot, Publisher and Advertising Agent*, 26.
35. Maume, *The Long Gestation*, 156.
36. *Irish Times*, 3 & 6 March 1915; *Freeman's Journal*, 3 March 1915.
37. O'Brien, "'With the Irish in France'."
38. cf. note 7 above; *Freeman's Journal*, 3 March 1915.
39. *HC Deb.*, 10 March 1915, vol 70 cc1423-4.
40. In 1952 O'Kelly recalled that, ' ... some weeks expired before we had another newspaper and then, again provided with money by the I.R.B, we started *Nationality*. We could not get a printer in Dublin to take the risk of publishing such a paper so we went to Belfast and there we [employed] a man named Davidson who had a good sized printing establishment with suitable printing machinery which could turn out our paper weekly—as many copies as we wanted. I explained to him what we wanted and he was prepared to do the job at a price. We paid him his price which was not very much in excess of the printing rates in Dublin at that time. Davidson was well-known to the police authorities. Re was a loyal Orangeman, one hundred percent pro-British, but as the newspaper was, for him a profitable business he took his chance and continued loyally printing the paper for us up to, as far as I remember, the Rising of 1916 when, of course, the paper ceased publication. We had, however great difficulty from time to time in sending our copy for the paper to

Belfast' (See n.7 above; *Irish Press*, 10 July 1961, for O'Kelly writing that Griffith only agreed to take I.R.B. money 'provided he were given a free hand').

41. *Nationality*, 8 June 1918.

Bibliography

Cook, E. *The Press in War-time, with Some Account of the Official Press Bureau*. London: Macmillan, 1920.

Curran, W. H. *The Life of John Philpot Curran, Late Master of the Rolls in Ireland*. 2 vols. London: Constable, 1819.

Curry, J. "*The Worker*: James Connolly's 'Organ of the Working Class'." In O'Brien and Larkin, 75–88.

Davison, N., V. Altman O'Connor, and Y. Altman O'Connor. "'Altman the Saltman" and Joyce's Dublin: New Research on Irish-Jewish Influences in Ulysses." *Dublin James Joyce Journal* 6/7 (2013–2014): 44–72.

Keller, P. 1979. *States of Belonging: German-American Intellectuals and the First World War*. Cambridge, MA, USA: Harvard University Press.

Kelly, M. J. *The Fenian Ideal and Irish Nationalism 1882–1916*. Suffolk: Boydell & Brewer, 2006.

Kenny, C. "'An Extraordinarily Clever Journalist': Arthur Griffith's Editorships, 1899–1919." In O'Brien and Larkin, 16–20.

Kenny, C. 2011. *Irish Patriot, Publisher and Advertising Agent: Kevin J. Kenny (1881–1954)*. Bray: Bray, Co. Wicklow: Ox.

Kenny, C. *An Irish-American Odyssey: The Remarkable Rise of the O'Shaughnessy Brothers*. Columbia, MO: University of Missouri Press, 2014.

Kenny, C. "Arthur Griffith: More Zionist than Anti-Semite." *History Ireland* 24, no. 3 (2016): 38–41.

Kenny, C. "Sinn Féin, Socialists and 'McSheenys': Representations of Jews in early Twentieth-century Ireland." *Journal of Modern Jewish Studies* 16, no. 2 (2017): 198–218.

Klekowski, E., and L. Klekowski. *Americans in Occupied Belgium, 1914–1918: Accounts of the War from Journalists, Tourists, Troops and Medical Staff*. Jefferson, NC: McFarland, 2014.

Larkin, F. "Arthur Griffith and the *Freeman's Journal*." In Rafter, 174–185.

Lyons, G. *Some Recollections of Griffith and His Times*. Dublin: Talbot Press, 1923.

Maume, P. *The Long Gestation: Irish Nationalist Life 1891–1918*. Dublin: Gill and Macmillan, 1999.

Maye, B. *Arthur Griffith*. Dublin: Griffith College Publications, 1997.

McGee, O. *Arthur Griffith*. Sallins, Co. Kildare: Merrion Press, 2015.

Meehan, C. "'The Prose of Logic and of Scorn': Arthur Griffith and *Sinn Féin*, 1906–1914." In Rafter, 186–199.

Monger, D. "Press/Journalism (Great Britain and Ireland)." In *1914–1918-Online: International Encyclopedia of the First World War*, edited by U. Daniel, et al., Berlin: Freie Universität Berlin, 2014.

Newsinger, J. "'A Lamp to Guide Your Feet': Jim Larkin, the *Irish Worker* and the Dublin Working Class." *European History Quarterly*, 20 (1990): 63–99.

O'Brien, M., and F. Larkin, eds. *Periodicals and Journalism in Twentieth-century Ireland: Writing Against the Grain*. Dublin: Four Courts Press, 2014.

O'Brien, M. "'With the Irish in France:' The National Press and Recruitment in Ireland 1914–1916." *Media History* 22, no. 2: 159–173.

Ó Drisceoil, D. "Keeping Disloyalty within Bounds? British Media Control in Ireland, 1914–19." *Irish Historical Studies* 38 (2012): 52–69.

O'Keeffe, K. *A Thousand Deadlines: The New York City Press and American Neutrality, 1914–17*. The Hague: Springer, 1972.

Pennell, C. "Presenting the War in Ireland, 1914–1918." In *World War I and Propaganda*, edited by T. Paddock, 42–64. Leiden: Brill, 2014.

Putnis, P., and K. McCallum. "Reuters, Propaganda-inspired News and the Australian Press During the First World War." *Media History* 19, no. 3: 284–304.

Rafter, K., ed. *Irish Journalism before Independence: More a Disease than a Profession*. Manchester: Manchester University Press, 2011.

Rockett, K., L. Gibbons, and J. Hill. *Cinema and Ireland*. New York: Syracuse University Press, 1988.

Appendix 1. Table of Sources in *Scissors and Paste*

	All sources (and their incidence) of news items and news analysis	
BM	*Benziger's Magazine* (NY)	1
BN	*Belfast Newsletter*	1
CaB	*Catholic Bulletin*	3
CaP	*Catholic Press* (Sydney)	3
CaT	*Catholic Times*	3
CL	*Clarion* (Manchester)	1
CNa	*Clonmel Nationalist*	1
CNe	*Central News* (agency)	1
CoT	*Connacht Tribune*	1
CSM	*Christian Science Monitor*	2
DCi	*Daily Citizen* (London)	6
DCr	*Daily Chronicle* (London)	20
DDE	*Daily Express* (Dublin)	1
DE	*Daily Express* (London)	4
DI	*'Daily' [Irish] Independent*	13
DM	*Daily Mail* (London)	51*
DN	*Daily News* (London)	46
DT	*Daily Telegraph* (London)	3
EE	*Enniscorthy Echo*	2
EH	*Evening Herald* (Dublin)	17
EM	*Evening Mail* (Dublin)	16
EN	*Evening News* (London)	1
ES	*Evening Standard* (London)	1
ET	*Evening Telegraph* (Dublin)	3

(Continued)

Appendix 1. (*Continued*)

	All sources (and their incidence) of news items and news analysis	
Extel	Exchange Telegraph (agency)	1
F	*Forward* (Glasgow)	13
FJ	*Freeman's Journal* (Dublin)	11
GCA	*Guy's Cork Almanac*	1
GL	*Globe* (London)	2
GR	*Grocer* (British)	1
GT	*Great Thoughts* (British)	1
H	Hansard (parliamentary debates)	2
I	The *Ironmonger* (London)	1
IJ	*Irish Journalist*	1
II	*Irish Independent.* See at DI above.	
IMS	*Irish Messenger of the Sacred Heart* 1	
IN	*Irish News*	1
InC	*Indiana Catholic*	1
IoC	*Interocean Catholic* (Utah)	2
IT	*Irish Times*	17
IV	*Irish Volunteer*	2
JB	*John Bull* (British)	2
L'É	*L'Éclair* (Le Midi, France)	1
LL	*Labour Leader* (British)	16
LW	'London World'	1
M	The *Month* (Jesuits, British)	3
MCr	*Meath Chronicle*	2
MCy	*Motor Cycling* (London)	1
MG	*Manchester Guardian*	2
MN	*Mayo News*	1
MP	*Morning Post* (London)	56*
MRec	*Missionary Record* (Oblates)	1
MRep	*Midland Reporter* (Irish)	2
MT	*Midland Tribune* (Irish)	1
NAG	The *New Age* (British)	1
NAT	*Nation* (London)	1
NW	*Northern Whig* (Belfast)	1
NYA	*New York American*	30
NYF	*New York Freeman's Journal*	1
NYS	*New Yorker Staats-Zeitung*	1
NYTi	*New York Times*	3
NYTr	*New York Tribune*	2
PA	Press Association	1
PB	Press Bureau	1
R	*Rifleshot*	3
Reut.	Reuters (agency)	1
S	*Star* (London)	1
SB	*Sydney Bulletin*	5
SC1	*Southern Cross* (Buenos Aires)	1
SC2	*Southern Cross* (Adelaide)	2
SCh	*Sunday Chronicle* (Manchester)	8
SDT	*Sydney Daily Telegraph*	1
SFD	*San Francisco Daily News*	1
SFE	*San Francisco Examiner*	2
SFL	*San Francisco Leader*	1

(*Continued*)

Appendix 1. (*Continued*)

	All sources (and their incidence) of news items and news analysis	
SHJ	*Seraphic Home Journal* (USA Capuchin Order)	1
SJS	*Saint Joseph's Sheaf* (Dublin)	1
STi	*Sunday Times* (Sydney)	1
T	*Times* (London)	71*
TB	*Tit-Bits* (British)	1
TP's	*TP* [O'Connor]'s *Weekly* (London)	3
TS	*Tipperary Star*	1
WD	*Weekly Dispatch* (London)	1
ws	without source (snippets)	5

*Not including other reports from DM and T in issue 2, and DM, MP and T in each of issues 3–22, cited in 'From the German wireless' feature filling up to two columns on page 3.
(Literary and historical sources of the non-news items are not listed here).

FIGHTING AND WRITING
Journalists and the 1916 Easter Rising

Mark O'Brien

The relationship between journalists and the Irish rebellion of Easter 1916 is a complex one. While the Rising was led in large part by a miscellany of poets, editors and journalists (many of whom feature prominently in the Rising's historiography) many lesser-known journalists acted as planners and participants in the insurrection. As well as assessing the contribution of these lesser-known journalists to the events of 1916 and the Rising's impact on journalistic life in Dublin, it explores how a representative organisation—the Irish Journalists' Association—acted as a cover for the clandestine insurgent-related activities of many journalists. It finds that the IJA played a key role in facilitating the expression of radical views by this cohort of journalists who could not express their radicalism through their everyday posts on the mainstream media and, by so doing, it played a key, though hitherto unacknowledged, role in the events of Easter 1916.

Introduction

The historiography of the 1916 Rising is well established and, amid its centenary, ongoing.[1] Home rule for Ireland was enshrined in the Government of Ireland Act 1914 but was shelved following the outbreak of the First World War—a decision that averted a clash between the Ulster Volunteer Force, formed to prevent home rule being implemented, and the Irish Volunteers which had been established to ensure the realisation of a Dublin parliament. The reaction of both organisations to the war would reverberate through Irish history for decades afterwards. While the Ulster Volunteer Force enthusiastically viewed the conflict as an opportunity to demonstrate its fidelity to the British Crown, the call by Irish Parliamentary Party leader John Redmond for all Irish Volunteers to enlist in the British Army and fight for the freedom of small nations split the organisation. While the majority supported Redmond and established themselves as the National Volunteers, a sizeable minority rejected his call. And, while Redmond's fortunes became tied to a seemingly never-ending war effort, the fortunes of those who opposed enlistment became manifest in the age-old dictum that Britain's difficulty was Ireland's opportunity. On Easter Monday 1916 a number of groups—including the Irish Republican Brotherhood (a secret oath-bound organisation dedicated to the establishment of an Irish republic), the Irish Volunteers and the Irish Citizen Army—seised several buildings in Dublin's city centre and declared an Irish Republic.[2] After a week of intense fighting, during which the city centre was shelled by a British gunboat, the insurgents surrendered.

While much has been written about how the leaders of the Rising, such as James Connolly and Padraig Pearse, plied their trade as editors of and contributors to newspapers associated with the trade union and revolutionary movements many other journalistic supporters of the independence movement worked in what might be termed the mainstream press and it is the activities of this cohort of journalists that this article examines.[3] Unable, given their posts in mainstream newspapers such as the *Freeman's Journal* and the *Irish Independent*, to give voice to their political radicalism in print, these journalists instead expressed their radicalism through their activities within the Irish Journalists' Association. As a representative association it gave a veneer of respectability to their clandestine activities—activities that have, until now, remained unexamined within the historiography of the Rising. Most likely, this omission in the journalist historiography is a result of a perceived lack of sources relating to these individuals. Indeed, beyond the works of Darrell Figgis, Desmond Ryan and Desmond FitzGerald there is very little in terms of memoir on the part of journalists who took part in the Rising.[4]

There are, however, other sources now available that shed light on the activities of these lesser-known journalist-insurgents. Many were members of a little known and long forgotten organisation, the Irish Journalist's Association (IJA), and while its records were destroyed in the Rising, some fragmented documents remain. The IJA published a monthly journal—*The Irish Journalist*—most copies of which were lodged with the National Library of Ireland. In addition, newspaper reports of its meetings frequently list the IJA's membership: this in turn allows for the press obituaries of its prominent members to be located.[5] Some of the journalist-insurgents made witness statements to the Bureau of Military History which was established in 1947 to collect and preserve the oral testimony of those who took part in the Rising.[6] But perhaps most useful of all there are digital newspaper archives that allow researchers to search for memoir-type articles written by these journalists. Indeed, in his correspondence with the Bureau of Military History, one such journalist, Piaras Béaslaí, informed the Bureau that all he had to say about his involvement in the Rising could be found in the various series of memoir-type articles he wrote for the *Irish Independent* between 1953 and 1957.[7] While the dependence on newspaper articles may not be ideal from a historian's point of view, when they are added to other sources they can play an important role in shedding light on areas of historical inquiry. They are, in fact, an oft-neglected piece of the wider historiographical jigsaw and as digital newspaper archives become more prevalent and their search functionality become more refined, there are, as Bingham has observed, 'few who deny the value of newspaper content for understanding politics, culture and society'.[8]

Journalistic Life in Dublin Pre-1916

The political positioning of the mainstream press in Ireland in the period under consideration has been well ventilated. While the *Freeman's Journal* was linked closely with John Redmond's Irish Parliamentary Party and the *Irish Independent* supported constitutional nationalism and home rule, both the *Irish Times* and the *Daily Express* were strongly opposed to home rule.[9] The idea of individual journalists expressing an opinion, in print, contrary to their paper's position on any given issue was simply not possible. As recalled by prominent Fenian, John Devoy, it was, at this time, 'one of the anomalies of daily journalism in every country (including America) that the editorials are largely written by men who don't agree with the policy of the paper, but write to order'.[10] Whatever about politics, poor employment conditions and poor pay among journalists in Britain and Ireland prompted journalists to organise. In Britain the Institute of Journalists, the membership of which included newspaper proprietors, was established in 1884. This was followed in 1907 by the National Union of Journalists (NUJ) which sought to represent the interests of rank and file journalists. While the NUJ sought to establish a foothold in Ireland it was quickly displaced by the establishment of the Irish Journalists' Association (IJA) in 1909. Membership of the IJA was confined to those whose 'income was, and for three years, derived from journalism as a main source of livelihood' and it specifically excluded newspaper managers, directors or proprietors.[11] Representing almost exclusively journalists in Dublin, by 1911 it had recruited 106 members.[12] In October 1914 it launched a monthly publication, *The Irish Journalist*, within which members debated frankly such issues as the professional standing of journalists, employment conditions, pay rates, the lack of opportunities for female journalists, the practice of senior journalists rewriting reporters' copy for London titles without sharing the fees received, and the issue of whether the organisation should be a trade union or an independent representative body separate from the wider trade union movement. The prospect of home rule and what this would mean for journalists also loomed large. The first edition of the *Irish Journalist* observed that home rule would mean 'much in the way of progress and prosperity in every direction for our neglected and impoverished country' and expressed the hope that the arrangements for reporting debates in the new parliament would be given careful consideration.[13] Such was the importance placed on this issue by the IJA that a deputation from the organisation met with Irish Parliamentary Party leader John Redmond to discuss the issue before the First World War broke out. Indeed, as late as July 1916, despite the unsuccessful post-Rising negotiations between Redmond and the British Prime Minister David Lloyd George about the immediate implementation of home rule, the IJA still envisaged a Dublin parliament that would require detailed planning in terms of 'the scale of pay, the size of staffs, the duration of labour demanded, details such as the holding of "boxes" in the Houses and of "gallery" tickets by journalists [and] the amount of copy to be esteemed a fair day's or night's work in Parliament'.[14]

But despite the IJA's enthusiasm for home rule, many of its members were also members of organisations that initiated the 1916 Rising and the IJA would act as an organising mechanism for these journalists to express their radicalism by utilising the respectability of the IJA to help organise the Rising. Indeed, some of the planning for the Rising took place at the IJA's headquarters, located at 65 Middle Abbey Street, which was in close proximity to the central site of the Rising, the General Post Office on Dublin's O'Connell Street. Both buildings—the GPO and the IJA's headquarters—were occupied by the rebels during the Rising and both buildings were shelled and destroyed by the British gunboat *The Helga*. Among those who combined membership of the IJA with membership of the revolutionary movements that instigated the Rising were Piaras Béaslaí of the *Freeman's Journal*, who along with being secretary of the IJA was a prominent member of the Irish Republican Brotherhood (IRB) and the Irish Volunteers; David Boyd of the *Evening Mail*, who was a member of the IRB and the Irish Volunteers and who took part in the importation of arms at Howth (Dublin) in July 1914; Seán Lester of the *Daily Express* who, along with sitting on the IJA's executive committee, was a member of the IRB and the Irish Volunteers; William O'Leary Curtis, who combined his sub-editorial duties at the *Irish Independent* with his IRB activities; Joseph Harrington and Michael Knighly of the *Irish Independent*, both of whom were members of the Irish Volunteers; and Larry de Lacy, IRB member and editor of *The Irish Volunteer*, who, in 1915, fled from Dublin to New York to avoid an arrest warrant issued under the Defence of the Realm Act.[15] Other IJA members—such as Thomas F. O'Sullivan of the *Freeman's Journal*—passed sensitive information to the revolutionary movement in the lead up to the Rising. The IJA members who have left most in terms of sources that outline the interplay between journalism and clandestine revolutionary activities are Piaras Béaslaí and Michael Knightly, while David Boyd and Seán Lester have left more fragmentary accounts of their activities.

Journalists and the Rising

Born into a Belfast Presbyterian unionist family, David Boyd (1892–1965) joined the IRB in 1911 'having come under the influence of fellow Protestant journalists active in the revolutionary movement, most notably Seán Lester and Ernest Blythe'.[16] Having moved to Dublin, he joined the Irish Volunteers in 1913. While working as a journalist with the unionist *Evening Mail* he was one of a select group of Irish Volunteers sent in July 1914 to secure the Dublin coastal town of Howth so as to facilitate the landing of arms and ammunition. In his memoirs—published as a series of newspaper articles in 1961—the officer commanding this group, future Irish president Seán T. O'Kelly, recounted how having been summoned to a house he was given charge of twenty-five men armed with crude batons whose job it was 'to see that neither the coast guard nor the police interfered with the landing of the arms'.[17] In a 1961 interview published by the *Evening Herald*, Boyd confirmed that he was present at Howth on 'reconnaissance' for the revolutionary movement and that he was 'one of a select few who had been given prior intelligence of the arrival' of the arms.[18] Recalling the events many years later, Boyd recounted that when a large party of Irish Volunteers arrived at Howth and realised that 'gun-running was in progress they were marched at the double, and in their excitement, broke ranks'. On the return march, when the now armed Volunteers encountered a cordon of police and military personnel, Boyd witnessed the demand that the arms be surrendered and the retort from the Volunteers that they had 'as much right to carry arms as they had in the North of Ireland'. He also witnessed the bayonet charge by the military that injured several Volunteers and dispersed the march.[19] Following the Rising, Boyd went on the run and ended up in Waterford city where he secured a post on the *Waterford Standard*, a newspaper he subsequently acquired and edited until its demise in 1953.[20]

Also from Northern Ireland, Seán Lester (1888–1959) joined the unionist *North Down Herald* in 1905 where he established a close friendship with fellow journalist Ernest Blythe —a leading light of the Irish language movement. Having joined the IRB in 1908 Lester moved to Dublin and took up the post of chief reporter of the *Daily Express* (a sister title of the *Evening Mail* both of which were owned by Henry L. Tivy, who also owned the *Cork Constitution*). Lester did not take part in the Rising itself due to the confusion surrounding the Easter Sunday manoeuvres. But his activities within the revolutionary movement were well known and Dublin Castle 'took an embarrassing interest in his movements, and on more than one occasion brought pressure to bear to have him dismissed by employers'.[21] Indeed, correspondence between Tivy and Lester indicate a terse relationship. While Tivy appreciated Lester's qualities as chief reporter he expressed frustration with Lester's activities—especially after the Rising had resulted in damage to his Dublin newspapers' premises. In one letter Tivy expressed his concern about Lester associating with those whom he referred to as living 'in a sphere of high temperament'.[22] In another letter, Tivy expressed consternation at Dublin Castle's tendency 'to class me as a Sinn Féiner whereas the fact is that I should be glad to do my bit in kicking the carcass of every Sinn Féiner and other rebel in Ireland into the [river] Liffey'.[23] When Lester informed Tivy that he has secured a new post at the nationalist *Freeman's Journal* Tivy responded by noting that it would be 'a relief' if Lester left his paper.[24]

Born in Liverpool to Irish parents, Percy Frederick Beazley (1881–1965), was better known by his gaelicised name Piaras Béaslaí. As a child he spent several summers with relatives in Ireland and as an Irish language enthusiast he was prominent within the Liverpool branch of the Gaelic League.[25] Throughout the month of January 1953 the *Irish Independent* published a detailed series of his recollections. Entitled 'A Nation in Revolt' the series gives a detailed account of his activities as an insurgent-journalist.[26] As a member of the Gaelic League and the IRB Béaslaí was among a group of individuals that established the Irish Volunteers in 1913. This group subsequently accepted an offer from William Sears, proprietor of the *Enniscorthy Echo*, to publish a weekly newspaper. First published in February 1914 *The Irish Volunteer* was edited by IRB member and *Enniscorthy Echo* journalist Larry de Lacy and given official recognition on the strict condition that 'proofs of all the editorial matter be sent in advance' to Béaslaí for approval—a condition adhered to until the paper ceased publication in October 1914.[27] At this time, Béaslaí was on the staff of the Irish Parliamentary Party's organ, the *Freeman's Journal* and was well aware that its proprietors 'regarded the starting of the Volunteers with suspicion and disfavour'. He very soon received 'personal proof' of the disfavour with which his Volunteer activities were viewed:

> Early in February 1914 my connection with the editorial staff of that newspaper was abruptly terminated without explanation and I became a freelance journalist. I still did occasional work for the 'Freeman' acting as substitute for members of the staff who were engaged in more lucrative 'special' work, but this of course was a private matter between myself and them, not coming under the cognisance of the Board of Directors.[28]

But despite moving in the inner-circles of the IRB and Irish Volunteers, Béaslaí recalled that he knew nothing of the plans to land arms at Howth in July 1914 (he was on tour with an acting troupe at the time). It was, he reflected, 'galling to think that our comrades had been in action against the British while we had been down south play-acting'.[29] On his return to Dublin he informed senior IRB figure Seán McDermott that if the war (which had just begun) came 'to an end without any armed effort for freedom' then he would leave the IRB. In response, McDermott made it clear that 'an insurrection at a suitable date had been decided on'.[30] John Redmond's call for Irish Volunteers to join the British Army met with a chilly response from *The Irish Volunteer* which observed that 'England's wars were no concern of the Volunteers [which had been] established to defend the rights of the Irish people'. A repudiation of this editioral position by the now Redmond-dominated Irish Volunteers executive committee also ended offical recognition of that journal.[31] Following the split from Redmond, Béaslaí was elected to the executive committee of the reconstituted Irish Volunteers and, in October 1914, was asked by Joseph Plunkett to submit any plans that he might have for occupying and defending positions in Dublin city or county. He was also instructed to collect such plans from any other officers that he might know. Béaslaí subsequently used the IJA headquarters as a drop-off point for other officers to deliver their plans. Among those who travelled to the headquarters to do so—as early as February 1915—was Tomás Ashe, commander of the Fingal Brigade, who dropped off maps of Fingal marked with strategic positions.[32]

As his parents lived in Liverpool Béaslaí had a legitimate reason to travel to Britain frequently. In December 1915 he was dispatched to Birmingham to secure the purchase of a large consignment of rifles. However, when he arrived at the firm he was told that the deal was off because the firm had just sold a large quantity of arms to Turkey—then at war with Britain—and had been reprimanded by the British government. Béaslaí was 'amused and astonished at the whole business—on the one hand at the laxity of the British government and on the other at the combination of business honesty and unscrupulous national treachery shown by these amiable and patriotic English businessmen'.[33] In late-January 1916 he was visited at the IJA offices by Seán McDermott who asked him to go to Liverpool to pass on a coded message to a contact who was helping to organise the ill-fated attempt by Germany to supply arms for the Rising. He was also instructed to ask the contact to enquire whether the Germans could, along with rifles and ammunition, supply machine guns and officers who could use them. On Good Friday, Béaslaí used the IJA offices to host a meeting of the officers of his Irish Volunteers unit at which plans for seising specific buildings were outlined and discussed.[34] The following day, Béaslaí was visited at the IJA headquarters by Michael Knightly of the *Irish Independent* who informed him that the paper had been visited by a British army officer who had instructed the editor not to print any report of the capture and sinking of a German ship off the Irish coast. Béaslaí immediately sought out Seán McDermott—but McDermott had already heard the news courtesy of another IJA member, Thomas F. O'Sullivan—a journalist with the *Freeman's Journal* who was prominent within Gaelic Athletic Association circles and who was friendly with many of the IRB leaders. O'Sullivan had also overheard military officers giving the non-publication instructions to his editor and had passed on the information to Seán T. O'Kelly. O' Kelly, who later described O'Sullivan as 'a sympathiser with our movement', undertook to find McDermott and inform him of developments.[35] Nonetheless, the Rising went ahead on Easter Monday. Following the Rising, Beasley was sentenced to three years' penal servitude but was released in the amnesty of 1917, whereupon he resumed his duties as secretary of the IJA.[36]

Michael Knightly's testimony to the Bureau of Military History throws further light on the IJA's premises being used as a location to plan the activities of 'F Company' of the First Battalion of the Irish Volunteers (Béaslaí's unit). Described in his obituary as 'a close personal friend of Mr de Valera, the late President Griffith, General Michael Collins, Mr Austin Stack and other prominent figures in the Sinn Féin movement' Knightly began his career with *Kerry News* and the *Cork Free Press* before joining the *Irish Independent* in 1913—the same year he joined the Irish Volunteers.[37] In his testimony, Knightly recounted how some days prior to the Rising, he disturbed a meeting taking place at the IJA headquarters. Having arrived at the building he was denied admission. When he was eventually allowed entry he was introduced to several senior Irish Volunteers officers who had been consulting Dublin street maps. He was also pointedly asked whether he would be 'turning out on Sunday'. Knightly replied that, as he was due in Cork to report on a teachers' conference, if the reference to Sunday related to 'an ordinary parade' he would not turn out, but that if it related to 'anything worth losing a job over' he would turn out. The reply from Béaslaí—'jobs won't count'—confirmed to Knightly that the plans being made related to an imminent insurrection.[38] When no mobilisation was enacted on Easter Sunday, Knightly made plans to travel to Cork on Easter Monday but when news reached Independent Newspapers that the GPO had been seised Knightly went there and, having been admitted advised Seán McDermott that he had heard in the newsroom that the British military were moving artillery to Dublin. According to Knightly, McDermott's response was 'Damn it, only for MacNeill yesterday we would have the whole country with us'.[39] Having remained in the GPO until Thursday, Knightly was conveyed to Jervis Street Hospital suffering from a severe throat infection. Post the Rising, Knightly was interned in Frongoch camp in Wales and, on his release, returned to his post at the *Irish Independent*, where he was asked by the paper's editor, T. R. Harrington, whether, if another event similar to the Rising were to occur, he would take part in it. Knightly's reply—that he would 'with more heart than on the previous occasion'—prompted Harrington to retort that he would 'build a special asylum for you people ... and put you all in it'.[40]

Reporting the Rising

Due to their location in Dublin's city centre some newspapers suffered damage during the Rising. The premises of Independent Newspapers on Abbey Street were occupied by the rebels though it remained relatively undamaged. In contrast, the premises of the *Freeman's Journal* on nearby Princes Street suffered extensive damage from shelling. Similarly, the premises of the *Daily Express* and the *Evening Mail* on Parliament Street were seised by the rebels after they failed to take Dublin Castle and were damaged in the ensuing fighting. Things were somewhat different for the *Irish Times* which was then located between O'Connell Street where the GPO was held by the rebels and Trinity College on College Green which was held by British forces. On the first day of the Rising, while all other newspaper buildings were seised by the rebels, production of the *Irish Times* continued as normal. But, despite being caught unawares by the Rising, the government was quick to implement censorship measures to prevent news of the Rising from spreading. On Easter Monday evening, after the *Irish Times* had been printed, its editor, John Healy, received a request from the government to delay its issue to the public with the result that 'the *Irish Times* actually issued to the public on that date was in greatly reduced form'. Its leading article observed that it had 'never been published in stranger circumstances than those which obtain to-day'; an attempt had been made 'to overthrow the constitutional government of Ireland [and] to set up an independent Irish Republic in Dublin'.[41] Caught between two strategic positions its staff found themselves trapped in the building for the best part of a week. To ease the cabin fever the general manager, John J. Simington, somehow secured a barrel of porter that was rationed out amongst the staff.[42] In his later dispatches as Irish correspondent of the London *Times,* John Healy gave an insight into the production of the paper during that week:

> On Monday night I went to my own newspaper, and until Friday night I was virtually a prisoner in its office. We were the only newspaper in Dublin which tried to 'carry on', and we succeeded until Thursday. On that day we were reduced to a 'folio of four pages'. Dublin was utterly cut off from the outside world. Of what was happening in Dublin we knew only what could be gleaned by the brief excursions of brave men who faced death every time they left the office door. We learned afterwards that the General Officer then commanding had sent at least one brief *communiqué* to the English Press, but this was denied to the only newspaper in Dublin.[43]

Despite being able to publish on most days, the paper's reportage was limited by the declaration of martial law, the imposition of press censorship, the inability to communicate with its London office, the dangers faced by journalists who ventured out of the building, and the fact that the police had instructed Healy to turn off all lighting within the building. On the fourth day of the Rising it declared that there was 'little or no news (we admit frankly) in the only newspaper; that, however, is not the newspaper's fault, and it may claim, perhaps, as a merit that it comes out at all'. Strangely, it was forced to recommend activities other than reading a newspaper to its readers: a father could 'cultivate a habit of easy conversation with his family … put his little garden into a state of decency' or do some 'useful mending and painting about the house'. Reading the works of Shakespeare was also highly recommended.[44]

Given that its premises on Middle Abbey Street had been seised by the rebels and 'were destroyed by the military operations' the *Irish Journalist* did not re-appear until August 1916 and that edition noted that the IJA's secretary Piaras Béaslaí had been been sentenced to three years' penal servitude for his role in the Rising—a sentence that the journal noted 'has had an injurious effect on our Organisation'. It also observed that Béaslaí 'was not the only journalist involved in the Rising, with which so many of the finest intellects of our country were associated. Numbers of other equally brilliant young Pressmen and literary men have been identified with the movement which culminated in an effort to establish an Irish Republic and are to-day bravely paying the penalty in English dungeons and British detention camps'. Among the journalists it listed as being interned in Britain were Robert Brennan and William Sears of the *Enniscorthy Echo*, Arthur Griffith of *Nationality*, John Joseph Scollan of *Hiberian*, James Murphy and Brian O'Higgins of the *Saturday Post*, William O'Leary Curtis and Michael Knightly of the *Irish Independent*, and Herbert Moore Pim of *The Irishman*. In an attempt to strike a balance between those journalists who supported and those who opposed the Rising it noted that it was the duty of the IJA 'without committing iself to approval or disapproval of the Rising, to take steps with the object of seeing that our colleagues in convict establishments are treated as political offenders and not as common criminals'. Indeed, it noted that not all Dublin journalists had been supportive of the Rising and intriguingly, though cryptically, observed that had an Irish Republic been established 'four journalists would have been asked to answer a charge of high treason'.[45] But whatever differences existed among Dublin journalists in relation to the Rising there existed some solidarity also. Somewhat pleasingly the *Irish Journalist* noted that one unnamed Dublin newspaper had been offered the financially lucrative task of supplying shorthand reporters to the trial of Eoin MacNeill, the chief of staff of the Irish Volunteers who had not taken part in the Rising. However, all the newspaper's journalists 'had refused to earn the usual professional fees on the ground that the trial was of a political character, and involved the prisoner's life. They therefore felt that they would not be justified in accepting the guineas which under other circumstances they would be only too glad to earn'. As a result of this stance special reporting staff 'had to be imported to do the work'. It also critcised the censorship imposed on the press that lingered long after the Rising by noting that 'the people least qualified to censor Journalists' work are half-educated military officers and thick-skulled Co. Inspectors of police'.[46]

Reporting on the Rising had been, the journal noted, 'a comparatively safe affair'. From the second day (Tuesday) onwards journalists were prevented by the military from venturing into the firing line and were not permitted to pass the militray cordons for some days after the suppression of the revolt. This, the journal pointedly remarked, was just as well 'as Dublin reporters have never been paid the salaries of war correspondents'. But several journalists were killed during the Rising. The execution of Francis Sheehy Skeffington—a pacificst, ardent opponent of military recruitment in Ireland and editor of the suffrgette publication *The Irish Citizen*—shocked Dublin to its core. Arrested while walking home from an unsuccessful meeting to organinse a civic guard to prevent looting in the city he was taken to Portobello Army Barracks. Later that evening he was forced to act as a human shield for an army raiding party led by Captain J. C. Bowen Colthurst.[47] Amid a raid that involved the shooting of several civilians by Bowen Colthurst, two more journalists—Patrick McIntyre (who had edited an anti-union organ, *The Toiler*, during the Great Lockout of 1913, and who was then involved in a little-known organ *The Searchlight*) and Thomas Dixon (editor of a gossip-themed publication entitled *The Eye-Opener*) were arrested and, along with Sheehy Skeffington, were taken back to Portobello Barracks where, the following morning, Bowen Colthurst assembled a firing squad that executed all three journalists together. For his actions Bowen Colthurst was found guilty of murder by a court matrial but was simultaneously declared to have been insane at the time of the killings. Following a short period of detention at Broadmore Mental Asylum he was released whereupon he emigrated to Canada.[48] On the killing of Sheehy Skeffington the *Irish Journalist* had strong words:

> One of the saddest tragedies in connect with the Rising was the murder of Mr F. Sheehy Skeffington, M.A., by the military officer, Bowen Colthurst. Mr Skeffington was a man of the highest intellectual attainments, a brilliant writer, with a loveable personality. He was strongly opposed to physical violence in any cause, and was actively engaged in preventing looting when he was arrested by the military. The officer who ordered his execution was found guilty of murder, but held insane. By this verdict his life was saved. His death, however, or that of a dozen other military officers, would have been a poor equivalient for the loss of the brave young journalist who was the champion of all weak causes.[49]

In a later issue, referring to the establishment of a Royal Commission to investigate the circumstances of Sheehy Skeffington's killing it observed that 'no report can exaggerate or minimise the appalling character of the cold-blooded atrocity'. Skeffington had, it declared, been 'murdered without the slightest justification or provocation'.[50] However, the journal made no mention of the two other journalists killed alongside Sheehy Skeffington. While it may be that their politics or journalistic activities were not to the liking of the IJA it is curious—given that they had been killed just as arbitrarily as Sheehy Skeffington—that the journal did not mention them in the spirit of professional solidarity. Similarly, no mention was made of the executed leaders of the Rising, many of whom had been involved in various aspects of journalism: Pádraig Pearse had been editor of *An Claidheamh Soluis* (the newpaper of the Gaelic League); James Connolly had been editor of the *Irish Worker* (a trade union newspaper); Seán McDermott had been manager of *Irish Freedom* (the IRB's newspaper); Éamonn Ceannt had been a contributor to *Irish Freedom*; Thomas Mac-Donagh and Joseph Mary Plunkett had been regular contributors to the *Irish Review* (a literary magazine); and Michael O'Hanrahan had been a contributor to Arthur Griffith's newspaper *Sinn Féin*.[51] While the journal was most likely seeking to strike a balance between IJA members who supported and those who opposed the Rising, it is extraordinary that no mention was made of the fate of Pearse and his companions given their prominence in literary and journalistic life in Dublin. The *Irish Journalist* did, however, record the death of Patrick Reynolds of the *Evening Mail*, who 'recevied three bullet wounds in Dame St on Easter Monday'. Reynolds was, the *Evening Mail* observed, 'one of the innocent victims of the rebellion': as he had tried to make his way out of the firing line he had been caught in the crossfire between the rebels, who had seised the newpaper's building on Parliament Street, and the soldiers who had attacked it from Dublin Castle.[52]

Discussion / Conclusion

The historiography of the 1916 Rising has tended to focus on the primary protagonists, and in so far as examining journalism and the Rising, has tended to focus almost exclusively on the primary protagonists' endeavours as editors of and contributors to literary magazines and newspapers associated with the trade union and revolutionary movements. But, as demonstrated, many lesser-known journalists who worked on the mainstream press acted as planners and participants in the insurrection and, unable to express their political radicalism in the newspapers for which they worked, they instead expressed their radicalism through their activities within the Irish Journalists' Association. While the activities of these journalists appear to have been known to the police it is clear that their involvement in the IJA provided some cover for their clandestine activities. The IJA's headquarters—which was used to plan some aspects of the Rising—were never raided by the police. If it had been raided then such an event would undoubtedly have been reported in the *Irish Journalist* and would have resulted in motions at condemnation at the IJA's annual meeting. Indeed, the police may have been aware of the adverse national—and international—press reaction should it raid the headquarters of a representative organisation for journalists.

Post the Rising the altered political landscape resulted in an altered press landscape. As public opinion swung behind the insurgents the Irish Parliamentary Party was swept aside in the 1918 general election by the physical force tradition in the guise of Sinn Féin. In a similar vein, the weaker organs of the daily press, specifically the *Freeman's Journal* and the *Daily Express*, ceased publication amid the Anglo-Irish conflict of the early 1920s. The fractious nature of the Irish independence movement was reflected in the civil war that followed independence, which in turn was followed by a specific press project—the establishment of the *Irish Press* in 1931—which gave voice to the faction that had unsuccessfully sought the rejection of the Anglo-Irish Treaty of 1921. In the early decades of the state's existence political battles were also press battles, with the *Irish Independent* and the *Irish Times* supporting the pro-Treaty faction and the *Irish Press* supporting the anti-Treaty faction—with both sides differing on the state's constitutional relationship with Britain. As has been noted elsewhere it was not until the advent of an Irish television service in 1961—a service bound in law to be objective and impartial in its coverage of news and current affairs—that the Irish press industry became less partisan in its political coverage.[53]

As for the IJA itself, post the Rising it was riven by division over its future direction. From the surviving records it appears that there existed two distinct camps—one populated by older journalists who did not take part in the Rising which wished to keep the IJA as a representative organisation separate from the wider trade union movement, and another populated by younger journalists who had taken part in the Rising or were involved in movements such as the Gaelic League which advocated that the IJA should register as a trade union. At its February 1916 AGM a motion that the IJA register as a trade union movement had been passed but at a subsequent meeting it had been agreed—to avoid a split—that a plebiscite of all members be held. However, the final edition of the *Irish Journalist* recorded that the Rising had prevented this plebiscite from taking place.[54] Thereafter the only record of what happened to the IJA resides in newspaper archives. One newspaper report recorded that a meeting of Dublin journalists 'unanimously decided' to request the association to summon an AGM 'to put into effect the terms of a resolution of 1919 [sic] forming the association into a trade union'.[55] This, presumably, should have read '1916'. In 1919 it affiliated to the Dublin Printing and Kindred Trades Alliance and in 1924 merged with the Dublin and Irish Association branch of the Institute of Journalists, heralding an end to a journalist representative association that played a key-role in the 1916 Rising.[56]

Disclosure Statement

No potential conflict of interest was reported by the author.

Notes

1. See Caulfield, "Easter Rebellion"; Williams, "The Irish Struggle"; Edwards and Pyle, "1916"; Coogan, "1916"; Townshend, "Easter 1916"; Wills, "Dublin 1916"; McGarry, The Rising"; Coleman, "The Irish Revolution"; Foster, "Vivid Faces" and Ferriter, "A Nation".

2. Many of the IRB's leaders were prominent in the Irish Volunteers and it was this inner-circle that instigated the Rising. When the leader of the Irish Volunteers, Eoin MacNeill, was told belatedly of the plans for a Rising on Easter Sunday, he issued an order cancelling the Sunday manoeuvres that were to be held countrywide as a prelude to the Rising. However, the IRB inner-circle decided to go ahead with the Rising in Dublin on Easter Monday. As a result of this confusion the Rising, which was meant to occur nationwide, was mostly confined to Dublin.

3. For more on Connolly's journalism see Curry, "The Worker"; for more on Pearse's journalism see Uí Chollatáin, "An Claidheamh Soluis".

4. See Figgis, "Recollections"; Ryan, "Remembering Sion" and FitzGerald "Memoirs".
5. The *Irish Times*, January 20, 1911 carries a comprehensive account of the IJA's first AMG and a list of its prominent members.
6. See http://www.bureauofmilitaryhistory.ie/
7. Bureau of Military History Witness Statement, no. 675.
8. Bingham, "Digitization of Newspaper Archives," 225.
9. For more on the *Freeman's Journal* see Larkin, "A Great Dail Organ"; for more on the *Irish Independent* see O'Brien and Rafter 2012; for more on the *Irish Times* see O'Brien 2008. The *Daily Express*, a Dublin Unionist newspaper, ceased publication in 1921.
10. Foley, "Colonialism and Journalism in Ireland," 380.
11. *Irish Journalist*, January, 1915.
12. *Irish Times*, January 20, 1911.
13. *Irish Journalist*, October, 1914.
14. *Irish Journalist*, May–August, 1916.
15. *Irish Journalist*, November, 1915.
16. Keating, "Muscovite Days and Nights," 116.
17. *Irish Press*, July 7, 1961. This paper published a series of O'Kelly recollections throughout July 1961.
18. *Evening Herald*, July 29, 1961.
19. *Evening Herald*, July 29, 1961.
20. In 1929 Boyd became the first, and only, editor to be prosecuted under the Censorship of Publications Act 1929 in relation to his reporting of a court case. See Keating, "Waterford Standard."
21. Griffin, "The Wild Geese," 244.
22. Gageby, "Last Secretary General," 9 (letter from Tivy to Lester, August 19, 1916).
23. Gageby, "Last Secretary General," 11 (letter from Tivy to Lester, August 22, 1916).
24. Gageby, "Last Secretary General," 11–12 (letter from Tivy to Lester, undated). Lester later served as the last secretary general of the League of Nations.
25. *Irish Press*, June 23, 1965.
26. The *Irish Independent* later published a second series of recollections, 'A Veteran Remembers' from May 16 to June 10, 1957.
27. *Irish Independent*, January 6, 1953.
28. *Irish Independent*, January 7, 1953.
29. *Irish Independent*, January 9, 1953.
30. *Irish Independent*, January 12, 1953.
31. *Irish Independent*, January 12, 1953.
32. *Irish Independent*, January 15, 1953.
33. *Irish Independent*, January 13, 1953.
34. *Irish Independent*, January 16, 1953.
35. *Irish Press*, July 11, 1961.
36. *Irish Independent*, June 18, 1917. In 1918 Béaslaí was elected to the First Dáil and served as the IRA's director of publicty during the Anglo-Irish War 1919–21. For more on Béaslaí's later life see Maume, "Béaslaí".
37. *Irish Independent*, December 21, 1964.
38. Bureau of Military History Witness Statement, no. 833, 2.

39. Ibid., 3.
40. Bureau of Military History Witness Statement, no. 834, 6. During the Anglo-Irish War 1919–21 Knightly passed information, including photographs of Dublin Castle officials, to the republican movement. He was imprisoned during the conflict, went to London as part of the staff of Treaty delegation, and served as press censor during the Second World War. See *Irish Independent*, February 19, 1955.
41. *Irish Times*, April 25, 1916.
42. O'Brien, "Irish Times," 48.
43. *The Times*, May 1, 1916.
44. *Irish Times*, April 27, 1916.
45. *Irish Journalist,* May–August 1916.
46. *Irish Journalist,* May–August 1916.
47. Maume, "Skeffington".
48. Maume, "Colthurst".
49. *Irish Journalist*, May–August 1916.
50. *Irish Journalist*, September–October 1916.
51. Ó Conchubhair, "Dublin's Fighting Story".
52. *Evening Mail*, August 4, 1916.
53. O'Brien, "The Fourth Estate", 116.
54. *Irish Journalist*, September–October 1916.
55. *Irish Independent*, October 28, 1918.
56. *Irish Times*, January 13, 1919; *Irish Times,* January 19, 1925.

Bibliography

Bingham, Adrian. "The Digitization of Newspaper Archives: Opportunities and Challenges for Historians." *Twentieth Century British History* 21, no. 2 (2010): 225–231.

Caulfield, Max. *The Easter Rebellion*. London: Muller, 1964.

Coleman, Marie. *The Irish Revolution, 1916–1923*. Harlow: Pearson, 2013.

Coogan, Tim Pat. *1916: The Easter Rising*. London: Cassell & Co., 2001.

Curry, James. 2014. "The Worker: James Connolly's Organ of the Working Class." In *Periodicals and Journalism in Twentieth-Century Ireland*, edited by Mark O'Brien and Felix M. Larkin, 75–88. Dublin: Four Courts Press.

Edwards, Owen Dudley and Fergus Pyle, eds. *1916: The Easter Rising*. London: MacGibbon & Kee, 1968.

Ferriter, Diarmaid. *A Nation and not a Rabble: The Irish Revolution, 1913–23*. London: Profile Books, 2015.

Figgis, Darrell. *Recollections of the Irish War*. London: Ernest Benn Ltd., 1927.

FitzGerald, Desmond. *Memoirs of Desmond FitzGerald, 1913–1916*. London: Routledge & K. Paul, 1968.

Foley, Michael. "Colonialism and Journalism in Ireland." *Journalism Studies* 5, no. 3 (2004): 373–385.

Foster, Roy. *Vivid Faces: The Revolutionary Generation in Ireland, 1890–1923*. London: Allen Lane, 2014.

Gageby, Douglas. *The Last Secretary General: Seán Lester and the League of Nations*. Dublin: Town House and Country House, 1999.

Griffin, Gerald. *The Wild Geese: Pen Portraits of Famous Irish Exiles*. London: Jarrolds, 1938.

Keating, Anthony. "Muscovite Days and Nights: A Small Town Irish Newspaperman's Soviet Travelogue of 1934." *Nordic Irish Studies* 13, no. 2 (2014): 115–135.

Larkin, Felix M. "A Great Daily Organ: The *Freeman's Journal*, 1763–1924." *History Ireland* 14, no. 3 (2006): 44–49.

Maume, Patrick. "Béaslaí, Piaras." In *Dictionary of Irish Biography*, edited by James McGuire, and James Quinn, Vol. 1, 386–389. Cambridge: Cambridge University Press, 2009.

Maume, Patrick. "Colthurst, John Bowen." In *Dictionary of Irish Biography*, edited by James McGuire, and James Quinn, Vol. 2, 697–699. Cambridge: Cambridge University Press, 2009.

Maume, Patrick. "Skeffington, Francis Sheehy." In *Dictionary of Irish Biography*, edited by James McGuire, and James Quinn, Vol. 8, 981–983. Cambridge: Cambridge University Press, 2009.

McGarry, Fearghal. *The Rising: Ireland, Easter 1916*. Oxford: Oxford University Press, 2010.

O'Brien, Mark. *The Fourth Estate: Journalism in Twentieth-Century Ireland*. Manchester: Manchester University Press, 2017.

O'Brien, Mark. *The Irish Times: A History*. Dublin: Four Courts Press, 2008.

O'Brien, Mark and Kevin Rafter, eds. *Independent Newspapers: A History*. Dublin, Four Courts Press, 2012.

Ó Conchubhair, Brian, ed. *Dublin's Fighting Story 1916–21*. Cork: Mercier Press, 2009.

Ryan, Desmond. *Remembering Sion: A Chronicle of Storm and Quiet*. London: A. Barker, Ltd., 1934.

Townshend, Charles. *Easter 1916: The Irish Rebellion*. London: Allen Lane, 2005.

Uí Chollatáin, Regina. 2014. "An Claidheamh Soluis agus Fáinne an Lae: The Turning of the Tide." In *Periodicals and Journalism in Twentieth-Century Ireland*, edited by Mark O'Brien and Felix M. Larkin, 31–46. Dublin: Four Courts Press.

Williams, Desmond. *The Irish Struggle, 1916–1926*. London: Routledge & K. Paul, 1966.

Wills, Claire. *Dublin 1916: The Siege of the GPO*. London: Profile Books, 2009.

CENSORSHIP AND SUPPRESSION OF THE IRISH PROVINCIAL PRESS, 1914–1921

Christopher Doughan

Press censorship was introduced in both Britain and Ireland at the start of World War I. As a more radical form of nationalism rapidly gained popularity in Ireland following the 1916 Rising the censorship was extended beyond the duration of the war. The censorship was mainly deployed to restrict the reporting of the more militant pronouncements of Irish republicans. This article explores how the censorship impacted on provincial newspapers, which constituted the greater part of the Irish print media. It specifically examines the censorship framework and considers if it was applied in an impartial and even-handed manner. It also outlines the cases of those provincial newspapers that were either suppressed or were subjected to attacks by Crown forces that resulted in prolonged closure. Finally, this article provides a broad assessment of the effectiveness of press censorship in Ireland during this period.

Introduction

Years of turbulence is the title of a collection of essays published in 2015 dealing with what is referred to by some historians as the revolutionary period of Irish history.[1] The precise start and end date of this period might be a subject for debate but most would agree that it roughly covers the decade or so up to the end of the Irish Civil War in 1923. Regardless of exact dates, it is a particularly apt title to describe a span of time that witnessed the outbreak of World War I, the Easter Rising, the emergence of a decidedly separatist form of nationalism (represented by the Sinn Féin party), the War of Independence, the Anglo-Irish Treaty, and, ultimately the Irish Civil War. The events of these yeas broadly coincided with the emergence of the popular press as both a powerful and influential medium. Accordingly, Irish nationalists of various hues sought to utilise the print media to promote their agenda. However, this was also a time when many states attempted to exercise a degree of control over the output of the print media, particularly newspapers, to an extent not previously witnessed. The outbreak of World War I in September 1914 prompted this dramatic change and it threw the relationship between government and print media into sharp focus. The introduction of the Defence of the Realm Act (DORA) in Britain at the start of the war 'gave the British state a range of extraordinary draconian powers' that applied to all forms of communication but had far-reaching effects on the print media especially.[2] Consequently, in Britain, and by extension in Ireland, it meant that the broad desire of the authorities to exert a certain level of influence over the popular press swiftly changed to a determination to do so.

This article explores how one section of the Irish print media, the provincial press, fared in such a rapidly changing environment. In this respect, it specifically focuses on the nature of the censorship under which it had to operate during these years. It examines the regulations that applied and the relationship between the Chief Press Censor (who had to apply such regulations) and provincial newspapers. Examples of censored material are scrutinised and compared to appropriate items that went uncensored. The examples of censored items are selected in order to best illustrate the nature of the material that the British authorities wished to prevent from appearing in print. The cases of provincial titles that were suppressed are also considered. Finally, this article briefly outlines the cases of those provincial newspapers that were forcibly shut down by Crown forces, usually in violent circumstances. However, it is not possible to fully comprehend such instances of censorship and suppression without firstly examining the political background.

At the start of World War I the pre-eminent force in Irish nationalist politics was the Irish Parliamentary Party led by John Redmond. Although Redmond supported the British war effort and encouraged Irishmen to enlist in the British army his support, as Keith Jeffery notes, was not unconditional. Redmond also wished to gain political advantage by finally securing home rule for Ireland.[3] To others, such as Patrick Pearse and 'other members of the militant and clandestine IRB [Irish Republican Brotherhood]' the war provided 'the opportunity for an Irish insurrection'.[4] Their planned insurrection took place at Easter 1916 but garnered minimal public support and was a complete military failure. Nonetheless, it marked a dramatic turning point in Irish nationalist politics.

During the course of the following few years a far more separatist form of politics came to the fore. This resulted from a variety of factors starting with the swift execution of the rebel leaders of 1916 but the introduction of military conscription during 1918 was probably one of the most significant. The principal beneficiary was the Sinn Féin party whose policies, which 'offered a smorgasbord of variously risky or risk-free ways of resisting, subverting or simply ignoring British rule', were well-suited to turning such a situation to its advantage.[5] Following its landslide victory at the general election of December 1918 Sinn Féin reached its apogee 'with the formal opening of the first Dáil Éireann or Irish parliament' in January 1919.[6] 'Such an event', as Townshend points out, 'would have seemed all but fantastic' less than a decade previously when 'republicanism in Ireland was a marginal political movement'.[7] However, this event coincided with the opening stage of a more violent campaign for Irish independence.

Despite its election victory many of Sinn Féin's more militant members were frustrated by the lack of progress towards Irish independence. Ultimately, this led to a guerrilla war, carried out principally by the Irish Republican Army (IRA), being waged against British rule that lasted until the truce called by the British government in July 1921. The ensuing Anglo-Irish Treaty six months later granted 'all that the constitutional Sinn Féiners had sought before 1916, but a rebellion and a guerrilla war were needed to bring about'.[8] Certain aspects of the treaty created difficulties for the elected members of Dáil Éireann but the most divisive was the necessity to take an oath of allegiance to the British monarch.[9] Ultimately, divisions over the treaty 'split the Irish body-politic' and led to a bitter civil war that lasted from June 1922 to May 1923.[10]

It was in the midst of such dramatic developments that 'the press reached the zenith of its influence in political and social life in Great Britain and Ireland'.[11] This came about due to a variety of developments that mainly took place during the latter part of the nineteenth century. These included reduced taxes on newspapers, advances in communications and print technology, improved transport links, and most importantly, marked increases in levels of literacy that resulted in a far greater amount of people having the ability to read. The considerable extent to which these factors applied to Ireland contributed to the increasingly influential role of newspapers across the Irish populace. Accordingly, it was during the last two decades of the 1800s and the first two decades of the 1900s that the Irish provincial press underwent its most notable period of growth. During this time newspapers professing nationalist sympathies came to dominate this section of the print media. John Horgan recognises this development as being 'based partly on rising educational and income levels among the Catholic population, and partly on developing forms of political self-expression from the Land War in the 1880s onwards'.[12]

Although newspaper circulation figures do not exist for the late nineteenth and early twentieth centuries their popularity is illustrated by the launch of nationalist titles on a scale not previously witnessed. In this respect the 1880s marked the start of a period when many such titles were established across the country. Some of these only lasted a few decades but many displayed a remarkable degree of longevity. Amongst the latter group are papers that have survived into the twenty-first century such as the *Leinster Leader* (launched in 1880), *Western People* (1883), *Limerick Leader* (1889), *Mayo News* (1892), *Longford Leader* (1897), *Fermanagh Herald* (1902), *Kerryman* (1904), *Connacht Tribune* (1909), and *Donegal Democrat* (1919). This upsurge in the amount of provincial papers meant that almost half of the provincial papers published in Ireland between 1914 and 1921 had only been established within the previous thirty years or less.[13]

The increasingly influential position of the broader print media was clearly a cause for concern to the authorities. In this regard the British government introduced the Peace Preservation bill as far back as 1870 which included specific measures to control the output of the press.[14] In the case of the provincial press the concern was even greater. As Marie-Louise Legg observed, the official attitude appeared to be that 'the further away the reading public were from the capital the more influential the provincial press'.[15] However, if the authorities displayed a strong inclination to control the press in the latter part of the nineteenth century it paled in comparison to the efforts expended to ensure a compliant press following the outbreak of war in 1914.

The start of World War I was marked by what Adam Hochschild refers to as 'a blizzard of regulations' that 'shaped what could appear in print'.[16] The government's determination to control the press was perhaps best exemplified by Lloyd George who was happy to state 'that he would not hesitate to prosecute someone for publishing the sermon on the mount if it interfered with the war effort'.[17] As matters transpired, however, there was little requirement for extreme measures. As Alice Goldfarb Marquis noted, 'the press willingly censored itself', possibly the most pertinent example of such self-censorship being the non-publication of casualty lists before May 1915.[18] Such willingness was undoubtedly stimulated by the government treating newspaper proprietors and editors to 'breakfast, lunch, tea, dinner and golf weekends in the company of the powerful'.[19]

The comparatively lower circulation of Irish newspapers meant that such a convivial relationship with the authorities was hardly likely to exist. Nonetheless, there was a certain level of engagement. The most visible example of this was a function hosted by the Lord Lieutenant, Baron Wimborne, at the Viceregal Lodge in the Phoenix Park in Dublin in October 1915 for editors of the Irish press. The main purpose of the event was to consult with representatives of the print media 'as to the lines on which their co-operation could most effectively be given to the recruiting campaign' that had been on-going throughout Ireland during 1915.[20] The other most striking, though not so visible example of the engagement between the authorities and Irish newspapers took place in January 1916. This was a tour of the western front that was arranged for seven members of the Irish press. The most prominent of these were John Edward Healy, editor of the *Irish Times*, and William J. Flynn, managing-editor of the *Freeman's Journal*, though the group also included one provincial newspaper editor, Thomas J.W. Kenny of the *Connacht Tribune*.[21] The inclusion of an editor such as Kenny in this group may possibly suggest a relatively affable relationship between the authorities and the provincial print media but any such notions were dispelled rather quickly as events unfolded after the Easter Rising. Wartime censorship regulations and the rise of Sinn Féin from 1917 onwards combined to ensure press-state relations became considerably more complicated thereafter.

Press Censorship in Ireland

Press censorship in Ireland, as in Britain, was originally incorporated into the Defence of the Realm Act (DORA) though this was superseded in Ireland by the Restoration of Order in Ireland Act (ROIA) as the situation in the country grew increasingly militant between 1919 and 1921. Nonetheless, there is some evidence from well before this time to indicate a considerable degree of unhappiness at the restrictions on newspapers. The Irish Journalists Association was an organisation formed in 1909 with the aim of addressing a wide variety of the concerns of working journalists. In the early months of the war the organisation's monthly newsletter, the *Irish Journalist*, showed minimal restraint in articulating its disdain for the censorship regulations. The restrictions on the press were described as 'probably the strictest, most rigid, and most autocratic the press of these countries has ever experienced'.[22] To further compound matters the censorship had been conducted in an 'arbitrary and high-handed, manner, strongly marked by egregious incompetency and ridiculous absurdity'.[23]

Despite this antipathy there is little evidence of any significant conflict between Irish newspapers and the authorities prior to the Easter Rising of 1916. The situation began to change following the rebellion and grew more fractious with the growing popularity of Sinn Féin. In the wake of Easter 1916 the post of press censor specifically for Ireland was created. It was filled by Lord Decies who had accompanied General Sir John Maxwell to Ireland in the immediate aftermath of the Rising.[24] Even though his job was to enforce a highly unpopular measure Decies enjoyed quite a warm relationship with the Irish provincial press. Ian Kenneally has noted how he was only too happy to engage in conversations about horse racing with many editors.[25] This was a subject in which Decies had a passionate interest, his horse, Ballaghtobin, having won the Irish Derby in 1915.[26] The *Killarney Echo* described Decies as a 'courteous, affable, and capable gentleman, with whom it was easy to arrange matters on a reasonable and satisfactory basis'.[27] Upon his resignation in 1919 the *Nationalist and Leinster Times* of Carlow was happy to state that 'Lord Decies acted all through in a most courteous and tolerant manner' and felt 'certain that all sections of the Irish press regret his departure'.[28]

Decies himself displayed a readiness to recognise the talents of those who were diametrically opposed to the government he represented. In one of his regular press censorship reports he acknowledged that the Sinn Féin organ, *Nationality*, was 'extremely well written and edited' by Arthur Griffith, and further conceded that 'much that is written is undesirable but extremely difficult to censor'.[29] Upon stepping down from the post in 1919 Decies wrote to Irish newspapers to express 'my deep appreciation of, and thanks for, the unfailing courtesy which during my term of office I have at all times received from the Irish press'.[30] Decies was succeeded as Press Censor by Major Bryan Cooper, who had acted as his assistant in the role. Although he only occupied the position for three months, following which the office of the Press Censor was terminated, there is at least some evidence that Cooper similarly earned the respect of the provincial press. Despite his paper being suppressed during Cooper's tenure as Press Censor, the abrasive E.T. Keane of the *Kilkenny People* believed Cooper to be 'an honourable man who would not consciously do what was unfair or unjust'.[31]

The clear respect that newspaper editors held for Decies and Cooper did not detract from the unpopularity of the measures that they had to enforce. Numerous instructions relating to the application of such measures were issued to all Irish newspapers in the few years following Easter 1916. These included directives prohibiting the publication of articles that could discourage recruitment, material that could prejudice the successful operation of Crown forces, reports of what were regarded as seditious speeches, and generally the publication of any items that might cause or spread 'disaffection'. During the summer of 1916 Decies commenced his contact with Irish newspapers. In one of his earliest circulars he advised all newspaper editors 'that resolutions or speeches passed or made at the meetings of corporations, county, urban or rural district councils and boards of guardians should be most carefully considered before publication'.[32] This set the tone for the next three years as the press were frequently reminded that certain statements made at political gatherings of any sort risked breaching Defence of the Realm regulations and could not be published.

Prior to the North-Roscommon by-election of February 1917 Decies warned Irish newspapers that 'reports or speeches or other political propaganda' that was 'likely to cause disaffection or otherwise offending against the Defence of the Realm regulations was 'in now way exempt from the operation of these regulations'.[33] The press was again reminded of its obligations under the Defence of the Realm Act during the lead-in to the general election of December 1918. In late November Decies advised that speeches made during the campaign that constituted 'an incitement to armed rebellion or that 'inflame public opinion against the military' could not be published.[34] On the eve of the election he further instructed that the publication of 'pamphlets, leaflets, election addresses, or other literature' relating to the election similarly risked breaching the regulations.[35]

Any reference to the 'late rebellion' of Easter 1916 was also a subject that risked official censure. As early as June 1916 papers were advised to give 'careful consideration' before publishing material related to the 'late rising in Dublin'.[36] The growing sympathy for the executed leaders was evidently a cause for concern to the authorities. By June 1917, Decies was warning that the publication of 'statements which either justify the late rebellion or advocate the policy of armed rebellion in Ireland' were in violation of the Defence of the Realm Act 'and cannot be permitted to appear'.[37] This came at an early stage in a sequence of Sinn Féin victories in a series of by-elections between February 1917 and August 1918. It is clear that many of the ensuing directives from the Press Censor's office appeared to be attempting to stem the rising popularity of the party. A circular to editors from July 1917 cautioning against 'the publication of reports of speeches, seditious articles, or other matter' was undoubtedly directed at Sinn Féin rallies around the country.[38] Another directive from February 1918 specifically referred to 'certain speeches made lately by prominent members of the Sinn Féin party' and 'earnestly requested' editors to consider whether such speeches contravened the Defence of the Realm regulations before deciding to publish.[39]

The death of Thomas Ashe while on hunger strike in September 1917 clearly provoked a fear at the potential level of republican propaganda that could be generated. Within two days of Ashe's death Decies wrote to Irish newspapers to warn them that the 'greatest care' should be taken in publishing reports of his death. Decies further claimed that many reports had already appeared in the press, 'the accuracy of which may be questioned', and recommended that any letters received by newspapers regarding the issue should firstly be submitted to his office.[40] The specific target of the censorship appeared to become plainly obvious in December 1917 when Decies informed the press 'that the publication of all reports of parades, drilling and route marches, of the Sinn Féin Volunteers should not be published'.[41] If there was any lingering doubt as to the primary objective of the censorship it was surely dispelled in March 1918 when Decies declared that many of the speeches made at Sinn Féin meetings across Ireland constituted 'the most violent anti-English propaganda' and emphasised the necessity for the press restrictions to be 'maintained over the reproduction of oratory of this description'.[42] Decies obviously believed that such a policy was proving successful as he observed, rather inaccurately, in August 1918 that 'the restrictions of censorship are proving an increasing embarrassment to the seditious activities of Sinn Féin'.[43]

Censored and Non-censored Material

During his time as Press Censor many Irish newspapers submitted a variety of items to his office in order to ascertain if publication of such items was permissible. Quite often permission to publish was not granted though there is little indication that any specific paper was refused permission more frequently than others. However, what press censorship reports for this period clearly confirm is that it was reports of speeches made at Sinn Féin rallies and meetings, rather than editorial commentary, that the Press Censor did not allow to be published. In this context, it is understandable how newspapers may have felt aggrieved as they were merely reprinting statements made by representatives of an organisation that was rapidly gaining the support of the Irish electorate. Nonetheless, a cursory consideration of some of the censored material provides a clear explanation of why the British authorities sought to curb the dissemination of the public pronouncements of Irish republicans. In July 1918, the *Kilkenny People* was refused permission to publish a report of a Sinn Féin meeting in the city at which one of the party's candidates referred to 'John Bull with his big hand, is prancing about on his war horse before the nations of the world'. The speaker added that 'there is a small nation at his hall-door whom he has plundered and pirated for hundreds of years'.[44] Statements made at Sinn Féin rallies tended to grow more militant during the lead-in to the general election of December 1918. At a meeting in Ennis, County Clare, a local priest spoke in support of Eamon de Valera's candidacy:

> Rev, Father Breen said ... the English chains have clanked too loudly in and too gratingly in Clare. Clare has been too steeped in English tyranny not to recognise that its duty is to get rid of the oppressor ... Clare knows well the varied system of English tyranny and pines for the day to be rid of it all.[45]

Unsurprisingly the *Clare Champion* was refused permission to publish this section of the speech. Sinn Féin's subsequent election victory only seemed to embolden the organisation and its public proclamations grew increasingly strident. At a Sinn Féin meeting in Tagmahon, County Wexford, in January 1919 one speaker enthusiastically declared that 'there may be another war, and it may be a stronger war'. Another speaker suggested that 'it would be better for the young men of Ireland to face the firing squad and be shot than that they should be held up as the only civilised nation in Europe without its freedom'. The *Wexford People* was prohibited from publishing both extracts.[46] The following month the *Enniscorthy Echo* experienced similar censorship when it was denied permission to publish the following section of a report of a Sinn Féin meeting:

> [At a public meeting in the Town Hall, New Ross, under the auspices of the O'Hanrahan Sinn Féin club, Rev. Wm. Harpur, chairman, said] 'If Sinn Féin failed to attain its end the Irish Volunteers would take their place. The Irish Volunteers failed in 1916 in the material sense, but they succeeded in the real sense of the word .... Did they think that the men were rotting in the jails in England today for the sake of parliamentarianism?[47]

Sinn Féin vice-president Father Michael O'Flanagan particularly occupied the attention of the Press Censor. In May 1918 Decies wrote to Irish newspapers with an instruction that a recent speech by O'Flanagan at Ballyjamesduff was not for publication.[48] In July 1918 the *Wexford People* was denied permission to publish the text of one of O'Flanagan's speeches in which he claimed that any attempt to impose conscription would be met with 'guerrilla warfare' carried out by 'bands of men up and down the country with little communication between one another'.[49] Three months later O'Flanagan's unrestrained remarks were again provoking the disapproval of the Press censor. During a lengthy address to Sinn Féin rally in Trim, County Meath, he labelled England 'a hypocrite' who was 'professing to fight for freedom' when 'she was merely throwing dust in the eyes of the world'. The *Meath Chronicle* was refused permission to publish most of the speech.[50]

The highly militant nature of many of these comments make it relatively easy to understand why the British authorities would wish to prevent them from appearing in print. Some of the other examples of censored material might seem rather trivial by twenty-first century standards yet they clearly demonstrate the determination of the British authorities to prevent the spread of any republican propaganda. This is best exemplified by two cases from September 1918 and March 1919 that provide what might be regarded as light relief, by twenty-first century standards if not by contemporary standards. In the former case the *Irish Independent* was refused permission to report that mottoes such

MEDIA CONNECTIONS BETWEEN BRITAIN AND IRELAND

'Join de Valera's IRA' and 'Up the Rebels' had been painted on walls and public buildings around the town of Letterkenny, Co. Donegal.[51] In the latter case the *Irish Times* was not allowed to report that a Sinn Féin meeting in Mullingar had advocated the non-payment of dog licences until all Irish political prisoners had been released.[52] While such examples of censored material provide a certain historic amusement value they are rendered even more strange when compared to some of the items that apparently escaped the attention of the authorities during this period.

In the very early stages of World War I the *Leitrim Observer* launched a stinging attack upon any notion of Irishmen enlisting in the British army:

> Why does he [Kitchener] not make an appeal to all the 'swanky' tennis players, golfers, and cricketers in 'appy Hengland' [*sic*] to join his new army? Those English 'Joonies' who sing Rule Britannia in time of peace, and who read novels and play cricket in war time when Irishmen are fighting their battles, they should be compelled to enlist. Certainly, the average Englishman is only a coward. He is good for nothing only eating beef, drinking beer and sleeping.[53]

This outburst attracted no official censure. Possibly the authorities were somewhat less vigilant at such an early stage of the war allied to the fact that a small rural newspaper located in a sparsely populated Irish county may not have been considered a major threat. While this may explain why the *Leitrim Observer* did not attract any official attention it is quite puzzling how, five years later, a series of eight articles written by Kevin O' Higgins of Sinn Féin went unchecked by the Press Censor.

These were published in the *Nationalist and Leinster Times* during the summer of 1919 and contained liberal doses of the type of language that Decies seemed intent on preventing from appearing in print. O'Higgins claimed that Ireland was ruled by 'an alien usurping government' and was held 'by the Lewis gun'.[54] He also referred to England's 'army of occupation' that has 'tried to smash this nation with canons' and 'exterminate it with artificial famine'.[55] O'Higgins maintained the favoured Sinn Féin ploy of likening British tactics in Ireland to those of Germany in World War I. He decried 'the Prussianism of English rule' and claimed that Britain's 'atrocities in Ireland make the worse deeds of the Prussians in Belgium look like peccadilloes'.[56] This belligerent tone continued throughout the summer of 1919 with O'Higgins frequently referring to the 'occupation' of Ireland and asserting that 'the history of England is dotted with broken treaties' and that it had equipped itself 'with all the most modern instruments of destruction to butcher and dragoon the inhabitants of Ireland'.[57] The militant tone did not diminish in the last of this series of articles as O'Higgins cited 'the rule of the English sword in Ireland' that propped up 'a Union begotten by force and fraud'.[58] Quite remarkably the *Nationalist and Leinster Times* suffered no censure for publishing these articles.

In October 1920, an editorial appeared in the *Kilkenny People* that exhibited just as much hostility as any of the articles written by O'Higgins. In this case the leading articles took aim at the Chief Secretary, Sir Hamar Greenwood, in the aftermath of a series of reprisals by Crown forces. Greenwood was labelled 'the Canadian Pussyfoot' who was a 'beautiful liar' and subsequently referred to as an 'accomplished liar' and then simply as 'Liar Greenwood'. The remarkably pugnacious editorial concluded by comparing Greenwood to 'the chimpanzee in the Zoological Gardens' and suggested that the chimpanzee would 'do his dirty work in a cleaner way than Greenwood does it'.[59] The *Kilkenny People*, similar to the *Nationalist and Leinster Times*, was not censured for its bellicose tone.

Suppressions and Attacks

The *Kilkenny People* editorial appeared well over a year after the Office of the Press Censor in Dublin had ceased operation. Nonetheless, this certainly did not mean Irish newspapers could afford to be any less circumspect in what they chose to publish. Only a month before the *Kilkenny People* poured scorn on the Chief Secretary the authorities at Dublin Castle had written to the Irish newspapers to remind them of their responsibility to refrain from publishing statements 'calculated to aggravate disorder and disaffection'.[60] While the *Kilkenny People* did not suffer in this instance it had twice been suppressed previously during a somewhat problematic relationship with the Office of the Press Censor.

The first suppression lasted from July 1917 until October 1917 and resulted from what Lord Decies regarded as repeated infringements of the Defence of the Realm regulations.[61] The paper had been under the radar of the authorities since shortly after the Easter Rising and the suppression came at a time when it was emerging as a strong supporter of Sinn Féin. Its editor-proprietor was the combative E.T. Keane and it was his decision to publish certain items that the Press Censor's office had already deleted from the proofs of the paper that resulted in the second suppression from August 1919 to September 1919.[62]

Several other provincial newspapers were suppressed for varying periods of time while the Office of the Press Censor operated in Dublin. The most notable of these were the *Southern Star, Clare Champion, Weekly Observer* (based in Newcastlewest, County Limerick), *Westmeath Independent, Waterford News*, and *Meath Chronicle*. One of the main batch of suppressions occurred in April 1918 when Decies deemed that several titles had 'seriously transgressed the Defence of the Realm regulations'.[63] The *Sligo Champion* was included in this group but was not subjected to any penalty. The other titles were all suppressed, but for differing lengths of time. The *Clare Champion* was only allowed resume publication five months later. The *Southern Star, Mayo News*, and *Weekly Observer* endured month-long suppressions while the *Westmeath Independent* resumed publication one week later. The *Waterford News* was suppressed for three months in February 1919 for publishing 'statements likely to cause disaffection'.[64] The paper, purchased by Edward Downey in 1907, had developed Sinn Féin sympathies in the aftermath of Easter 1916.[65]

The publication of the prospectus for the Dáil Éireann loan in September 1919 led to the brief suppression of several provincial newspapers.[66] The most notable of these were the *Limerick Leader, Midland Tribune, Kerryman*, and *Munster News*. Some suppressions resulted from the productions of Sinn Féin election leaflets at the newspapers' printing works. This was the reason for the suppression of the *Meath Chronicle* in December 1918.[67] It was also why the *Ballina Herald* was briefly banned around the same time. Although classified as a neutral organ it had started out as a unionist paper in the nineteenth century.[68] This led the *Connaught Telegraph* to acerbically remark that 'the only unionist paper in the county has been suppressed'.[69] A similar reason may also have led to the suppression of the *Southern Star*, based in Skibbereen, County Cork, in August 1918 but this was only one of several suppressions endured by the paper.

In total the *Southern Star* was suppressed on four separate occasions between 1916 and 1919. The first of these was a month-long suppression that was imposed in November 1916. There is very little evidence of a specific reason for the suppression though the *Irish Independent* reported at the time that that it was due to the publication of an article that was critical of the police.[70] Just over a year later the *Southern Star* was acquired for £570 by a large group of Sinn Féin supporters, one of whom was Michael Collins.[71] The second suppression followed only four months after the acquisition when it was one of the five aforementioned titles deemed by Lord Decies in April 1918 to have contravened the Defence of the Realm regulations. The suppression lasted four weeks during which time Decies wrote to the paper's editor to refer him to the many circulars issued by the Office of the Press Censor with regard to what was or was not permissible to print.[72] The third and lengthiest suppression lasted from August 1918 until April 1919. Michael Collins, in a letter to a local Sinn Féin activist, expressed his belief that the ban on the paper stemmed from the publication of Sinn Féin election leaflets.[73] Whatever the reason for the suppression it seems clear that it was not instigated by the Press Censor. This is apparent from a letter sent by the paper's business manager, Seamus O'Brien, to Ernest Blythe, then editor of the paper but imprisoned at Belfast since his arrest in March 1918. In the letter, O'Brien revealed that 'Lord Decies knew nothing of the suppression and did not seem to like the idea of the military authorities taking the full power into their own hands'.[74] The fourth and final suppression resulted from the publication of the Dáil Éireann loan prospectus in October 1919.[75] Although other papers that similarly published the prospectus were allowed resume publication fairly quickly the ban on the *Southern Star* was only lifted in March 1920.[76] Over the four suppressions between 1916 and 1921 the paper was banned for a total of almost 61 weeks.

The *Southern Star* suffered more than most provincial newspapers during this period yet it avoided any violent attack on its premises that was the fate of several other titles around the country. In this respect the second suppression of the paper was somewhat ominous as it signalled that Crown forces were beginning to adopt a more robust attitude to Irish newspapers. From 1920 onwards this became a more notable feature of the Anglo-Irish conflict. In some cases, it took the form of reprisals and might have appeared quite arbitrary. However, it was generally titles that were supportive of Sinn Féin that were targeted. In August 1920, the printing plant of Quinnell and Sons (publishers of the *Killarney Echo*, *Kerry News*, and *Kerry Weekly Reporter*), Tralee, was burned down following an attack on the police in the town.[77] The following month the office and printing machinery of the *Galway Express* were destroyed by Crown forces. The attack on the paper followed an incident at the city's railway station that led to the death of an English policeman and a local man.[78] Three years previously the paper, originally a unionist organ, had been purchased by Sinn Féin interests in the city.[79]

The next paper to come under the radar of Crown forces was the *Westmeath Independent* only a few weeks later. Owned by Church of Ireland member, Thomas Chapman, it had increasingly aligned itself with the Sinn Féin cause in the wake of Easter 1916.[80] Its brief suppression in April 1918 probably reflected such sympathies but it suffered much more serious consequences in October 1920 when Crown forces destroyed its printing works. The paper only managed to resume operations in February 1922.[81] A short few weeks later the *Leitrim Observer* was subjected to a similar attack. The *Irish Times* reported that the owner, Patrick

Dunne, and his sister Eliza, were held at gunpoint while 'the machinery and plant' were reduced to a mass of wreckage'.[82] Patrick Dunne held clear republican sympathies which may well have led to his arrest only three weeks later following which he was interned at Ballykinlar camp in County Down. The paper remained out of print until January 1923.[83]

Dunne was one of several provincial newspapermen that were arrested and imprisoned between 1916 and 1921. The most notable of these were William Sears of the *Enniscorthy Echo* and P.J. Doris of the *Mayo News*.[84] Maurice Griffin of the *Kerryman* was also detained briefly in August 1916 and it was his newspaper that attracted the unwanted attention of Crown forces in April 1921.[85] Following the IRA killing of Major John Alastair McKinnon at the golf links outside Tralee the printing works of the *Kerryman* were destroyed during a series of aggravated reprisals in the town.[86] Although the *Irish Independent* reported at the time that it would be six months before the *Kerryman* could resume publication it was August 1923 before the paper reappeared.[87]

Conclusion

The attack on the *Kerryman* newspaper was the final noteworthy event in this particular facet of the Anglo-Irish conflict prior to the declaration of a truce just over two months later. The manner in which the British authorities applied censorship over the previous five years was uneven and inconsistent at best, and at worst appeared prejudiced and frequently violent in nature. Quite possibly this reflected the highly disordered nature of British administration in Ireland at the time. This was characterised by British journalist Hugh Martin, as Ó Drisceoil observes, as 'chaos upstairs, downstairs and in my Lady's chamber with Brute Force sitting in the drawing room'.[88] The highly disjointed enforcement of censorship was possibly an extension of this, even though the Chief Press Censor, Lord Decies, and his successor, Major Bryan Cooper, fostered a mutually respectful relationship with provincial newspapers.

It is quite clear that censorship was primarily deployed to halt the rise of Sinn Féin. This is plainly discernible from the various instructions issued to Irish newspapers from around June 1917 onwards and was effectively confirmed by Decies in August 1918. The samples of censored material from a variety of newspapers further supports this argument. Across the country papers were regularly instructed to curtail their reporting of Sinn Féin meetings and rallies. This particularly affected provincial titles where such localised reports appeared with the greatest frequency. However, there was inconsistency in the implementation of the regulations.

While some of the most innocuous comments made at such meetings were deemed unsuitable for publication other, more provocative items, remained uncensored. This was most clearly apparent in the series of articles written by Kevin O'Higgins that appeared in the *Nationalist and Leinster Times*. The inconsistency was also reflected in the suppression of newspapers. Although several titles were similarly judged to have breached Defence of the Realm regulations in April 1918 the duration of their suppressions ranged from one week (*Westmeath Independent*) to five months (*Clare Champion*). This unevenness surfaced again in relation to publication of the Dáil Éireann loan prospectus when the *Limerick Leader*, *Midland Tribune*, and *Munster News* were only briefly banned while the *Southern Star* was only allowed resume publication several months later.

While the Office of the Press Censor operated in Dublin, newspapers at least had some form of guidance regarding the regulations. Even if it was only a facade for the restriction of Sinn Féin publicity it is reasonably clear that Decies sought to be fair to all publications. However, the closure of this office in September 1919 left provincial papers in a precarious position as they were still legally obliged not to publish material that might spread 'disaffection'. The increased levels of violence from 1920 onwards only further imperilled their situation. Newspapers found themselves caught up amidst the reprisals carried out by Crown forces. Yet however random these reprisals appeared, it was primarily recognised Sinn Féin organs such as the *Galway Express*, *Westmeath Independent*, *Leitrim Observer*, and *Kerryman* that were subjected to attack that resulted in lengthy and enforced closures.

There is little doubt that the censorship and suppression of the 1916–21 period was an extremely taxing time for Irish nationalist newspapers, many of which were only in the early stages of their development. It was a time characterised by uncertainty, instability, and insecurity. Ultimately the attempt to influence the output of the print media proved most ineffective as support for Sinn Féin continued to increase and rarely wavered prior to the Anglo-Irish Treaty of 1921. If anything, the censorship was counter-productive as republican propaganda cited the banning of newspapers as attacks on a free press. The commemorative issues of many of the provincial newspapers suppressed during these years almost proclaim their suppression as a badge of honour. Ultimately this may be the most telling commentary of all on how newspapers regard attempts to tell them what they may or may not publish.

Disclosure statement

No potential conflict of interest was reported by the author.

Notes

1. Ferriter and Riordan, eds., *Years of Turbulence*.
2. Ó Drisceoil, "Keeping Disloyalty within Bounds," 54.
3. Jeffery, *Ireland and the Great War*, 14.
4. Ibid., 47.
5. Townshend, *Easter 1916*, 11.
6. Laffan, *Resurrection of Ireland*, 266.
7. Townshend, *The Republic*, xiii.
8. Laffan, *Resurrection of Ireland*, 351.
9. Ibid., 351.
10. Kennedy, "Anglo-Irish Treaty," 642.
11. Larkin, "Double Helix," 125.
12. Horgan, *Irish Media*, 6.
13. Doughan, "The Printed Word," 257–61. 68 of the 135 provincial papers being published during these years had been established after 1880.
14. Legg, *Newspapers and Nationalism*, 109.
15. Ibid., 132.

16. Hochschild, *To End All Wars*, 222.
17. Ibid., 222.
18. Marquis, "Words as Weapons," 477.
19. Ibid., 478.
20. *Freeman's Journal, Irish Times*, 29 Oct. 1915.
21. O'Brien, "With the Irish in France," 165.
22. *Irish Journalist*, 1, no. 1 (October 1914).
23. Ibid., 1, no. 2 (November 1914).
24. *Irish Independent*, 2 Feb. 1944.
25. Kennealy, *The Paper Wall*, 7.
26. *Irish Press*, 3 Feb. 1944.
27. *Killarney Echo*, 17 May 1916.
28. *Nationalist and Leinster Times*, 3 May 1919.
29. Press Censorship Report, September 1917, CO904/166/1, UK National Archives (hereafter cited as Press Censorship Report).
30. *Freeman's Journal*, 29 Apr. 1919.
31. *Kilkenny People*, 13 Sept. 1919.
32. Lord Decies to All Editors, 17 Aug. 1916. Press Censorship Records 1916–1919, 3/722/15-128, National Archives of Ireland (hereafter cited as Decies to all editors)
33. Decies to all editors, 1 Feb. 1917, 3/722/15-128.
34. Decies to all editors, 30 Nov. 1918, 3/722/21-71.
35. Decies to all editors, 5 Dec. 1918, 3/722/18-1.
36. Decies to all editors, 5 Jun. 1916, 3/722/15-128.
37. Lord Decies to Editors, All Newspapers, Ireland, 25 June 1917. Kenny Papers, 5.3, Dublin City University (hereafter cited as Decies to Irish newspapers)
38. Decies to Irish newspapers, 19 July 1917.
39. Decies to all editors, 15 Feb. 1918, 3/722/21-71.
40. Decies to Irish newspapers, 27 September 1917.
41. Decies to Irish newspapers, 5 December 1917.
42. Press Censorship Report, March 1918, CO904/166/2.
43. Press Censorship Report, August 1918, CO904/167/1-89.
44. Press Censorship Report, July 1918, CO904/167/1-11.
45. Press Censorship Report, December 1918, CO904/167/1-378.
46. Press Censorship Report, January 1919, CO904/167/2-427.
47. Press Censorship Report, February 1919, CO904/167/2-508.
48. Decies to Irish newspapers, 27 May 1918.
49. Press Censorship Report, July 1918, CO904/167/1-508/9.
50. Press Censorship Report, October 1918, CO904/167/1-299.
51. Press Censorship Report, September 1918, CO904/167/1-242.
52. Press Censorship Report, March 1919, CO904/167/2-546.
53. *Leitrim Observer*, 19 Sept. 1914.
54. *Nationalist and Leinster Times*, 31 May 1919.
55. Ibid., 7 Jun. 1919.
56. Ibid., 14 Jun. 1919.
57. Ibid., 28 Jun. 1919.

58. Ibid, 2 Aug. 1919.
59. *Kilkenny People*, 2 Oct. 1920.
60. *Irish Times*, 4 Sept. 1920.
61. Seditious literature, censorship, publication of offensive articles, CO904/160/6-485, UK National Archives (hereafter cited as Seditious Literature).
62. Seditious Literature, CO904/160/6-485.
63. Press Censorship Report, March 1918, CO904/166/2.
64. *Freeman's Journal*, 14 May 1919; *Western People, 125th Anniversary 1883–2008* (18 November 2008);
65. *Irish Independent, Irish Times*, 12 Feb. 1937.
66. This loan took the form of bonds issued by Dáil Éireann in order to raise funds for the apparatus of the Irish Republic that it was attempting to establish in defiance of British rule.
67. *Freeman's Journal*, 4, 9 Dec. 1918.
68. *Newspaper Press Directory and advertisers' guide 1917*, p.207; *Western People, 125th Anniversary 1883– 2008* (18 November 2008);
69. *Connaught Telegraph*, 28 Dec. 1918.
70. *Irish Independent*, 14 Nov. 1916.
71. Ibid., 26 Dec. 1917; *Southern Star 1889–1989: Centenary Supplement* (11 November 1989).
72. Decies to editor, *Southern Star* 22 Apr. 1918, 3/722/20-66.
73. Collins to Kelly, 18 November 1918, Irish Volunteers Papers, P16, University College Dublin.
74. O'Brien to Blythe, 15 January 1919, Ernest Blythe Papers, P24/1028, University College Dublin.
75. Inspector General's and County Inspectors' monthly confidential reports, October 1919, CO904/110-250, UK National Archives.
76. *Freeman's Journal*, 19 Mar. 1920; *Irish Independent*, 27 Mar. 1920;
77. *Irish Independent*, 16 Aug. 1920.
78. *Connacht Tribune*, 11 Sept. 1920.
79. *Freeman's Journal*, 21 Sept. 1917; *Irish Independent*, 22 Sept. 1917;
80. Wheatley, *Nationalism and the Irish Party*, 241.
81. *Westmeath Independent: 150th Anniversary Special Supplement* (July 1996).
82. *Irish Times*, 11 Nov. 1920.
83. *Leitrim Observer: 1890–1990—One hundred years of history in the making* (28 November 1990); *Leitrim Observer*, 30 Nov. 1968;
84. *Enniscorthy Echo*, 30 Mar. 1929; *Mayo News*, 6 Mar. 1937;
85. *Cork Examiner*, 30 Aug. 1921.
86. *The Kerryman 1904–2004* (5 August 2004).
87. *Irish Independent*, 21 Apr. 1921.
88. Ó Drisceoil, "Keeping Disloyalty within Bounds," 52; Martin, *Ireland in insurrection*, 40.

References

Doughan, Christopher. "The Printed Word in Troubled Times: A Historical Survey of the Irish Provincial Press, 1914–1921." Unpublished PhD thesis, Dublin City University, 2015.

Ferriter, Diarmaid, and Susannah Riordan, eds. *Years of Turbulence: The Irish Revolution and Its Aftermath: In Honour of Michael Laffan*. Dublin: University College Dublin Press, 2015.

Hochschild, Adam. *To End All Wars: A Story of Protest and Patriotism in the First World War*. London: Pan Books, 2012.

Horgan, John. *Irish Media: A Critical History Since* 1922. London: Routledge, 2001.

Jeffery, Keith. *Ireland and the Great War*. Cambridge: Cambridge University Press, 2000.

Kennealy, Ian. *The Paper Wall: Newspapers and Propaganda in Ireland 1919–1921*. Cork: Collins Press, 2008.

Kennedy, Michael. "The Anglo-Irish Treaty." In *Atlas of the Irish Revolution*, edited by John Crowler, Donal Ó Drisceoil, and Michael Murphy, 642–648. Cork: Cork University Press, 2017.

Laffan, Michael. *The Resurrection of Ireland; the Sinn Féin Party, 1916–1923*. New York: Cambridge University Press, 1999.

Larkin, Felix M. "Double Helix: Two Elites in Politics and Journalism in Ireland, 1870–1918." In *Irish Elites in the Nineteenth Century*, edited by Ciaran O'Neill, 125–136. Dublin: Four Courts, 2013.

Legg, Marie-Louise. *Newspapers and Nationalism: the Irish Provincial Press,1850–1892*. Dublin: Four Courts,1998.

Marquis, Alice Goldfarb. "Words as Weapons: Propaganda in Britain and Germany During the First World War." *Journal of Contemporary History* 13, no. 3 (July 1978): 467–498.

Martin, Hugh. *Ireland in Insurrection: An Englishman's Record of Fact*. London: Daniel O'Connor, 1921.

O'Brien, Mark, "With the Irish in France: the National Press and Recruitment in Ireland 1914–1916." *Media History* 22, no. 2 (2016): 159–173. doi:10.1080/13688804.2016.1141043

Ó Drisceoil, Donal. "Keeping Disloyalty Within Bounds? British Media Control in Ireland, 1914–9." *Irish Historical Studies* 38, no. 149 (May 2012): 52–69.

Townshend, Charles. *Easter 1916: The Irish Rebellion*. London: Allen Lane, 2005.

Townshend, Charles. 2013. *The Republic: The Fight for Irish Independence, 1918–1923*. London: Allen Lane.

Wheatley, Michael. *Nationalism and the Irish Party: Provincial Ireland 1910–1916*. Oxford: Oxford University Press, 2005.

'A BIT OF NEWS WHICH YOU MAY, OR MAY NOT, CARE TO USE'
The Beaverbrook-Healy friendship and British newspapers 1922–1931

Elspeth Payne

As the formal Anglo-Irish union ended, Tim Healy, Irish nationalist politician turned Free State Governor-General, and Lord Beaverbrook, politician and press baron, entered their second decade of friendship. Whereas existing scholarship privileges the place of this Beaverbrook-Healy nexus in pre-independence high politics, this article uses correspondence preserved in the Beaverbrook papers to rectify neglect of the post-1922 era and reintegrate the relationship into Anglo-Irish and British media history. The article demonstrates how this enduring informal connection functioned as a vital forum for the exchange of material relating to British and Irish affairs and examines its influence on news content. Tracing the construction of individual stories and overall editorial lines, this case study also facilitates a broader re-evaluation of the process of content production and, by analysing feedback relayed in the letters, provides fresh insight into the place of the British press in the new Irish Free State.

Introduction

In August 1922 Lord Beaverbrook, the Canadian-born British politician and press baron, wrote to Tim Healy, Irish nationalist and soon to be Free State Governor-General, declaring 'I miss seeing you so much and it is a pity that we should be separated by an expanse of water'.[1] Healy was equally smitten. His letter of May 1923 closed 'I think of you constantly every day'.[2] At a time when the Anglo-Irish relationship was in a state of flux, this friendship formed in the House of Commons in 1910 was still going strong.[3] Upon Healy's seventy-second birthday in 1927 Beaverbrook's telegram professed 'my love and affection for you is ageing but like good wine growing mellow and I hope more pleasing to you'.[4] The feelings were still mutual. In the same year Healy wrote 'You can understand that an old man who has got tired of himself, shd [should] be pleased that he has not grown tired of others'.[5] In 1931, three days before Healy died, Beaverbrook's exchanges with Elizabeth Healy confirmed 'I looked upon your father as my dearest friend'.[6] Their enduring friendship is at the heart of this article.

By 1923 Beaverbrook owned controlling shares in the *Daily Express, Sunday Express* and *Evening Standard*.[7] While the *Evening Standard* targeted a limited elite London-based readership, Beaverbrook secured a growing share of the exploding press sales of the nineteen-twenties for his tabloid titles.[8] Across this rapid expansion and intense press competition, second only to the *Daily Mail,* the *Daily Express* boasted a circulation of 850,000 in 1925 and 1,693,000 in 1930. The newspaper of record, the *Times*, claimed equivalent figures of 190,000 and 187,000 respectively.[9] In 1928, a decade after launching, sales of the now-profit making *Sunday Express* reached 440,000.[10] In the competition for consumers, these British newspapers actively courted the expanding, and until 1933 duty-free, Free State market.[11] Although exact numbers are frustratingly elusive, in 1926 the *Mail* and the *Express* had a combined Free State circulation of 49,119. At just under 50,000 less than the bestselling Irish equivalent, this denotes a significant readership. In 1931 the two rival tabloids secured Free State sales of 60,707.[12]

Capturing the politics of Beaverbrook's publications in a few pages, let alone a few sentences, is a near impossible task. Although broadly conservative in outlook, shaped by the fluctuating allegiances, whims and feuds of their proprietor, the titles were loyal to no one party or politician.[13] Irish editorial policy epitomises this media autonomy. Credited by Beaverbrook and subsequent scholars to Healy's influence, the recruitment of his newspapers to the nationalist cause marked a reversal of the publications' traditional unionist sympathies and contradicted established personal allegiances.[14] In the decade that followed, both proprietor and publications continued to position themselves as allies of the new Free State.

The importance of the Healy-Beaverbrook nexus in the pre-independence period has been documented extensively. It is not hard to see why. From covert host of meetings during the third home rule crisis to secret advisor in the 1921 treaty negotiations, as a proselyte to the Irish cause Beaverbrook played an active role in shaping the final days of union. The source of Beaverbrook's conversion—friendship with Healy—encouraged and facilitated these clandestine manoeuvrings. Across this upheaval Beaverbrook entrusted Healy with oversight of the Irish message of his newspapers and subsequently secured his appointment as Governor-General.[15] Looming large in the men's own recollections, this thrilling high political drama has similarly lured subsequent scholars.[16] Although the friendship continued to flourish, waning academic interest in an apparently settled and increasingly obscured Irish question has left what happened next in the Beaverbrook-Healy saga largely unanswered.[17]

Piecing together fragments preserved in private correspondence, this article continues their story. It begins by exploring the importance of the relationship and the elite contacts it facilitated as a connection between Britain and Ireland after 1922. Removing the friendship from the typical confines of high political narratives and biography, it then considers the implications of this link for the construction of news content. With a growing Irish readership of British publications in this period, the final section uses the letters to reconcile Free State demand with the traditional narrative of government censorship. Marrying the insights of the rarer sustained commentary—in particular, exchanges on the topic of religion—and the tantalising glimpses afforded by their more frequent one-line remarks, an often-hidden side of news production is recovered. Demonstrating how an intimate alliance furnished one individual with the undisclosed and unofficial power of editor, censor and content contributor, the article offers a different kind of newspaper history.

I

'Thanks for the political news'. So read Healy's letter to Beaverbrook on 30 January 1922. The correspondence, having scolded his friend for not providing more information on the 'one man I wd [would] have liked to hear about ... yourself', moved swiftly on to more pressing business concerns.[18] The service that Beaverbrook had provided to prompt this gratitude lasted substantially longer. From a cheerful account of the 'holiday spirit' of the *Daily Express* offices during the 1926 General Strike to a critical review of Lloyd George's 1928 industrial programme, Beaverbrook remained a window into British affairs.[19] Notably, upon British Conservative Prime Minster Andrew Bonar Law's resignation in May 1923, Healy solicited Beaverbrook's thoughts on the Boundary Commission.[20] Despite being provided for in the 1921 Treaty, the representative body charged with reviewing the border that partitioned Ireland was yet to be established. Confident that any recommended redistribution would render the Northern Irish state untenable, thereby securing a united Ireland, the Commission was a long-term pet project of the Irish Governor-General. While restoration of peace in the Free State had removed one barrier, Stormont's boycott continued to impede progress.[21] Healy was cognisant that the change of regime at Westminster might bring the issue back on to the political agenda. Professing himself to be 'so out of English politics I hardly know what advice to give now on this head', Healy instead relied upon Beaverbrook's superior counsel. Adding that he was 'glad to hear that you [Beaverbrook] dined with L. [Lloyd George] & hope you will steer him as the right course to take', Healy entrusted his friend with influencing potential policy makers.[22] Earlier that year, Healy had sought to utilise Beaverbrook's intimate associations with Bonar Law to secure the return of Sir Hugh Lane's art collection from London to Dublin's National Gallery.[23] In 1922 as civil war dawned in the Free State, Healy's appeal for the pardoning of Joseph O'Sullivan—assassin of famous British army officer turned security advisor and Ulster Unionist Member of Parliament, Field Marshall Sir Henry Wilson—had again relied upon Beaverbrook's sway over 'distinguished' persons.[24] Hampered by unfavourable political climates, neither the O'Sullivan or Lane request were successful.[25] Nevertheless, the very act of asking is indicative of Healy's continued faith in his intense friendship with Beaverbrook.

In return, Healy kept Beaverbrook abreast of Irish-related developments. Indeed, Healy's O'Sullivan appeal rested on the conviction that absolution for the man who had lost a limb at Flanders might sway the Labour-inclined Irish diaspora vote at the next British election while alleviating wider revulsion and risk of reprisal. As treaty tensions simmered, Healy's letters predicted that, popular with only a 'claque' in a few electoral districts, Éamon de Valera would be 'squelched' at the Free State polls in 1922.[26] Two years later, countering reports in the *Daily Mail*, Healy instructed that although admittedly 'not a strong man', President Cosgrave was 'sticking on very pluckily and showing great adroitness in the Dail [sic]'.[27] In 1925 Healy wrote gleefully relaying rumours rife in Ireland that Beaverbrook planned to purchase the *Irish Independent*.[28] The accuracy of these accounts is of little interest here. Coming from the man who had converted Beaverbrook to the Irish cause in the first place, Healy's authoritative offerings retained their ability to shape the press baron's evolving views.

This facet of the relationship was particularly valuable in Beaverbrook's Empire Free Trade Crusade. With Healy's correspondence freely offering encouragement and feedback on the endeavour, Beaverbrook engaged his supportive friend to secure necessary information on relevant Free State developments. In February 1930 Beaverbrook's employee conveyed such a request:

> Lord Beaverbrook has been informed that Mr. Cosgrave has introduced into the Free State a special system for regulating the price of margarine.

> It seems very difficult to get any information on this side, so I wonder if you would be kind enough to send Lord Beaverbrook any information you possess on this subject.[29]

Healy readily obliged. He forwarded the letter to the Free State agricultural minister Patrick Hogan with instructions to contact Beaverbrook directly.[30] Healy had already confirmed, rightly or wrongly, that Hogan was in favour of the scheme and had recommended an interview with the minister.[31] His response also provided unsolicited information identifying the Dublin Gas Directors as probable backers, declaring these men to be symptomatic of the wider business community and labelling the Northern Irish finance and agricultural ministers as theoretical but not practical supporters.[32] Although the Free State did not feature heavily in the campaign, receiving no mention in Beaverbrook's *My Case for Empire Free Trade*, in their capacity as intermediaries the two men continued to connect Britain and the now-dominion Ireland.

The Beaverbrook-Healy nexus functioned as a hub out of which new contacts were made. From job requests to letters of introduction, contemporaries identified and successfully exploited the effectiveness of this communication line. Beaverbrook and Healy were themselves conscious builders of this network. Notably, during W. T. Cosgrave's visit to London in February 1923, Healy compelled Beaverbrook to make contact with the Free State President.[33] It was possibly this personal connection that prompted Cosgrave's civil war *Daily Express* articles and informed the paper's overwhelmingly positive presentation of the president.[34] Four years later Cosgrave would join Healy on a private yacht chartered by Beaverbrook for a social weekend on the Irish Sea.[35] Fast-forward thirty years and Beaverbrook and Cosgrave were communicating directly as friends in their own right. Across the nineteen-sixties Beaverbrook sent gratefully received copies of his published works. Cosgrave assisted in the locating of Irish material for future publications, provided relevant material he held, and confirmed 'Do not hesitate to question me on anything'.[36] Offering warm remarks in lieu of attending the twentieth anniversary dinner of Beaverbrook's 1940 Club, Cosgrave's tribute to the press baron included fond recollections of their nautical adventure and the mutual friend who had set them up in the first place.[37] Prominent Irish nationalist politicians Eamon Duggan, Kevin O'Higgins and William O'Brien and Irish newspaper proprietor William Lombard Murphy were similarly introduced to Beaverbrook via Healy.[38]

Correspondingly, Beaverbrook connected Healy with key employees working on his publications. Upon the engagement of a Mr Russell as the *Daily Express*'s Irish correspondent in 1923, Beaverbrook wrote introducing his new employee and confirming that his protégée was 'entirely favourable to the Free State cause, and in no circumstances will he betray you, or act in any way contrary to your interests'.[39] Healy's response disclosed that a face-to-face meeting with Beaverbrook's 'Cambridge boy' had subsequently taken place.[40] A year earlier, Beaverbrook had similarly presented the *Daily Express*'s C. J. Ketchum to Healy and urged the two to meet.[41] While Russell wrote under the anonymous title of '"Daily Express" Special Correspondent', Ketchum, with articles published under his own name, was something of a celebrity journalist. Some form of enduring relationship between Healy and Ketchum subsequently developed. On Healy's resignation in 1928, it was Ketchum who interviewed the former Governor-General and produce a series of articles on Healy's five-year term in office.[42] When the *Express*'s serialisation of Emil Ludwig's *Life of Christ* sparked outrage in the Free State three months later, the two were still in touch as Ketchum endeavoured to minimise the damage caused by the allegedly blasphemous biography.[43] Later, detailing the high points of his own career, Ketchum included a 'dinner with Tim Healy, and an interview on the future of his country'.[44]

These Irish correspondents were part of a wider journalistic network to which Healy had access. Healy was in frequent communication with a Mrs Alexander.[45] Alexander in turn relayed the necessary information to the relevant editor.[46] Exchanges with other members of Beaverbrook's staff were not uncommon. Beaverbrook was the crucial but not the only facilitator of this. These links were perhaps also possible thanks to Healy's pre-existing relationship with R. D. Blumenfeld, editor of the *Daily Express* from 1909 until 1929 and editor-in-chief of the publication from 1924 until 1932.[47] Letters went alongside face-to-face meetings. Notably, in 1928 Healy informed Alexander 'We have had Mr. Blumenfeld and the bunch of the English journalists here. They enjoyed their visit to Killarney and the weather was good.'[48] No further information on the visit remains. Why the journalists were there, who organised it, and what they did while in the Free State has been lost. Two years earlier, fearing the increasing dominance of American attitudes, Beaverbrook had organised an educational tour of the British Isles for a group of Canadian schoolteachers.[49] Possibly Beaverbrook now engineered the journalists' trip to remedy lingering misconceptions of Ireland. Perhaps Blumenfeld wanted to meet his old Irish contact. Or maybe this was just a holiday. Whether for business or pleasure this was a further opportunity to forge new contacts.

Like the original friendship it was born out of, and functioning in much the same way, the creation of this wider hub of contacts benefitted both engineers. Securing privileged access to prominent Irish individuals suited Beaverbrook's appetite for politics and society as well as the demands of his newspapers. Here was a route to insight and influence as well as a potential scoop. Linking up his staff with the well-positioned Free State Governor-General held similar advantages. In return, direct contact with these journalists provided Healy with access to exclusive, mass readership platforms. The personal link thereby provided an important wider unofficial connection between British and Irish societies in the post-independence era.

II

What did this transnational relationship and its offshoots mean for British news content? It perhaps explains the prominence and favourable tone of stories relating to Healy in the *Daily Express*. Healy's appointment to the position of Free State Governor-General, for example, merited front page and editorial space. Here he was depicted as a physician with the 'Healying Touch'.[50] As valued guides to affairs in their respective nations, and with intense faith in one another, these political and social exchanges between trusted confidants also conceivably went further to mould the wider attitudes of both recipients. Given Beaverbrook's control over publication ideology and content, and Healy's association with Beaverbrook's employees, these interactions could inform the outlook of the *Daily Express, Sunday Express* and *Evening Standard*.[51] Healy's accounts of the unthreatening and unpopular de Valera or the still-feisty Cosgrave plausibly shaped tabloid assessments of these politicians and their wider political landscape. They may in part explain the *Express's* sustained confidence in the latter, disdain for the former, and general propensity not to panic over the changes in the Free State of the nineteen-twenties. Not produced or consumed in a media vacuum, these articles could in turn influence the lines taken by rival publications. Tracing concrete impact on philosophies is somewhat problematic. Although important in content creation, they are often elusive in the individual article. Struggles to understand cause and effect are compounded by the multitude of factors driving the nuances of often complicated and at times convoluted press discourses written by multiple journalists. This phenomenon is also noted in Bingham, Gender, Modernity and the Popular Press, 16–17.

Specific cases of the direct impact of this continued mechanism for the communication of ideas and information can be traced through the preserved correspondence. Most directly Healy wrote articles for Beaverbrook's publications. Healy offered a letter on the Battle of the Boyne to mark its anniversary in 1924.[52] A year later he provided a column on the retirement of the chairman of the Port of London Authority, Lord Devonport. In accordance with the author's instructions, this piece was published unsigned in the *Express* on 31 March 1925.[53] Further examples of content by Healy can be found in the *Express* including articles, exclusive interviews and, as directed by Beaverbrook, Healy's serialised memoirs.[54] Newspaper articles by and interviews with notable figures, of benefit to both contributor and publisher, were not unusual; Healy was not exceptional in this respect. Healy's participation and successful publication were feasibly encouraged, however, by his connection with Beaverbrook. Moreover, given the demanded anonymity of the Devonport article, these named contributions are potentially symptomatic of a more common hidden phenomenon. Indeed, discretion would again be paramount in 1929 with instructions to the *Express's* editor-in-chief that 'he must treat the source [Healy] of the information privately'.[55]

Similarly obscured in the newsprint are the topics Healy recommended for publication. In December 1926 Healy wrote to Beaverbrook detailing the fraudulent scandal around the collapse and looming liquidation of the Workman Clark Belfast shipyard, 'a bit of news which you may, or may not, care to use'. The same letter offered 'Another bit of Belfast news', alleging that the Northern Irish leaders of opinion feared the ramifications of a British Labour government on the subvention their existence relied upon.[56] Beaverbrook's response suggests he was paying attention to such leads, or at least claiming to, assuring Healy: 'I have asked Blumenfeld to look up at once the Workman and Clark story and also the subvention to the Northern Government'.[57] Without Healy's intervention these stories may not have reached the tabloid proprietor or editor. Healy was perhaps eager to forward these particular rumours as they reflected poorly on the six counties. In 1931 he was again keen to relay news of the Royal Mail 'socalled [sic] Moratorium' in the region, declaring it to be 'the most audacious yet attempted since the Workman &

Clarke [sic] swindle'.[58] Other updates communicated by Healy in the post-1922 period were seemingly encouraged by disdain for Northern Ireland. His appeal for O'Sullivan's life in 1922 had claimed 'The Orangemen in the 6Cos [six counties] take life so easily that my feelings may be blunted'.[59] Healy's feedback on Canadian Prime Minister Robert Borden's proposed federal solution to the Irish problem in 1924 similarly rested on the conviction that while able to dupe the press and British sentiment, for loyalists 'Killing Catholics ... is a better sport than cockfighting'. Healy warned that 'drunk, they [loyalists] curse England'.[60] Convinced that an 'overture of murder' was being orchestrated in Belfast to sabotage the Boundary Commission, Healy presented Beaverbrook with damning accounts of contemporary Northern Irish politics.[61]

Healy's article suggestions were not always so highly politically charged. In May 1927 he provided a shorthand account of community singing in Dublin.[62] In July 1929 it was instructions issued from Holyhead: 'Noticed at Euston large bales of <u>Sunday Express</u> loaded into van for Ireland. Think a good "snap" of this c' [could] be taken & interest public'.[63] Beaverbrook confirmed that he would 'see that the photograph is taken at once'.[64] In June 1930, Healy recounted the tale of Lord Ashton's contested will. A note on the top of the letter stating 'This was read to Baxter' indicates this successfully made it into the hands of the then editor-in-chief of the *Daily Express*.[65] Healy's endeavours were not restricted to Irish affairs. Mayan discoveries, a Spanish Jesuit's new battery and information on China secured from a returned missionary were just as faithfully relayed.[66]

Beaverbrook actively courted these contributions. With Healy's expressed Empire Free Trade enthusiasm, Beaverbrook sought an article of endorsement for the *Sunday Express*.[67] Upon receiving Healy's letter on the dispersal of the Duke of Leinster's residence, Beaverbrook enlisted Healy to secure the necessary notes on the collection for a piece in the *Evening Standard*.[68] Other requests were unprompted. In July 1924 Beaverbrook asked Healy to ascertain the contribution of the Guinness Brewery to the Free State revenue and its projected domestic and export trade. Not atypically, this inquiry included reassurance that 'he [Beaverbrook] will not deal with it any way which would appear hostile to the Free State, but as a matter of interest'.[69] This process also extended to less highbrow topics. Permission was sought, for example, to print news of Healy's son's election as Master of the Coombe Hospital.[70] Beaverbrook's explicit fidelity to the Free State allowed this supply line of information to flourish.

The extended network of contacts utilised this route to manipulate news content. As the details of the first Free State national loan were being finalised in October 1923, Healy relayed a letter from the Free State Finance Minister Ernest Blythe. Blythe requested that, as 'English comment on our financial position will be extremely important', Healy should persuade Beaverbrook:

> that in the papers which he controls, sympathetic comments should be offered on the efforts of the Government here to effect economies which would enable the Budget to be balanced ... and generally to conduct our finances on sound and conservative lines.[71]

Beaverbrook complied, arranging for the content of Blythe's forthcoming statement in Dáil Éireann and support for the loan to be printed across the *Express, Evening Standard* and the *Daily Mail*.[72] The Irish postmaster general similarly recruited Healy in July 1924 to promote the Tailteann Games in the *Express*. The application and, in accordance with Healy's wishes, publicity material, were dutifully relayed to Beaverbrook.[73] In reality the revived Irish sporting and cultural Olympics appear to have received limited tabloid coverage.[74] But the exchange itself is testimony to outsider understanding of the possibilities the Beaverbrook-Healy link held. For some, like Blythe, this assessment certainly paid off; he successfully influenced British press content.

In editing, Beaverbrook and his staff had the opportunity to modify these news offerings. It was not uncommon, however, for relevant proofs to be submitted to Healy for review. In 1927 this included Beaverbrook's forthcoming article staking Healy's claim to the title of 'greatest parliamentarian'. Although the returned draft recorded minor and primarily stylistic amendments—a word substituted for an appropriate synonym, an 'a' inserted or a 'the' deleted—these were changes nonetheless.[75] Crucially, the opportunity for more substantial revisions was there. Cover letters accompanying now lost manuscripts confirm this potential. In August 1923 Beaverbrook had requested Healy:

> read over the enclosed and tell me if you have any objection to its publication in the "Sunday Express". I am sorry to trouble you but I fear printing anything over my signature that may do you an injury. If you think I do harm, please suggest alterations.[76]

Expressing hope that his 'small changes improve it', with a few alterations Healy again sanctioned publication.[77] Earlier feedback scrawled on an already-critical account of papal envoy Monsignor Salvatore Luzio's peace mission during the civil war indicates that Healy did use his privileged position to do more than copy edit. Clarifying, for example, that 'Neither de Valera nor any of his men ever offered regret, qualification or explanation of these crimes since the revolt began' Healy's modifications bolstered the article's contention that Luzio had chosen the wrong ally in de Valera. Proposing the document end with a note that 'President Cosgrave may not have spent long at the classics, but he seems to have assimilated their wisdom more than some Roman scholars', Healy's pen likewise boosted the support expressed for the Free State government's rejection of the peace overture.[78] Beaverbrook's forthright devotion to Healy, and by extension the Free State, was presumably integral in the creation of this content in the first place. Bringing in Healy as an informal editor furnished the Governor-General with a direct means of ensuring these discourses were to his liking. If words are seen to be the constructors of meaning—the way in which we process and understand the world—then altering even a word, a phrase, or sentence matters.[79]

Although already published and interacting with the readership, Healy also offered Beaverbrook feedback on articles printed in his newspapers. On 11 October 1928 this extended to Lord Castlerosse, the Anglo-Irish architect of the *Sunday Express's* 'Londoners Log' feature. Healy challenged Castlerosse's claim that novelist Eimar O'Duffy had been inspired by Seán O'Casey in his latest work. Healy contended 'This will not be so. O'Duffy has already printed two or three clever novels, and is undoubtedly a man of wayward genius'.[80] Beaverbrook gratefully replied 'I am showing Valentine [Castlerosse] your statement about O'Duffy, and telling him to use it'.[81] By critiquing material already in circulation, Healy therefore had the power to modify subsequent content.

Whether a true reflection of correspondent priorities or the skewed picture painted by the surviving archival material, religious rather than exclusively Irish content offers the clearest example of Healy's influence at work. In December 1925, marked 'still more private', an upset Healy's letter opened 'With pain I read above in Fridays Express [sic]'. Attached was the sixth instalment in the series 'What do we believe?', a self-proclaimed 'mission of investigation of the religious beliefs of today' by James Douglas. Douglas's contention that the Christian notion of the virgin birth was an 'obsolete dogma' which 'ought never have been invented' had offended Healy's devout Catholic sensibilities.[82] Beaverbrook was quick to reassure his old friend that he did not approve of this view. Moreover, as Douglas was employed on the paper, Beaverbrook claimed that he would have refused him an audience had he known the content in order to protect the paper from association with dissent it did not endorse.[83] This was neither an isolated incident nor the most distressing.

Upon the publication of Ludwig's *Life of Christ* in the *Express* in 1928, a distraught Healy condemned the series, deploring:

> to suggest that the Mother of God (conceived without sin and therefore an Eve before the Fall) renounced her son on any occasion or declared him abnormal or unbalanced is horrible and shocking. It stabs at both [Mary and Jesus] with one thrust.

This 'poisoned arrow' of a generally heretical text was not, Healy asserted, rooted in any biblical text. He concluded the *Life* was the 'malignant daub of either a Jew or an Atheist'.[84] The *Life* had once again left Healy aggrieved. Beaverbrook's response, however, suggests that he had in fact taken on board Healy's feedback on the Douglas article. Beaverbrook confirmed 'I asked the "Express", when I heard publication was to be undertaken, if the Life was orthodox. I was assured it was so'. Moreover, while appearing in his letter more interested in the Newmarket races, Beaverbrook again took action in an effort to prevent a repeat scenario. Unable to read all instalments prior to print, Beaverbrook assured Healy that he would 'insist on Blumenfeld carrying out this task for the future'.[85]

Just two months later Healy would again contact his friend about the religious content of his newspapers. Worse than the 'Jewish liar', there was now some author with an 'Irish name', G. H. Daly, denying the 'Heaven & Hell arrangement'.[86] Beaverbrook consequently secured a promise from the *Sunday Express* and *Daily Express* that they were not to 'depart from the orthodox in the future'.[87] As this was the third complaint, the feedback mechanism clearly was not flawless. Nevertheless, Healy's reactions do seem to have had some impact on the paper. In March 1930, Healy wrote to Beaverbrook gushing 'The Express and its policy continues to interest all my friends here'.[88] Beaverbrook replied, 'The policy of that paper should interest you, because your interests are its chief concern'. He went on to recollect 'Only the other day there was printed something of a non-evangelical character. I reprimanded the Editor. I then heard he had sent word to his staff that Mr. Healy must not be offended again'.[89] Perhaps Beaverbrook was just placating or flattering his old companion. He may simply have been paying lip service to such assurances and claims as part of his habitual desire to please those closest to him. Possibly these anecdotes contained an element of Beaverbrook's trademark teasing, encouraged by the familiarity of theological clashes with Healy.[90] But as Healy subsequently seemed generally happy with the content, it is certainly plausible that his views were in fact valued and acted upon. After all, Beaverbrook delayed publication of his *Divine Propagandist* until after Healy's death to avoid upsetting his friend.[91] It is feasible that Beaverbrook also modified the religious outlook of his newspapers according to Healy's disposition. In doing so, the Beaverbrook-Healy friendship moulded wider, non-Irish, British press discourses.

III

Exploring the influence of the Beaverbrook-Healy nexus therefore facilitates better understanding of the processes of news content construction. Analysing this element of production also provides insight into the relationship of British national titles with the newly independent Free State. Endeavouring to get stories into Beaverbrook's newspapers, Healy and his Free State associates still perceived British press comment to be an important public forum. This was not about securing the 'quality' ear of the *Times* with the 'right' readership, but infiltrating the mass platform of the often-dismissed tabloids. Equally, Beaverbrook was still keen to print stories about the Free State. This required either a British readership perceived still to be interested in their neighbours, contrary to the dominant retrospective narratives, or an important Free State audience. The *Daily Express* had both.

Through his correspondence with Healy, Beaverbrook was able to get a better understanding of this Free State readership. We, in turn, can get a better feel for this imagined audience. Of Ludwig's *Life,* Healy reported 'The priests in Kilkenny asked the news-agent not to sell it & letters have appeared calling on the Govt. [sic] to exclude such papers from the country.'[92] At the height of the scandal Healy lamented 'Sorry the Ludwig purulences [sic] hit the *Express* here. I felt they wd [would]'. Healy cautioned Beaverbrook that the incident would probably feature in the forthcoming Evil Literature debates.[93] Of the later alleged Daly heresy, Healy again warned Beaverbrook that 'your property & outlay in Ireland are remorselessly undermined by some boyo who cares little for you or your enterprises'. He went on to suggest 'If you care for an Irish circulation, pay a Catholic Censor to read atheistic articles'.[94] Here was additional incentive, beyond his friend's feelings, to modify the religious tone of the *Express*. It was purportedly a central factor driving, or halting, Irish consumption of the title.

With the extensive scholarship surrounding the Committee of Evil Literature, this aspect to the British press's relationship in Ireland is part of a well-known narrative; fearing moral pollution, foreign content was subject to censorship and prohibition.[95] A letter from Healy a month before the Ludwig incident offers a dramatically different assessment of the paper's fortunes. Relaying an observation from Senator McLaughlin, Healy stated:

> his [McLaughlin's] Parish Priest in Buncrana (Donegal) recommended the <u>Express</u> to his flock, from the altar, for its Mexican articles. He added that it is beating the <u>Mail</u> in Derry & Donegal ... He finds news in the <u>Express</u> of a local sort, better than in the <u>Independent</u>.[96]

Contrary to the familiar storyline of Catholic condemnation, here was at least one pulpit endorsement. Moreover, with the paper apparently flying off the shelves in Donegal, any boycotts following the Douglas, Ludwig or Daly scandals do not appear to have lasted very long. The paper was still relevant to Irish audiences and not just for its Irish stories. Paradoxically, the British press was both enthusiastically condoned and consumed while simultaneously being vocally condemned and censored.

MEDIA CONNECTIONS BETWEEN BRITAIN AND IRELAND

Writing to Alexander a year later, Healy confirmed the potential popularity of the *Express* in the Free State. His letter praising H. V. Morton's coverage of the Dublin open air masses to mark the centenary of Catholic Emancipation noted, 'I went to several news agents [sic] for a copy of Monday's Express but could not obtain one. Sold out everywhere'. The pious but increasingly frail Healy had been unable to attend in person. Nevertheless, or possibly encouraged by this, Healy lauded Morton's piece as:

> superbly restrained and alike for Catholics and Protestants – England and Irish. But his mere bit of journalism for English readers nothing could have been more choicely voiced.

> Irish newspapers have spent columns upon the grand event but the Express condensed them into a tabloid which contained and preserved all the elements.[97]

Although the target audience for the article was an imagined English readership with a continued interest in Irish affairs, these eager Irish consumers perhaps agreed with Healy's assessment. Discussing material cut from his memoirs, Healy remarked:

> It is impossible for the English to know what wd [would] go in Ireland, as for the Irish – speaking "by & large" – to prophecy what wd [would] interest Britain. Not mere vanity but experience helps me to the conclusion that what London rejections, your editions in Ireland shd [should] embrace.[98]

Beaverbrook agreed. These reminiscences would be 'of much greater interest to the Irish readers of *Express*.[99] Nationality was therefore understood to dictate taste and accordingly distinctions were drawn between English and Irish readership. This sat, however, alongside a recognised transnational, and perhaps transcultural, appeal to well-crafted journalism.

Conclusion

The two friends were no strangers to controversy. Yet after 1922 the Beaverbrook-Healy relationship was largely accepted by contemporaries.[100] The privileged access and unprecedented position as unofficial editor it afforded the Irish Governor-General on foreign publications raised no eyebrows. Although leading politicians had protested the sensitive information leaked to Beaverbrook's British titles during the treaty negotiations, the exercise of the relay function of the Healy-Beaverbrook partnership across the subsequent decade was not scandalous.[101] Printed interviews and signed articles in Beaverbrook's paper were likewise not in themselves problematic. Only when comments were deemed to compromise the political impartiality demanded by Healy's position in office were concerns voiced. With Healy's speeches meriting similar reproach, here the newspaper was merely the medium of expression.[102]

The correspondence analysed in this article was just the tip of a much bigger iceberg. Littered throughout the Beaverbrook's papers are invitations to visit, reprimands for failing to do so and arrangements for face-to-face meetings. Although often social, the features identified in the letters were perhaps continued or even furthered at these reunions. Business ventures, legal advice and family updates were equally prominent in their written exchanges. This was not just, then, about politics or even the press, but a genuine, all-encompassing friendship. Indeed, 'My dear Tim' and 'My dear Max', or in one case 'Max, Honey', were the preferred salutations of letters adorned with lavish sentiments of mutual affection. Symptomatic of their sustained devotion, it is perhaps not surprising that, while not its exclusive or even primary function, their earnest relationship continued to bridge the gap between Britain and Ireland. This trusted connection and its offshoots held the potential to mould both individual and publication outlooks. It provided a direct means of gathering, verifying and contradicting information on the respective countries and a forum for proposing, amending and critiquing article content. With an eager but sensitive Irish readership as well as an interested imagined British audience, these were valuable exchanges. Returning to the Beaverbrook-Healy nexus thus demonstrates how an easily overlooked friendship was an informal yet integral component of the complex processes informing the construction of British media discourses. As Healy was the first in a succession of similarly intense attachments, re-examining Beaverbrook's links with confidants such as Arnold Bennett, Valentine Castlerosse, Stanley Morison and Michael Foot may be equally rewarding.[103]

Disclosure Statement

No potential conflict of interest was reported by the authors.

Funding

This work was supported by the Irish Research Council under the Government of Ireland Postgraduate Scholarship Scheme and by Trinity College Dublin under the R. B. McDowell Fellowship.

Notes

1. Aitken to Healy, 1 August 1922, BBK/C/163, Beaverbrook Papers, Parliamentary Archives. Awarded the peerage in 1917, the text of this article refers to William Maxwell Aitken by his title.
2. Healy to Aitken, 25 May 1923, BBK/C/163.
3. Callanan, *Healy*, 490–1.
4. Aitken to Healy, 17 May 1927, BBK/C/165.
5. Healy to Aitken, 19 April 1927, BBK/C/165.
6. Aitken to Elizabeth Healy, 23 March 1931, BBK/C/166b.
7. Beaverbrook also held a 49% stake in the *Daily Mail,* see Chisholm and Davie, *Beaverbrook,* 135, 207–8, 215–6.
8. Chisholm and Davie, *Beaverbrook,* 207–16, 240–1; Taylor, *Beaverbrook,* x–xi, 215.
9. Jeffrey and McClelland, "A world fit to live in", 29.
10. Chisholm and Davie, *Beaverbrook,* 230.
11. Cullen, *Eason and Son,* 347–58.
12. *Express/Mail* figures taken from Morash, *A History of the Media in Ireland,* 139 as cited in Rafter "Evil Literature," 411. Rafter also makes comparison with *Irish Independent.*
13. See Chisholm and Davie, *Beaverbrook*; Koss, *Rise and Fall*; Taylor, *Beaverbrook.*

14. See Aitken, *Politicians and the* press; Callanan, *Healy*, 556–9; Chisholm and Davie, *Beaverbrook*, 118, 176, 181; Taylor, *Beaverbrook*, 75, 187; Healy to Aitken, 7 April 1923, BBK/C/163.
15. Aitken, *Politicians and the Press*, 39–44; Callanan, *Healy*, 493–5, 551–9, 566–81, 598; Chisholm and Davie, *Beaverbrook*, 176–81, 118–20; Taylor, *Beaverbrook*, 80–2, 187–90, 204.
16. See Healy, *Letters and Leaders*; Aitken, *The Decline and Fall*; Aitken, *Politicians and the Press*.
17. Only 32 pages of Callanan's 627-page monograph, for example, address the Governor-General era. Callanan's account of office, alleged role in the Boundary Commission and O'Brien's conspiracy theories were invaluable in the preparation of this article.
18. Aitken to Healy, 30 January 1922, BBK/C/163.
19. Aitken to Healy, 24 May 1926, BBK/C/165; Aitken to Healy, 14 October 1928, BBK/C/166a.
20. Healy to Aitken, 25 May 1923, BBK/C/163.
21. For further discussion of Healy's involvement in Boundary Commission see Callanan, *Healy*, 565, 577–86, 610–3.
22. Healy to Aitken, 25 May 1923, BBK/C/163.
23. Healy to Aitken, 9 January 1923, BBK/C/163.
24. Healy to Aitken, 29 July 1922, BBK/C/163.
25. Aitken to Healy, 1 August 1922 and 10 January 1923, BBK/C/163.
26. Healy to Aitken, 15 February 1922, 25 March 1922, BBK/C/163.
27. Healy to Aitken, 28 March 1924, BBK/C/164.
28. Healy to Aitken, 2 November 1925, BBK/C/164.
29. Skevington to Healy, 27 February 1930, BBK/C/166b.
30. Healy to Skevington, 3 March 1930; Healy to Beaverbrook, 3 March 1930, BBK/C/166b.
31. Healy to Aitken, 27 July 1929, BBK/C/166b.
32. Healy to Aitken, 3 March 1930, BBK/C/166b.
33. Healy to Aiken, 8 February 1923, BBK/C/163.
34. For Cosgrave articles see *Daily Express*, December 21, 1922 and March 12, 1923.
35. Taylor, *Beaverbrook*, 234.
36. Cosgrave to Aitken, 12 June 1963, BBK/C/99.
37. 1940 Club invitation, 2 May 1960, BBK/C/99.
38. See Healy to Aitken, 24 July 1924, BBK/C/164; O'Brien to Aitken, 1 July 1923, BBK/C/163; Healy to Aitken, 22 September 1925, BBK/C/164.
39. Aitken to Healy, 20 February 1923, BBK/C/163.
40. Healy to Aitken, 7 April 1923, BBK/C/163.
41. Aitken to Healy, 31 March 1922, BBK/C/163.
42. *Daily Express*, February 3–7, 1928.
43. Healy to Aitken, 26 May 1928, BBK/C/166a.
44. *Daily Express*, February 16, 1931.
45. Correspondence suggests Mrs Alexander was Beaverbrook's secretary in this period.
46. See for example Healy to Alexander, 7 February 1927; Alexander to Healy, 8 February 1927, BBK/C/165.
47. Chisholm and Davie, *Beaverbrook*, 103.
48. Healy to Alexander, 1928, BBK/C/166a.
49. Aitken to Healy, 24 May 1926, BBK/C/165.
50. See *Daily Express*, December, 4, 6–7, 1922.

51. See Taylor, *Beaverbrook*, x–xiii, 177, 249, 265 and Chisholm and Davie, *Beaverbrook*, 210, 213, 216–17, 229.
52. Aitken to Healy, 14 July 1924, BBK/C/164.
53. Healy to Aitken, 21 March 1925; Healy to Alexander, 23 March 1925, 26 March 1925, 30 March 1925; Alexander to Healy, BBK 25 March 1924, 27 March 1925, BBK/C/164.
54. See for example *Daily Express*, 24 August 1922, 30 August 1922, 6 July 1923, 13–19 November 1928. For exchanges on memoirs see for example Aitken to Healy, 18 March 1925, 31 March 1925, BBK/C/164; Aitken to Healy 14 July 1926, 17 July 1926; Alexander to Healy, 8 February 1927, BBK/C/165; Healy to Aitken, 29 March 1928, BBK/C/166a.
55. Aitken to Healy, 8 October 1929, BBK/C/166b.
56. Healy to Aitken, 23 December 1926, BBK/C/165.
57. Aitken to Healy, 25 December 1926, BBK/C/165.
58. Healy to Aitken, 30 January 1931, BBK/C/166b.
59. Healy to Aitken, 29 July 1922, BBK/C/163.
60. Memo, 17 November 1924, BBK/C/164.
61. Healy to Aitken, 25 March 1922, BBK/C/163.
62. Healy to Aitken, 5 May 1927, BBK/C/165.
63. Healy to Aitken, 6 July 1929, BBK/C/166b.
64. Aitken to Healy, 8 July 1929, BBK/C/166b.
65. Healy to Aitken, 7 June 1930, BBK/C/166b.
66. Healy to Aitken, 12 July 1926, BBK/C/165; Healy to Aitken, 7 October 1927, BBK/C/165; Healy to Aitken, 26 March 1930, BBK/C/166b.
67. Aitken to Healy, 13 July 1929, BBK/C/166b.
68. Healy to Aitken, 26 October 1925, 19 November 1925, 23 November 1925, 25 November 1925; Aitken to Healy 20 November 1925, BBK/C/164.
69. On behalf of Aitken to Healy, 17 July 1924, BBK/C/164.
70. Aitken to Healy, 28 December 1928, BBK/C/166a.
71. Blythe to Healy, 31 October 1923, BBK/C/163.
72. Aitken to Healy, 1 November 1923, BBK/C/163. See *Daily Express*, November 5, 1923; *Daily Mail*, November 22, 24, 30, 1923.
73. Healy to Aitken, 12 July 1924 and Walsh to Healy, 9 July 1924, BBK/C/164.
74. Assessment based on a reading of the *Daily Express*, August 1–19, 1924. For relevant content see *Daily Express*, August 7, 12, 18, 1924.
75. 'The Tim Healy Debate', [1927], BBK/C/165.
76. Aitken to Healy, 31 August 1923, BBK/C/163.
77. Healy to Aitken, 6 September 1923, BBK/C/163.
78. 'A Roman Candle', [1923], BBK/C/163.
79. See Fowler, *Language in the News*.
80. Healy to Aitken, 11 October 1926, BBK/C/165.
81. Aitken to Healy, 12 October 1926, BBK/C/165.
82. Healy to Aitken, 20 December 1925, BBK/C/164. For offending article, see *Daily Express*, December 18, 1925. For series, see *Daily Express*, December 2–24, 1925.
83. Aitken to Healy, [1925], BBK/C/164.
84. Healy to Aitken, 7 May 1928, BBK/C/166a.
85. Aitken to Healy, 11 May 1928, BBK/C/166a.

86. Healy to Aitken, 17 July 1928, BBK/C/166a.

87. Aitken to Healy, 26 July 1928, BBK/C/166a.

88. Healy to Aitken, 26 March 1930, BBK/C/166b.

89. Aitken to Healy, 28 March 1930, BBK/C/166b.

90. See Taylor, *Beaverbrook*, 237, 281; Chisholm and Davie, *Beaverbrook*, 232.

91. Callanan, *Healy*, 626; Chisholm and Davie, *Beaverbrook*, 245; Taylor, *Beaverbrook*, 649–50.

92. Healy to Aitken, 15 May 1928, BBK/C/166a.

93. Healy to Aitken, 26 May 1928, BBK/C/166a.

94. Healy to Aitken, 17 July 1928, BBK/C/166a.

95. See Horgan, *Irish Media*; Martin, *Censorship*; Rafter, "Evil Literature".

96. Healy to Aitken, 24 April 1928, BBK/C/166a.

97. Healy to Alexander, 26 June 1929, BBK/C/166b.

98. Healy to Aitken, 2 March 1928, BBK/C/166a.

99. Healy to Aitken, 10 March 1928, BBK/C/166a.

100. British links in general, not with Beaverbrook specifically, placed Healy at the centre of Irish nationalist colleague and confidant William O'Brien's conspiratorial *The Irish Free State: secret history of its foundation*. Charged with relaying false and unfulfilled British assurances regarding the task of the Boundary Commission, O'Brien presented Healy as instrumental in securing the 1921 settlement and thereby the betrayal of Ireland. Remaining unpublished, the provocative theory necessarily lacked subscribers. See Callanan, *Healy*, 576, 581, 613–6.

101. Callanan, *Healy*, 570.

102. Callanan, *Healy*, 612, 622–3.

103. Taylor, *Beaverbrook*, 237.

Bibliography

Aitken, William Max. *Politicians and the Press*. London: Hutchinson, 1925.

Aitken, William Max. *My Case for Empire Free Trade*. London: [s.n.], 1930.

Aitken, William Max. *The Decline and Fall of Lloyd George: And Great was the Fall Thereof*. London: Collins, 1963.

Beaverbrook Papers, Parliamentary Archives.

Bingham, Adrian. Gender, Modernity and the Popular Press in Inter-War Britain. Oxford: Oxford University Press, 2004.

Callanan, Frank. *T. M. Healy*. Cork: Cork University Press, 1996.

Chisholm, Anne, and Michael Davie. *Beaverbrook: A Life*. London: Pimlico, 1993.

Cullen, L. M. *Eason and Son: A History*. Dublin: Eason and Son, 1989.

Fowler, Roger. *Language in the News: Discourse and Ideology in the Press*. London: Routledge, 1991.

Healy, Tim. *Letters and Leaders of My Day*. 2 vols. New York: Frederick A Stokes, 1929.

Horgan, John. *Irish Media: A Critical History Since 1922*. London: Routledge, 2001.

Jeffrey, Tom Jeffrey, and Keith McClelland. 1987. "A World Fit to Live in: The Daily Mail and the Middle Classes 1918–39." In *Impacts and Influences: Media Power in the Twentieth Century*, edited by James Curran, Anthony Smith, and Pauline Wingate. London: Routledge.

Koss, Stephen. *The Rise and Fall of the Political Press in Britain*. London: Fontana, 1990.

Martin, Peter. *Censorship in the Two Irelands, 1922–39*. Dublin: Irish Academic Press, 2006.

Morash, Christopher. *A History of the Media in Ireland*. Cambridge: Cambridge University Press, 2010.

Rafter, Kevin. "Evil Literature: Banning the News of the World in Ireland." *Media History* 19, no. 4 (2013): 408–420.

Taylor, A. J. P. *Beaverbrook*. London: Hamilton, 1972.

TUNED OUT? A STUDY OF RTÉ'S RADIO 1 PROGRAMMES *DEAR FRANKIE/WOMEN TODAY* AND BBC 4'S *WOMAN'S HOUR*

Finola Doyle-O'Neill

In the conservative, Catholic milieu of 1920s and 1930s Ireland, it should come as no surprise that women's issues were not addressed on the national broadcaster, Radió Éireann. Women's voices were effectively 'tuned out' and it would not be until 1963 that some attempts were made to publicly address, however benignly, issues on female sexuality. This came in the form of Ireland's first radio agony aunt, Frankie Byrne and her programme Dear Frankie. *However, it wasn't until the 1970s that Irish radio really began to give women's concerns the attention they fully deserved. It began in earnest in the form of* Women Today, *a pioneering radio programme, broadcast on RTÉ Radio 1 from 1979 to 1984. The fact that it lasted just four years and did not enjoy the longevity of the BBC 4's flagship radio programme,* Woman's Hour, *serves as a useful comparator for the issue addressed in this article; namely the differing cultures experienced by women, both on and off-air, at the BBC and RTÉ between 1926 and 1984.*

Female Employees at Radió Éireann and the BBC Radio Network from 1926 to 1940s

2RN, Ireland's first national radio service, began broadcasting on New Year's Day 1926. Throughout its early years, programmes aimed specifically at women were limited to twice weekly 'talks' of 10 or 15 minutes duration. When ardent Gaelic League activist and dramatist, Mairéad Ní Ghráda, joined the station in 1926, she was given the title 'Woman Organiser and Relief Announcer.' Her duties required the organisation of programmes for women and children, while also being expected to work as an announcer, a translator of News on sight into Irish, and as a presenter of live 'gramophone concerts.'[1] Her successor as 'Woman Organiser' was Kathleen Beattie, a married woman, who, due to the Marriage Bar, could only be employed on a temporary basis, albeit that lasted 25 years! Ms Beattie duties included organising *Children's Hour* and providing 'general clerical assistance, interviewing members of the public, and acting as announcer from time to time.'[2]

Into this rather confined and undefined Women and Children's Department—dismissively referred to by one male producer as the 'WC Department'[3]—came the highly politicised Sidney Gifford. She was sister to Grace, who married the doomed 1916 leader, Joseph Mary Plunkett hours before his execution at Kilmainham Gaol. Sidney, a relatively well-known journalist, adapted the broadcasting pseudonym, John Brennan, and hers is remembered as a radical and lively voice in the early decades of Irish radio. Her talks as John Brennan, which began in 1926, were not confined to domestic matters, but also dealt with the Arts and Irish politics. Moreover, Irish suffragist, Hannah Sheehy Skeffington, co-founder of the Irish Women's Franchise League, as well as the aristocratic Irish literary

Revivalist, Maud Gonne, both contributed occasionally to the on-air programme schedule. However, there were no permanent female voices on-air in the early years of Irish radio.

In 1937, 2RN changed its name to Radió Éireann and by 1939 its Annual Report describes women's programming as those concerning 'all the subjects dear to the home-maker, including home-crafts, dieting, gardening, cooking, laundry work, care of babies, first aid etc.'[4] The wide-spread belief that women's concerns extended only to the domestic sphere, highlights the rampant misogynistic and discriminatory treatment of female presenters and their listeners. Moreover, just 1% of the station's output was listed as 'women's talks' and were slotted in under the generic rubric of Women and Children's programming.

At the BBC, there was also a focus on broadcasting as a 'domestication' of the airwaves. However, BBC Radio differed quite significantly from Radio Éireann in its deference to woman and their importance as a primary radio audience. Indeed the juxtaposition of the radio and the fireside was commonplace in British radio literature of the 1930s. This is evidenced in a Winter Issue of the *Radio Times* in 1935. An advert advised that one of the real pleasures in life was listening to radio while the fire glowed in the hearth.[5] This placement of the hearth and the wireless together as a focus of interior space and family pleasure, propels mothers and housewives centre stage as part of this broadcasting family. Moreover, daytime radio on the BBC expressly addressed the woman as monitor of the private sphere. Radio talks such as 'Motherhood and a Fitter Nation' and 'Colds, Tonsils and Adenoids'—broadcast in 1934[6]—used the airwaves to encourage women to forge closer links with the doctor and the hospital. The concept of radio as the 'constant companion' was adapted by the BBC to schedule daytime programmes around life of the busy housewife, a role that was held in considerable esteem by the BBC Radio Corporation.

Furthermore, within the Corporation itself, employment conditions for women were impressive. Subsequent to the passage of the Sex Disqualification (Removal) Act of 1919, women in Ireland and the UK were formally granted access to the professions. BBC Radio, initially at least, took a modern approach to women broadcasters. The station employed women from the very start, not only in support roles as telephonists, typists and catering staff, but by 1926, according to Kate Murphy in her book, *Behind the Wireless—An History of Early Women at the BBC*[7]—as 'doyennes' of radio. Many women stars were launched by the BBC, including the first female comedienne Helena Millais, known as 'our lizzie.' Mabel Constanduros was to follow in 1925 with her character 'Mrs Buggins' and then the most celebrated radio actor of them all was Gladys Young, who was first heard in a drama broadcast in May 1926.[8]

The inter-war years provided many opportunities for woman who wished to rise up the ranks of the BBC Corporation. From 1931 to 1947, Mary Somerville was Director of Schools Broadcasting and was even granted three months' maternity leave on full pay, followed by an additional three months on half pay in 1929. Even earlier, in 1927, Hilda Matheson became the first Director of Talks. Matheson had been head-hunted by BBC's Director General John Reith and she is credited with transforming the broadcasting of the spoken word. In 1929, she instituted the *Week in Westminster* radio programme, aimed at educating newly enfranchised women about the workings of parliament where all the speakers were female MPs. Two other vital areas of female control and power at the BBC were the appointments of Isa Benzie in 1933 as Foreign Director and Mary Adams as the first woman television producer in 1937. In addition to these women at the top echelons at the BBC, was Elise Sprott. Her role as Women's Press Representative ensured the feminine angle of the BBC was constantly in the news. Moreover, in spite of the introduction of a Marriage Bar in 1932, women deemed to be of special importance to the BBC Corporation were entitled to stay. Furthermore, these top women employees were very well remunerated compared to their sisters in other industries and in particular their counterparts in Radió Éireann. Hilda Matheson, as Head of Talks at the BBC, wrote to her then lover Vita Sackville-West in 1929: 'My BBC pays me a fat screw, £900 a year, which is more than any other woman I know gets and quite out of the way generous.'[9]

In contrast, Radió Éireann had never really considered the concept of the 'engaged female listener' and was certainly never concerned with female comediennes and such like. Indeed women who worked in the broadcasting service were treated as inferior to their male colleagues in terms of pay and conditions. The Civil Service Marriage Bar applied, but unlike the BBC, Radio Éireann's rigid imposition of the ban on married female staff resulted in many women, who might have had a promising future in broadcasting, never being allowed to fulfil that potential.

Rules were bent somewhat to allow The Radió Éireann Players—the radio drama group—to employ married women. However, they were paid less than men for many years, and there was no such thing as maternity leave. According to former RTÉ radio presenter Doireann Ni Bhriain,[10] whose mother was a Radio Éireann Player, as late as 1971, one woman producer recalls being grateful for being allowed to take paid annual leave to coincide with the birth of her child.

Equally the RTÉ Symphony and Light Orchestras employed married women, recognising eventually that their talent as musicians did not disappear on marriage. This recognition came only after many years of battling by the women musicians with their employers, and with the Department of Finance. In 1932, when the Station Orchestra was being expanded, a newspaper advertisement stated that women were to be paid £1 a week less than men (for the same work) and they might be required to resign on marriage.[11] When the orchestra was expanded again in 1935, the thorny issue of lower pay for women musicians was raised again. As one female letter writer to the *Evening Mail* asked: 'Did the women pay less for their musical training than men? Do they pay less for a musical instrument? Are rent and rates on a lower scale for women? Is income tax lower in their case?'[12]

Despite these grim conditions, the situation was considerably worse for female instrumentalists at the BBC. Prior to World War Two, the main orchestras and bands in the UK were filled entirely with male musicians. This would change in 1943 when the glamorous and gutsy Ivy Benson became a resident Dance Band Leader at the BBC. Her appointment provoked outrage from the all-male Dance Band Director's Union,[13] resulting in a detailed written complaint to Broadcasting House.

Paradoxically, the BBC's willingness to nurture female entertainers on-air, contrasted sharply with its hostile opposition, not only to female musicians but also to women announcers and newsreaders. The latter were tuned out of the BBC service in its early years as their voices were deemed to lack sufficient authority for the job.[14] When the voice of the first female announcer—that of Sheila Borrett—was first heard on the BBC Home Service in 1933, the *Radio Times* predicted: 'panic among the horsehair armchairs, with retired colonels muttering darkly over their muffins.'[15] In the event, it was not the colonels, but mostly women listeners who wrote in to complain, and the experiment was abandoned after three months.

The Beginning of Woman's Hour on BBC 2 and Women's Programmes on Radió Éireann from the 1940s to 1960s

At the BBC, women employees had become much more visible, as Britain's war-time efforts had meant that they were frequently called upon to fill available roles. This included training as engineers and filling in for absent male presenters. This change opened up new opportunities for women, and would lead to more challenging radio programmes presented by and especially created for women, including *Women's Hour*, which was created by BBC Controller of Light Programmes, Norman Collins. *Woman's Hour* was first broadcast on October 1946 on the BBC's Light programme, now called BBC 2. Though the product of a man's world-(created and presented initially by a man, journalist and ex-RAF intelligence officer, Alan Ivimey)—from its inception, it had always been distinctly *for* women. This was evident from its 2pm scheduling, after a woman's housework was finished but before the children came home from school. Early episodes featured items such as 'cooking with whale meat,' 'I married a lion-tamer' and 'how to hang your husband's suit.'[16] Yet, it deliberately departed from a 'domestication' of the airwaves and adapted its own unique approach to the female listener. According to broadcasting historian and former BBC Radio producer, David Hendy: 'In 1948 no other programme on the BBC would have discussed the menopause, as *Woman's Hour* did,'[17] causing quite a flurry of concerned memos from one senior Corporation figure, overcome by all the talk of hot flushes.

Yet, When Joan Griffiths took over as presenter of *Woman's Hour*, women were gaining recognition for their radio skills, resulting for example, with an MBE for Janet Quigley for her radio programmes *The Kitchen in Wartime, Calling all Women* and *The Factory Front.*[18]

Ireland's neutral status in the Second World War presented no such opportunities for Irish women to excel on air. Moreover, the Irish female listener contented herself to writing down lists of ingredients from Maura Laverty's much loved cookery talks on *Housewives' Half Hour* during the 1940s. This limited range of programming for women, coupled with a paucity of female presenters, continued to a large extent throughout the 1950s, though the canvas had broadened somewhat to include the Arts and wider social affairs. *Between Ourselves*, produced by Petronella O'Flanagan, had as one of its regular contributors, the eminent Irish writer, Kate O'Brien. The 30-minute *Scrapbook for Women*, a musical and literary programme stylishly scripted by Dan Treston, was another regular broadcast in that decade from the Womens and Children's Department.

It took until the 1960s for the station to cover more challenging programmes for women. Síle Ní Bhriain's weekly series 'A Woman's World' stands out as a pioneering insight into the lives of women. Additionally, the era of the lunchtime sponsored programmes had arrived, many aimed at the housewife and the family. These included radio soap operas such as the *Kennedy's of Castleross* to the *Fruitfield Programme*, the latter providing responses to queries regarding housekeeping, cooking and gardening.

MEDIA CONNECTIONS BETWEEN BRITAIN AND IRELAND

Up to the late 1960s, the perception of the woman as homemaker and wife dominated the agenda. Although it was accepted she might have cultural interests too, these areas were not covered on Irish radio. Furthermore, the years in which many women were employed in factories and other low paid jobs, were also never reflected on the national broadcaster. Neither was there any indication that they might have a role to play in politics, or have any aspirations to positions of power or influence.

RTÉ Radio 1 reflected the level of debate that was taking place—or not taking place—on the conditions in which people lived. Broadcasting mirrored and was influenced by the social and political conditions of the time. In the realms of Church and State, there was a very limited amount of questioning of authority. This was reflected on radio where any discussion of women's lives confined itself to un-contentious issues. There is a telling moment in one of Sile Ni Bhriain's *A Woman's World* series in the 1960s, when she tentatively and politely enquires of a male interviewee from the Irish Productivity Committee,[19] whether he thinks it is fair that men, having been served an evening meal by their stay-at-home wives, should venture out to their clubs or for a game of golf, while the wife is left tied to the kitchen.[20] To his credit, the man in question suggests it may not be fair, though he lays the blame squarely on the shoulders of the women for not standing up for themselves! The airwaves of the 1960s—on radio at any rate—were not the place for questioning the status quo as far as women were concerned.

Moreover, the backroom teams at RTÉ were full of women providing secretarial, legal, library and other support to programme makers. If women wished to marry, the price they paid, under the marriage bar, was compulsory resignation from their jobs. Thus, almost all of the technical and production staff was male, allowing for very little on-air recognition of the personal and romantic lives of women—that is until the advent of the radio programme—*The Woman's Page*-sponsored by Jacobs biscuits, in 1963. This was presented by Frankie Byrne and was affectionately referred to as *Dear Frankie*.

Dear Frankie—1963–1985

Frankie Byrne was Ireland's first radio 'agony aunt' and this simple action of unburdening oneself to a relative stranger, albeit through letters and not phone-calls, was to provide the template for an even more successful radio talk show, RTÉ Radio 1's the *Gay Byrne show*.[21] *Dear Frankie* opened with the words, 'Welcome to *Woman's Page*, a programme for and about you.' The programme started out as a 15-minute question and answer format on household issues but soon it was to become compelling radio for people all over Ireland. Listeners sat in kitchens, workplaces and boarding schools during their lunch-break, pausing in silence, as letter writers shared problems of jealous husbands, lovelorn teenagers and concerned "Irish' mammies". The most unique feature of *Dear Frankie* is that it was the first of its kind on radio to set people talking, and it helped begin a national conversation on the lonely struggles of generations of Irish women. It gradually transformed itself from a household—tips format to an intimate programme on relationships. The letters received by Frankie portrayed a different, more diffident era. These letters, mainly from women, discussed issues such as how to prod a reluctant boyfriend into popping the question, or how to get husbands to help out in the home. One such letter, which is certainly reflective of a different Ireland, was sent by a woman asking if 'she could get pregnant by sitting on her boyfriend's knee?'[22] Frankie Byrne advised her to have a chat with her mother.

The 1970s

By the 1970s Frankie Byrne's practical advice—which was limited by the strict moral guidelines set down by RTÉ—faced little challenge from *Here and Now,* a daily current affairs and features show which began on RTÉ Radio 1 in 1971. No concessions were made for the fact that the majority of the listeners were women, and the material covered was unimaginative and frivolous. *Here and Now* was succeeded by *Day by Day*, a daily current affairs show which was willing to give airtime to what were finally beginning to be called 'women's issues.' Hitherto unarticulated topics were now forming part of broadcasting discourse. The agenda being set by the Women's Liberation Movement was finding its way into programmes and opening up debates on subjects such as contraception which, throughout the 1970s, was still illegal in the Republic of Ireland.

For the first time, in the 1970s, radio began to open the airwaves to reflect the existence of women in roles other than those of homemaker and housewife. In 1972, the newly re-named RTÉ (to include the new television service), appointed Olivia O'Leary as its first woman journalist to cover 'hard' news. More developments came in 1979 when Caroline Murphy became Ireland's first woman sports reporter. Her appointment provoked a journalist in the *RTE Guide* to remark that 'it would take some time before people could get used to the idea of a female voice in sports programmes.'[23]

In Britain, on the other side of the microphone, women such as Monica Simms, were rising right to the top of BBC Radio 4. Simms was editor of *Woman's Hour* between 1964 and 1968, and went on to become Controller of Radio 4 from 1978 until 1983. In front of the microphone, 1972 was the year that the first female newsreader's voice was heard—that of Hylda Bamber. She was removed after six months. However, in a similar scenario to Ireland, by 1974, Women's liberation was in full swing in Britain and Sheila Tracy was appointed as the first permanent female newsreader on Radio 4.

The *Women Today* Radio Programme

By 1973 the marriage bar had finally been removed but it wasn't until 1979 that a group of like-minded people in RTÉ Radio decided it was time for a programme devoted specifically to women listeners. Producers Clare Duignan and Betty Purcell, reporter, Hilary Orpen, researcher Patrick Farrelly and presenter Marian Finucane were the pioneering team who launched *Women Today*. The show had been proposed by Clare Duignan to redress the inadequate representations of women in RTÉ broadcasting. Both Duignan and Purcell believed this daily spot on the national airwaves would allow women's voices to be heard and 'to take on all the patriarchal ideas that were still dominant in 1979.'[24] Subjects in the first season of broadcast included 'women in the Churches, depression, the psychological effects of miscarriage, broken engagements, an interview with Margaret Thatcher, lesbianism, women in education, sport, music.'[25] Here at last was the reflection on radio of the clamour for change being heard all over Ireland, and elsewhere. With a similar time-slot to

Woman's Hour, (which shall be dealt with in more detail later in this article), *Women Today* took on, head first, some of the basic women's rights issues of the day.

From its inception on 31 May 1979, *Women Today* discussed topics as diverse as women's sexuality, health and social standing. This approach was a difficult challenge to those at RTÉ who were more conservatively minded than the programme makers themselves. The minutes of the Editorial Committee's views on *Women Today*, make it clear that the committee faced a sustained challenge from both the public and from personnel within RTÉ itself. Opposition to a programme item on pornography was considered 'unsuitably scheduled at 2pm'[26]; An item on lesbianism received the following response: 'subjects like lesbianism should not be dealt with in daytime broadcast'[27]; An upcoming Programmes listing included: 'contraceptive methods, sexism in schoolbooks, sexual problems in women and medical advice.' Minutes of the Editorial meetings noted that '*Women Today* tended to deal too frequently with topics of minority interest.'[28]

Yet, *Woman Today* was unique in its focus on issues dealing with sexual behaviour and morality on daytime national radio. Its pioneering spirit came at a time in Ireland when television should have been at the forefront of ground-breaking programming. Instead, it was radio which engaged in the production of challenging ideas. These issues were already being discussed in the Irish media as part of the *Women's Pages* of newspapers and sparked by journalists such as Mary Maher, Mary Kenny and Nell McCafferty, all central to the burgeoning Irish Women's Liberation Movement of the 1970s.

Women Today encouraged women to talk. Woman spoke on air and in letters of the joys and pains of pregnancy and childbirth; the misery of difficult marriages; the exhilaration of sporting achievement; the frustrations of trying to break the male mould in traditional politics and the delight in succeeding. Most spoke of the unfairness which still caused women to be treated as unequal to men in so many spheres. There were many critics who believed the programme undermined family values, and accused it of being a danger to society. The *RTÉ Authority*[29] *Meeting Notes* regarding *Women Today*, highlight the heroic efforts of Michael Littleton, Head of Features and Current Affairs in RTÉ, to shield his team from the disquiet directed at the programme. His defence of its content was put in motion from his very first encounter with a young Betty Purcell, (later to become its series producer), when he offered her a job on *Women Today*. Littleton told Purcell to 'Do the best programme' she could and he would 'back her up.'[30] And he did. *Women Today* met with an avalanche of criticism, including from former Gaelic Athletic Association President and RTÉ Authority member, Con O' Murchú. He accused the show of becoming 'obsessed with Sex and obscenity.'[31] Minutes from both RTÉ Authority Meetings and Editorial Committee meetings offer insights into an Ireland not wholly ready for change, in particular where issues of a sexual nature were discussed so openly and as part of public discourse.

Moreover, there were times when the brashness and enthusiasm of *Women Today* rendered it somewhat provocative. For example, a group of women wrote to the *Evening Press* newspaper, complaining of the programme's 'morbid over-emphasis on sex,' with another listener in Sligo writing to presenter Marian Finucane, advising her to 'take care' and to 'not become an instrument of the devil.'[32] It is also quite noteworthy that at one Editorial Committee, a *Sunday Press* article was highlighted which criticised *Woman Today* for its inability to conduct 'altogether calmer and collected subjects covered on *Woman's Hour* on BBC Radio.'[33]

Those within RTÉ also queried its 2pm weekday slot, deeming it as unsuitable for a programme with such controversial content.[34] Attempts were made by some members of the Editorial Committee to move the programme to a late-night slot, with the suggestion that 'sensitive issues' would not be covered during the summer months while children were out of school. It was proposed that thorny issues would be held over 'to be taken up during the winter months.'[35] This suggestion of deferral was rebuffed by radio management who argued against a 'closed season' in broadcasting. BBC radio already had editorial guidelines in place which required the scheduling of programmes which 'contained explicit sexual content' to ensure that this content was 'relevant to the audience expectations of each radio network.'[36] The argument against a watershed for programme items on *Women Today* centred on the fact that from its first broadcast the programme contained explicit sexual discussions. Thus, clear content parameters were established and parents had the option of turning the programme off or tuning into the newly launched, RTÉ Radio 2. This was a youth station that began broadcasting on 31 May 1979, the same day as *Women Today* first went on air.

Yet, there was much support for the integrity of *Women Today*, even from Television managers who argued the programme had 'given a new dimension to women's programming', insisting that 'restrictions should be kept to a minimum as long as the team accepted management's reasonable wishes.'[37] Soon radio producers were enthusiastically offering a heady mixture of programmes on 'transvestites and wives, divorce and annulment; women's sexual problem.'[38]

The success of *Women Today* was largely due to the daily letters it received. These were central to the success of the programme. *Women Today* provided the platform for these emerging stories. Series producer Betty Purcell, in her book, *Inside RTÉ*,[39] explains the success of *Women Today*. She believed the programme 'consciously mirrored the subject matter' of the very vocal and active Women's Liberation Movement, of both which she and Hilary Orpen were members. It gave a platform to women who were put upon in the home or in the workplace. The programme also allowed access to real people with real voices, democratising the airwaves. Purcell also singles out the radio skills of the show's presenter Marian Finucane who had the ability 'to make the most intimate conversations happen over the airwaves.'[40]

After Marian Finucane's departure from *Women Today* in 1981, Doireann Ní Bhriain became its presenter. One of her strongest memories is of reading and writing letters. The programme's postbag reflected an extraordinarily range of views from women—and from men—for they too were listening and learning from *Women Today*.[41] Those who worked on the programme effectively provided an information service for women, not just on air but also off-air, responding to the endless stream of queries and cries for help which arrived on a daily basis. For women with small children during those years, the programme provided a real lifeline. Moreover, there must be some acknowledgement of how daring and courageous a move it was by RTÉ Radio[42] that the station was prepared to bring *Women Today* into the schedule in a prime-time listening slot, five days a week.

The 1980s

The 1980s would herald the confessional era. The air waves were filled with stories of institutional abuse and more intimate sexual stories and *Women Today* was at the coalface of all these revelations. This confessional genre of radio could be linked to the process of secularisation beginning to take force at that time in Ireland. This involved a renegotiation of sexual identities leading to competing versions from the Catholic Church and from the media. An increase in talk about the intimate sphere on radio was therefore not all together surprising at a time when new modes of behaviour were under negotiation. Doirenn Ni Bhriain,[43] refers to the public service agenda of the show and its role as a conduit for new ideas of how women could best contribute to society and instigate change.[44] *Women Today* would run until 1984, with its focus on issues such as family law, women and the church, domestic violence, illegitimacy and adoption. This latter programme on adoption in 1983, 'pulled back a curtain to reveal a large number of stories of heartbreak and loss, involving both mothers and their children, who had been given up for adoption.'[45]

Women Today inspired the setting up of women's support groups throughout the country. Media analyst, Brok Weber[46] highlights the functions of talk radio and its power to attract wide audiences. This notion of talk radio as a forum to negotiate important issues has become part of scholarly research and is pertinent to the role played by *Women Today* during its time on air. Putting women in touch with each other, providing information they could not otherwise have found easy access to, helping them to realise they were not alone, provided them with a real lifeline.

The ultimate agenda of *Women Today* had been to ensure that women's concerns gained as much attention as those of men. By the mid-1980s, this was finally beginning to happen in the form of *Lifeline,* presented each weekday by Marian Finucane, on RTÉ Radio 1. *Lifeline* gradually began to embrace the core listenership of *Women Today*, making women's issues part of the mainstream of Ireland's cultural and public life, similar to the activist role and impact of, *Women's Hour* in British life.

Woman's Hour from 1973 to 1984 and the Culture for Women at the BBC and RTÉ

By 1973, *Woman's Hour* had transferred from Radio 2 to Radio 4. In fact, there had been a dramatic shake-up of the BBC Radio network on 30 September 1967. This included the re-launch of BBC Radio 1 as a pop music station; the BBC Light Programme (launched in July 1945) was renamed BBC Radio 2 and the BBC Home Service (launched in September 1939) became BBC Radio 4.

Former *Woman's Hour* presenter, Sue MacGregor, recalls that the programme was now presiding over 'gynaecological talks, discussions on abortion, the pill, homosexuality, piles and incontinence ... divorce, single parenthood, physical and mental handicap.'[47] These were received with 'polite acknowledgement' rather than 'wholesale approval,'[48] with both editors and producers fully aware that too much talk of feminism and workplace revolutionaries would alienate its core listenership. This included all women, regardless of their sexual politics, who were welcomed into this 'unique mixture of jam, Jerusalem and genital warts.'[49]

Moreover, former *Woman's Hour* producer, Kate Murphy notes, that despite its early promise, by 1973, an internal BBC report highlighted wide-spread misogyny and discrimination in the BBC Corporation. The Report presented the uncomfortable news that less than 6% of senior posts were held by women. Murphy notes, as time evolved, 'the institutionalization and professionalization of the Corporation made it harder for women to obtain a top job.'[50] It took until the mid-1980s and the appointment of the BBC's first equal Opportunities Officer to help change the prospects of women on air at the BBC.

The culture for woman at RTÉ in the 1980s was not dissimilar to that of the BBC. In April 1981, the RTÉ Authority—the body formed to ensure proper governance of Ireland's radio and television stations—published a report called the *Working Party on Women in Broadcasting*. Its remit had been 'to consider job opportunities for women in RTÉ; the participation and representation of women in programmes; and the portrayal of women in advertisement.'[51] A section in the report which referenced the 'Participation of Women as Programme-makers and Presenters' made the following comments:

> A lone Martian, orbiting the earth, who happened to tune in to some hours of Irish radio or television, might well conclude that humankind is divided into two sexes in proportion of six-to-one.[52]

The Working Party also reported that women made up 'only 9% of radio producers' and 'inevitably these internal imbalances are reflected in programme output.'[53] Despite these misgivings, by 1984, *Women Today* was taken off the air, replaced as mentioned, by the daily phone-in radio show *Livline*, presented by Marian Finucane.

In contrast, the BBC's *Woman's Hour* was soaring to new heights and changing direction dramatically. By the 1980s, the average age of the *Woman's Hour* team had dropped by ten years, as single mother Sandra Chalmers became its editor in 1982. She was followed by Clare Selerie in 1986, and then Jenni Murray (2007)as its regular presenter. This young 'triumvirate'[54] in their thirties moved the programme agenda towards more subtle, but nonetheless, sexual frankness, albeit all three women denied they had any plans to turn the programme into a mouthpiece for feminism.[55] The world in Britain was changing for women and *Woman's Hour* reflected that change. The programme interviewed the country's first female Prime Minister, Margaret Thatcher, celebrated the Royal wedding of Charles and Diane with a quiz on royal occasions, and covered the emergence of female trailblazers, Kate Adie and Moira Stewart, in the world of broadcasting. *Woman's Hour* was also exploring new subjects of interest to women, reflecting changes in their lives. These included programmes on assertiveness, bulimia, job-sharing, cosmetic surgery, page 3 girls. The programme also welcomed more men on the show and notable interviewees in the early 1980s included the Archbishop of Canterbury and playwright Willy Russell. *Woman's Hour* examined all of the big issues of the day through a female lens. Its new editor, Sandra Chalmers, bought a 'fresh spirit'[56] to the programme. Soon it began to move from a reactive format to actually initiating the agenda itself. This was evidenced in programmes dealing with sensitive items, including those on families wrongly accused of child abuse to issues regarding IVF. By 1984, RTÉ's *Women Today* had ended its four-year tenure, as *Woman's Hour* continued to showcase the immense achievements of women throughout that decade and beyond.

Discussion and Conclusion

Some would argue that women's programming should never be severed from mainstream broadcasting. Yet, *Women Today* very consciously targeted the female listener. Ultimately, however, it did not achieve the longevity of the BBC's *Woman's Hour*, yet it very definitely met a palpable need at a very important time of change in the lives of many Irishwomen.

In contrast, *Woman's Hour* currently enjoys weekly listenership figures of 3.5 million, 40% of whom are male.[57] Danica Minic, in her article on *Woman's Hour*,[58] attributes the programme's longevity to its successful combination of identity, diversity, equality and transformative politics. This admixture has helped it evolve into a mainstream specialist programme, securing a daily broadcasting site to those interested in women's and gender issues. Minic acknowledges that the status of *Woman's' Hour* as a mainstream programme is only made possible by conditions that do not exist anywhere else. The BBC, with its wholly public broadcasting service is much better positioned than RTÉ-(with its dual-funded model and reliance on commercial as well as public funding)—to allocate resources to what many would now deem a specific subject area, with a gendered programme title. Therefore, *Woman's Hour* is a unique and resilient programme that few countries can emulate. This resilience was tested in 1990 when it was forced to change its time-slot from 2pm to 10.30am but it refused to change its name.

Nevertheless, *Women Today* was also unique. For four years it was a modern, audacious and relevant programme. Former programme producer Betty Purcell articulates it well when she says: '*Woman Today* provided—as indeed RTÉ is required to-, a necessary and a much-welcomed, if occasionally resisted, public service.'[59]

By the time it came off-air in 1984, *Women Today* had paved the way for another audacious and challenging daily radio show *Liveline*,[60] presented by Marian Finucane. This live phone-in programme granted access to all, to the airwaves. Its continuing success is due in no small part to the pioneering producers and presenters of *Women Today*.

Disclosure Statement

No potential conflict of interest was reported by the author.

Notes

1. Announcers Report and Program Schedule, 2 February 1926, RTÉ Archives.
2. Ibid.
3. Doireann Ní Bhrian interview with author, 15 November 2014.
4. RTÉ Annual Report 1939, 17.
5. Mitchell, *Women and Radio, Airing Differences*, 122.
6. Murphy, *Behind the Wireless*, 121.

7. Ibid., 251.
8. Ibid., 26.
9. Murphy, *Behind the Wireless*, 154.
10. The author in interview with Doireann Ni Bhriain, 5 October 2016.
11. Women in Irish Society Exhibition, RTÉ Archives.
12. *Evening Mail*, 3 May 1939.
13. *BBC News Magazine*, 'The 1940's Bandleader Who Braved Virulent Sexism,' 14 October 2014.
14. Hodgson, *For the Love of Radio 4*.
15. Ibid., 183.
16. Hodgson, *For the Love of Radio 4*, 186.
17. Hendry, *Life on Air*, 332.
18. Murphy, *Behind the Wireless*, 254.
19. Irish National Productivity Committee Minutes in, Irish State Administration Database, Dáil Éireann Vol. 190, 14 June 1961.
20. RTÉ Radio Archives.
21. This ran from 1973 to 1998, presented by Gay Byrne.
22. 'Dear Frankie', *Irish Independent*, 19 December 1998.
23. *RTÉ Guide*, 13–19 September 1971.
24. Purcell, *Inside RTÉ*, 43.
25. *RTÉ Guide*, 6–12 July 1979.
26. Editorial Committee Minutes, 8 June 1979.
27. Editorial Committee Minutes, 15 June 1979.
28. Editorial Committee Minutes, 24 August 1979.
29. The RTÉ Authority, its members appointed by the Government, was set up under the 1960 Broadcasting Act to monitor the content of RTÉ programming.
30. Purcell, *Inside RTÉ*, 45.
31. RTÉ Authority Minutes, 8 March 1980.
32. Purcell, *Inside RTÉ*, 47.
33. Editorial Board Minutes, 8 January 1981.
34. RTÉ Authority Minutes, 10 April 1980.
35. Editorial Committee Minutes, 14 September 1979.
36. *BBC Editorial Guidelines*, 2006.
37. Editorial Committee Minutes, 31 August 1979.
38. Editorial Committee Minutes, 14 September 1979.
39. Purcell, *Inside RTÉ*, 73.
40. Ibid., 61.
41. Doireann Ní Bhriain has kindly provided the author with copies of these letters from the *Woman Today* programme.
42. Radió Éireann becomes RTÉ under the 1960 Broadcasting Act, to incorporate the new television service.
43. Doireann Ni Bhrian in interview with the author, 14 November 2014.
44. RTE Archives—Women in Irish society Exhibition.
45. Purcell, *Inside RTÉ*, 95.
46. Brok Weber, 'A Loud Angry World on the Dial: 24 Hours of Talk Radio in a Town Meeting of the Alienated,' *New York Times*, 2 June 1992.

47. Ibid., 333.
48. Ibid.
49. Feldman, 'Twin Peaks,' 65.
50. Murphy, *Behind the Wireless*, 256.
51. RTÉ Authority Minutes, 8 February 1979.
52. A Working Party Report on Women in Broadcasting, April 1981.
53. Ibid., 16.
54. Hendry, *Life on Air*, 333.
55. Ibid., 333.
56. *Woman's Hour: From Joyce Grenfell to Sharon Osborne, Celebrating Sixty Years of Women's Lives*, 256.
57. *The Guardian*, Woman's Hour reaches 70th birthday—and no need for 'light dusting of powder,' 10 October 2016.
58. Minic, 'What makes an issue a Woman's Hour Issue?'.
59. Purcell, *Inside RTÉ*, 57.
60. *Lifeline* is now presented by Joe Duffy.

Bibliography

Feldman, Sally. 2000. "Twin Peaks: The Staying Power of BBC4's Woman's Hour." In *Woman and Radio-airing Differences*, edited by Mitchell C., 65. London: Routledge.

Hendry, D. *Life on Air: A History of Radio Four*. Oxford: Oxford University Press, 2008.

Hodgson, C. *For the Love of Radio 4*. Chichester: Summerdale, 2014.

Minic, D. "What Makes an Issue a Woman's Hour Issue?" *Feminist Media Studies* 8, no. 3 (September 2008): 301–315.

Mitchell, C. *Women and Radio, Airing Differences*. London: Routledge, 2000.

Murphy, K. *Behind the Wireless, A History of Early Women at the BBC*. London: Palgrave, 2016.

MurrayJ.. 2007. *Woman's Hour: From Joyce Grenfell to Sharon Osborne, Celebrating Sixty Years of Women's Lives, foreword by Jenni Murray*. 1996. London: John Murray.

Purcell, B. *Inside RTÉ: A Memoir*. Dublin: New Island, 2014.

TELEVISION AND THE DECLINE OF CINEMA-GOING IN NORTHERN IRELAND, 1953–1963

Sam Manning

This article assesses the impact of television ownership on cinema attendance in post-war Northern Ireland. It downplays a monocausal relationship between cinema and television, and emphasises the range of social, economic and political factors that led to cinema closures. While the coronation of Queen Elizabeth II acted as a catalyst for television ownership, it did not fundamentally alter patterns of cinema attendance. This research counters claims that cinema exhibitors were unresponsive to population shifts and examines the relatively large number of cinemas that opened in Northern Ireland in the 1950s. It then examines the impact of commercial television and documents the reasons for cinema closures in Northern Ireland's two largest cities: Belfast and Derry.

Introduction

Following the Second World War, cinema-going was the most popular form of commercial entertainment and UK cinema attendance peaked in 1946 with 1.6 billion admissions.[1] As post-war austerity gave way to increased affluence and a burgeoning consumer society, the composition of cinema audiences and the nature of cinema attendance changed. During the 1950s, rising incomes, population shifts, the growth of television, new forms of youth culture and a greater range of leisure activities all contributed to a rapid decline in cinema attendance. By 1963, UK cinema admissions fell to 367 million.[2] Cinema closures followed and these were more likely in areas where television was more firmly established. It is difficult to argue with Joe Moran's assertion that cinemas 'began seriously to decline in the late 1950s as their mainly working-class audiences acquired TVs on a large scale'.[3] However, the causes of cinema's decline have provided a source of debate for social scientists and historians. In 1962, economist John Spraos cited the closure of neighbourhood cinemas, increased travel distancs, less frequent public transport and higher admission prices as key factors.[4] Historians have subsequently followed this lead, avoiding monocausal explanations and placing greater emphasis on the changing nature of consumer capitalism and the arrival of the 'affluent society'.[5] Barry Doyle, furthermore, used Board of Trade statistics to show how regional variations in the introduction of television, alongside the size, age and location of existing cinemas, impacted the geography of cinema's decline in Great Britain.[6]

One flaw of these assessments is that they exclude Northern Ireland from their analysis, party since records of cinema attendance were collected separately from the rest of the UK. This article fills this lacuna and investigates the impact of television ownership on cinema attendance in Northern Ireland from the introduction of BBC television in 1953 to the opening of Ulster Television's (UTV) Strabane transmitter in 1963. Though Northern Ireland's population of 1.4 million was relatively small, this article offers further evidence of the geographical diversity of UK cinema attendance and builds on the work of historians who show the place-specific nature of cinema attendance.[7] It also bridges the gap between British and Irish studies of cinema-going and complements Kevin Rockett's existing work on film exhibition and distribution in Ireland.[8] Northern Ireland's lower wages and higher unemployment delayed the diffusion of television ownership, which was consistently lower than other regions in England, Scotland and Wales. This meant that cinema attendance remained strong until the mid-1950s. The evidence presented here suggests that independent exhibitors in Northern Ireland were more responsive to population shifts than their UK counterparts, constructing several new cinemas. This did not, however, prevent long-term declines in cinema attendance and the number of cinemas in Northern Ireland fell from 130 in 1958 to 107 in 1963.[9] While many Irish households received British television signal, Irish television (RTÉ) did not broadcast until 1961.[10] This was one of the reasons why cinema attendance declined later in the Irish Republic, where it peaked in 1954 with 54.1 million recorded admissions and fell to 30 million by 1965.[11]

Rex Cathcart and Robert Savage have traced the development of television services in Northern Ireland.[12] These accounts, however, do not consider television's impact on alternative leisure activities. In a previous article, I assessed how local geography, changes in the life cycle and the closure of cinemas influenced cinema-going practices in a working-class Belfast community.[13] While this included a discussion of the relative impact of BBC and ITV, the present article expands on these findings by placing them in a broader geographical context and introducing evidence from across the region. Records of Entertainments Duty kept by the Northern Ireland Ministry of Finance detail alterations in tax rates and contain the dutiable admissions for the majority of Northern Ireland cinemas, which provide a valuable insight into cinema attendance and audience habits.[14] While previous accounts have been overly reliant on statistical data, this article also uses a broad range of qualitative sources, such as local newspapers, trade journals and oral history testimony.[15] It follows the multi-method approach adopted by a group of Belgian cinema historians, who advocated the use of ethnographic methods alongside records of film programming and exhibition.[16]

The Introduction of Television and the Coronation of Queen Elizabeth II

The BBC television service opened in 1936, broadcasting to a limited audience in London and the Home Counties. The service was suspended in 1939, but after reopening in 1946, gradually spread throughout the UK regions. From 1948 to 1953, UK cinema admissions fell by 15.2% from 1.51 billion to 1.28 billion.[17] In the same period, Northern Ireland admissions fell by 13.97% from 32.98 million to 28.37 million.[18] From May 1953, the temporary Glencairn transmitter relayed the BBC signal from Scotland's Kirk O'Shotts transmitter to Belfast and the surrounding area.[19] On 2 June 1953, over twenty million UK viewers watched the television broadcast of the coronation of Queen Elizabeth II and it is rightly cited as a catalyst for increased television ownership. The number of UK television licences increased by 51.6% from 2.14 million in March 1953 to 3.25 million in March 1954.[20]

In Northern Ireland, the number of television licences increased dramatically from an extremely low base of 558 in 1953 to 10,353 in 1954.[21] Given the limited range of the television signal, 97.7% of these licences were held in Antrim or Down.[22]

Television sets were beyond the means of many working-class households and, in their 1954 survey of Belfast estates built by the Northern Ireland Housing Trust, Field and Neill found that only nine of 363 families had one in their home.[23] This meant that television footage of the coronation was experienced largely as a communal event. Approximately 20,000 Belfast residents watched television footage of the ceremony in private homes or public spaces.[24] Oral history interviews recorded with Belfast residents reveal that memories of the coronation were often linked to the absence of television in households and early experiences of television were often shared with friends and relatives. Jean McVeigh was born in 1943 and raised in a Roman Catholic Belfast household. Her house was so busy that she was sent to the local cinema:

> It was the only TV set in the entire city of Belfast apart from the one in the shop window up the street. And our house was absolutely packed with people to watch the coronation. So, my mother wanted rid of at least three of us and she gave me a shilling to take my brother Brendan and my younger brother David to the Broadway.[25]

The coronation was experienced often as both a televisual and a cinematic event. David McIlwaine visited friends in the seaside resort of Bangor, County Down, where he watched the ceremony. He recalled that 'it was really wonderful in 1953 to be able to see the coronation in black and white and on wee small screens. But, you could say, you could brag, I saw it on TV. And then you saw it in the cinema perhaps a week later'.[26]

Despite the communal nature of television broadcasts, low levels of television ownership meant that, alongside radio, press reports and local street parties, cinema screenings were central to coronation experiences. Cinemas went to great lengths to obtain and promote newsreels and full-length feature films of the coronation and it is likely that this footage was viewed by more residents than the television coverage. In Belfast, on the evening of the coronation, the managers of the Crumlin and the Gaumont drove 'to Nutt's Corner [airfield] to pick up the shots of scenes along the Coronation route for exhibition to their patrons at 10-30 o'clock the same night'. On 3 June, further sequences were 'flown over by special plane' and exhibited for the remainder of the week at both cinemas.[27] The Belfast Corporation considered the event so important that they arranged for 25,000 schoolchildren to view the coronation footage.[28] Matinees were organised at several cinemas and one report stated that the 2,000 children in attendance at the Royal Hippodrome 'cheered to the echo'.[29]

In 1953, the full-length Technicolor feature *A Queen is Crowned* (UK, 1953) was the highest grossing film at the British box-office.[30] It broke the attendance record at Belfast's Imperial cinema when it was screened nine times daily for five weeks.[31] The fact that the film was so popular in a centrally located cinema indicates that it appealed to patrons from both sides of the community. While the film clearly appealed to Unionist sentiment, the pageantry and spectacle of the occasion was also central to its attraction. As one *Belfast Telegraph* reviewer commented, 'Hollywood at its brightest and best has never produced anything as colossal'.[32] Nonetheless, its exhibition was controversial in other towns and bombs were planted to prevent screenings. On 15 June, a bomb destroyed the balcony of Newry's Savoy cinema.[33] While the cinema was repaired for the showing of *A Queen is Crowned*, the *Northern Whig* reported that '[p]olice were on duty outside and inside other police in civilian clothing mingled with the audience'.[34] In July, a further explosion at the Banbridge Picture House did not prevent it screening the film.[35] *A Queen is Crowned* was far more successful than ABC's rival film *Elizabeth is Queen* (UK, 1953) and shorter films such as Movietone's twenty-minute feature *Coronation Day* (UK, 1953). Despite this, the *Northern Whig* reported that patrons were 'in no mood to discriminate' between films, adding that 'anyone who finds the queue too long at one cinema makes his way to another'.[36] Screenings of these films were also combined with stage shows to enhance the spectacle of the event. ABC's in-house magazine reported that a stage show presented at the Belfast Ritz to accompany *Elizabeth is Queen* 'was the most successful they have ever run'.[37]

Cinemas in Northern Ireland also provided footage for those living in the Republic of Ireland, who had no access to television. Following threats from Sinn Féin and the Irish Anti-Partition League, no Dublin cinemas exhibited footage of the coronation. The *Cork Examiner* stated that there was 'a genuine interest among thousands of ordinary people who profess no allegiance to the Crown'.[38] Many Dubliners, therefore, took advantage of the Great Northern Railway's special fares and travelled from Dublin to Belfast to view Coronation films. On 10 June, 400 passengers boarded the early train from Dublin to Belfast. So many people turned up at the train station, that an extra train left fifteen minutes later, carrying a further 500 passengers.[39] One Belfast cinema manager claimed that he had received 3,000 letters and anticipated that 30,000 of the 50,000 patrons who would see the film in its first week would travel from the Irish Republic. 'They are falling over themselves to come here', he claimed.[40] This figure was likely an exaggeration and the manager of a large Belfast cinema claimed that he received around 1,000 patrons from across the border. The manager of a smaller cinema stated that 'we probably had about 300 Southerners here during the week. We had expected a great many more'.[41]

While the coronation led to increased sales of television sets, it did little to fundamentally alter patterns of cinema attendance in Northern Ireland. Recorded admissions even increased slightly from 28.37 million in 1953 to 28.84 million in 1954, which may have been a direct result of the popularity of coronation films.[42] Viewers may also have been perturbed by the lack of regional programming and Robert Savage states that 'when television arrived in Northern Ireland, it was primarily a relay station, transmitting programmes from London with very little home-produced material'.[43] Furthermore, the impact of increased television ownership was generational. In October 1952, one local resident told the *Belfast Telegraph*:

> I want to meet someone who will let me "look-in" on Coronation Day. Eventually I hope my home will have T.V. but as a young person and a cinema fan I do not think it will keep people from the pictures. It will be very nice to see shows at home but getting out and meeting friends has more attractions.[44]

For adolescents, the cinema still held an important social function, such as a space for courtship free from parental supervision. Meanwhile, John Spraos suggested that the convenience of home entertainment, the absence of repeat viewing costs and the diversion of household funds for rental and hire purchase agreements led homeowners away from the cinema, who were happier to spend their leisure time in a domestic setting.[45]

New Cinemas in Northern Ireland

While cinema attendance increased throughout the Second World War, building restrictions prevented the construction of new cinemas.[46] Though these restrictions were lifted in the mid-1950s, few cinemas were built as cinema attendance entered steep decline. The *Kinematograph Year Book* records that only 39 new UK cinemas opened between 1955 and 1958.[47] Given this low rate of cinema construction, it is remarkable that, in the same period, eight new cinemas opened in Northern Ireland. These were all located in Antrim and Down, the counties with the greatest levels of television ownership. Docherty *et al* noted that '[i]nstead of re-siting the cinemas and following the audience to the new housing estates, the film industry struck back at the technological level'.[48] Cinema exhibitors responded to declining attendances by asserting their technical superiority over television with new technologies such as 3D, CinemaScope, Todd-AO and VistaVision. In Northern Ireland, independent exhibitors were more responsive to population shifts than their counterparts in Great Britain, opening new cinemas in areas with the greatest levels of television ownership (see Figure 1). They could not, however, push back the tide of long-term decline and admissions fell significantly from the late 1950s.

From 1953 to 1957, UK cinema admissions fell by 28.75% from 1.29 billion to 915 million.[49] Despite the introduction of BBC television in Northern Ireland, the decline was

FIGURE 1.
New cinemas in Northern Ireland, 1955–1960

less precipitous and recorded admissions fell by 14.98% from 28.37 million in 1953 to 24.12 million in 1957 (see Figure 2).[50] It was not until July 1955 that the erection of the permanent Divis transmitter brought television signal to over two-thirds of Northern Ireland's population. Figure 3 shows that residents of Armagh, Fermanagh and Tyrone only obtained television sets in significant numbers from 1956 onwards. The majority of licences were still held in Antrim and Down, and, in December 1956, the *Belfast Telegraph* stated that 42,000 of Northern Ireland's 51,000 television licences were 'in the area of greater Belfast'.[51] In December 1957, the opening of BBC's Sheriff's Mountain transmitter brought television coverage to 96% of the population, including residents in Derry, Strabane, Newtownstewart, Dungiven and Limavady. By 1960, there were 142,789 licences in Northern Ireland and this figure increased to 206,000 in 1963.[52] These figures, however, should be treated with caution as there were a significant number of television owners who did not purchase television licences. In 1959, the *Belfast Telegraph* suggested that Northern Ireland had the highest proportion of unlicenced viewers in the UK and Media research company Television Audience Measurement estimated that as many as 23,000 television sets in Northern Ireland remained unlicensed.[53]

In post-war Belfast, slum clearance, new housing developments and employment changes resulted in centrifugal population shifts. Between 1951 and 1961, the population of Belfast County Borough fell by 6.3% from 443,671 to 415,856. In the same period, the population of County Antrim increased by 18.5% from 231,149 to 273,905, and the population of County Down increased by 10.7% from 241,181 to 266,939.[54] These post-war shifts, alongside relaxations on building restrictions, led to the construction of new cinemas to serve Belfast's suburban housing developments and satellite towns in Antrim and Down. In March 1955, the 1,050-seat Lido was the first cinema opened in post-war Northern Ireland. Its north Belfast location was near to many of the new housing

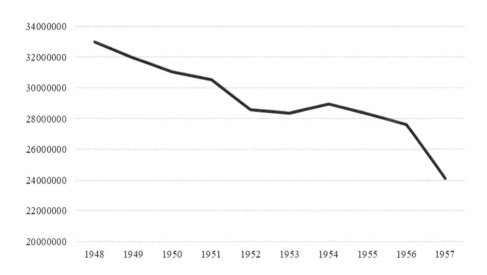

FIGURE 2.
Recorded admissions in Northern Ireland cinemas, 1948–57. Source: Reduction in rate of Entertainments Duty, 9 June 1958, Ministry of Finance, FIN/15/6/A/12, Public Record Office of Northern Ireland, Belfast

Year ending 31 March	Antrim and Down	Armagh	Fermanagh and Tyrone	Londonderry	Northern Ireland
1954	10,113	43	60	137	10,353
1955	23,535	34	68	171	23,808
1956	38,953	1,486	827	940	42,206
1957	56,198	3,343	1,729	2,078	63,348
1958	72,187	5,075	3,226	5,002	85,490
1959	86,094	6,896	5,092	8,506	106,588
1960	112,231	9,933	7,911	12,705	142,780

FIGURE 3.
Television licences in Northern Ireland, 1954–60. Source: British Broadcasting Corporation, *BBC Handbook*. London: BBC, 1955–61

developments built by the Northern Ireland Housing Executive. At its opening, former Lord Mayor Sir James Norritt stated that it 'filled a long felt want in that growing district of the city'.[55] In June 1955, the Tivoli, Finaghy, opened to serve the expanding suburbs of south Belfast. During its construction, Rank subsidiary company Odeon (N.I.) purchased the cinema from Irish Theatres. Despite efforts to construct a new Belfast city centre cinema, it was the only new cinema that the Rank Organisation opened in the period under review.

In December 1955, the 925-seat Iveagh cinema opened in Banbridge, County Down, with the capacity to screen CinemaScope and VistaVision films. The *Banbridge Chronicle* commented that its out-of-town location meant that it had the 'advantage of being built on a site which has a car park for about 100 cars'.[56] Cinema owner Derek Finney reassured patrons that 'the actual distance from town is not so great. It is only 400 yards from Bridge Street and about 450 yards from Church Square. I think most patrons will find it convenient'. He added that it was 'a great advance' on the existing Banbridge Picture House, 'which has more than served its day'.[57] Despite this statement, plans were announced to renovate the old cinema and introduce CinemaScope. Admissions at the Banbridge Picture House fell from 273,581 in 1952–3 to 76,495 in 1956–7.[58] In the latter year, admissions at the Iveagh totalled 288,123 and attendance figures at both cinemas totalled 364,618, demonstrating the extra demand for cinema seats in Banbridge.[59]

In September 1956, the Belfast-based Supreme Group opened two new cinemas in Northern Ireland. The 1,000-seat New Reo in Ballyclare, County Antrim, replaced the town's existing cinema and its owner stated that 'he hoped to serve a population of almost 10,000 in the Ballyclare area'.[60] The 1,000-seat Metro, Dundonald, was located just outside the Belfast city boundary. Its owner, T. J. Furey, claimed that while the competition of television and high levels of Entertainments Duty made the Metro a 'calculated risk', it 'had long been needed at Dundonald'.[61] At its opening, Secretary to the Northern Ireland cabinet Sir Robert Grandsen hoped that the people of this 'rapidly growing district … would appreciate what efforts were being made to bring the best in cinema entertainment their way'.[62] The Metro lasted only until March 1961, when the *Belfast Telegraph* reported that the building was available to let. It claimed that '[f]or two years after its opening the Metro attracted large crowds. But in 1958, when the general fall-off in picture-going began, it also felt the effect'.[63]

Rathcoole was one of the post-war housing estates constructed by the Northern Ireland Housing Trust. In 1955, one resident lamented that 'the estate empties at nine o'clock on Saturday morning and it's that way till late at night—all the entertainment's in Belfast'.[64] Cinema exhibitors saw this demand on the new estate and the 918-seat Alpha opened in April 1957. *Kine Weekly* reported that the Alpha 'is in the middle of a new housing estate with a present population of about 6,000. The area has a potential population of 10,000 to 12,000'.[65] The Alpha's facilities reflected its increasingly younger audience's diverse range of leisure activities. It contained a ground floor café and, in October 1959 it opened the first milk bar in a Northern Ireland cinema.[66]

In December 1957, the 400-seat Comber cinema was 'built on a site adjacent to the Comber Picture House ... to augment the facilities of the older cinema'. Its owners hoped to draw patrons 'from the new housing areas on the south-east side of Belfast, four miles away'.[67] Noel Spence grew up in Comber and commented that while 'the new cinema was very classy', the decision 'to build a new cinema in fifty-seven was kind of an act of faith with TV becoming a real menace—but they did it anyhow and for many years Comber cinema was very successful and very popular locally'.[68] *Kine Weekly* commented that many of the new cinemas were developed close to new housing estates and believed that independent exhibitors had greater freedom to expand their operations as 'the big circuits are tied closely to plans which must take into account the health of the industry in the United Kingdom as a whole'.[69] ABC and Rank opened relatively few new UK cinemas, even in areas of high population growth, and focused their efforts on modernising existing city centre sites.[70] In July 1958, the £27,000 New Antrim Cinema was the final new cinema building opened in the 1950s. *Kine Weekly* commented that the 'town of Antrim has grown appreciably in recent years and the directors are confident that despite the competition of television the venture will prove a success'.[71] Other cinemas renovated their premises and altered their programmes to compete with television. In December 1958, Belfast's Mayfair cinema reopened as Ireland's first news and cartoon cinema. Its owners stated that '[it] is one type of cinema which to-day is successfully competing against television. It offers something which can't be got on TV—coloured cartoon and coloured travelogues. The latter are becoming very popular'.[72]

The Decline of Cinema-going

Despite their investment in new cinemas, Northern Ireland exhibitors could not push back the tide of long-term declines in attendance. In September 1955, commercial television arrived in the London region with the launch of ITV. Regional franchises were then established across the United Kingdom. Prior to UTV's 1959 launch, a small minority of Northern Ireland viewers received signal from ITV's Winter Hill transmitter in Lancashire and, in 1956, reporter Robert Ray attended a 'commercial TV party' in Belfast's working-class Ardoyne district.[73] In 1956, *Kine Weekly* observed that while declines in cinema attendance were less than severe than in other UK regions, 'the sales figure of TV sets in Belfast is nearly 40,000—equivalent to the seating capacity in the city's cinemas'.[74] In Northern Ireland, the number of recorded admissions fell significantly from 1957, though this was as much to do with tax concessions for cheaper tickets as it was for actual declines in attendance.[75] There is no doubt, however, that audiences fell from the late 1950s as working-class families obtained television sets, often using rental and hire purchase.

To what extent was there a direct causal relationship between the increase in television ownership and cinema closures? The number of television licences in Northern Ireland increased from 42,206 in 1956 to 142,780 in 1960, when there were 33 licences per 100 families.[76] While this was still significantly lower than the equivalent figures for England, Scotland and Wales (see Figure 4) cinemas still closed from 1956 onwards. According to figures in the *Kinemataograph Year Book*, the number of cinemas in Northern Ireland increased from 120 in 1950 to 130 in 1958.[77] In contrast, from 1950 to 1959, the number of cinemas in Wales declined from 348 to 299, and in Scotland, from 600 to 464.[78] In Northern Ireland, high taxation, population shifts, dilapidated buildings, rising fixed costs, new housing developments and the possibility of converting cinema buildings for more profitable usage were all cited as reasons for cinema closures. After Belfast's Gaiety cinema ceased business in 1956, the *Irish Independent* claimed that it was 'the North's first casualty in the cinema versus television war'.[79] Despite this claim, it was only at the end of the 1950s that television was seen as the central threat to cinema attendance in Northern Ireland. By 1958, the increasing competition of television, the continuation of Entertainments Duty and recent increases in valuation rates meant that Northern Ireland exhibitors were 'looking to the future with only cautious optimism'.[80] *Belfast Telegraph* reporter Gordon Duffield claimed that the Belfast cinema industry was fighting for its life. While he highlighted television as cinema's 'great enemy', Duffield believed that Entertainments Duty placed an unfair burden on cinema exhibitors. He added that '[r]unning costs and overheads have increased by anything from 200 to 400 per cent. since before the war—yet cinema prices have gone up only a fraction of that figure'.[81]

UTV launched on 31 October 1959 and its Black Mountain transmitter served over 80% of Northern Ireland's population.[82] The introduction of UTV was a key turning point in the decline of cinema-going in Northern Ireland. Newspaper reports suggested that 'attendances dropped 20% in the first months of UTV' and from 1959 to 1960, Entertainments Duty payments from cinema tickets fell by 29.8%.[83] UTV offered new programme formats aimed primarily at working-class audiences. Robert Savage notes that, in its early years, UTV produced few programmes made in Northern Ireland and relied heavily

Year ending 31 March	England	Northern Ireland	Scotland	Wales	United Kingdom
1957	46.16	14.56	31.52	38.7	43.53
1958	52.8	19.63	39.51	46.24	50.31
1959	60.64	24.4	49.25	54.98	57.31
1960	67.57	32.55	58.97	62.86	64.45

FIGURE 4.
Percentage of families owning television licences, 1957–60. Source: British Broadcasting Corporation, *BBC Handbook*. London: BBC, 1958–61

on American and British imports.[84] In 1961, the headmaster of Knockbreda Secondary Intermediate School claimed that 6 out of 10 schoolchildren preferred television to the cinema, and 8 out of 10 preferred UTV to BBC programmes. Westerns, quizzes and children's programmes were particularly popular and one child stated that 'BBC programmes are for the older people and UTV for the younger people'.[85] Viewing figures confirm the popularity of UTV and, in the week ending 25 November 1962, the most viewed television programme was ITV game show *Take Your Pick*, which was watched in 83% of homes. In contrast, American western *Bronco* was the most popular BBC programme, which was seen only in 59% of homes.[86]

UTV's impact was felt most in Belfast, where twelve cinemas closed from October 1959 to the end of 1962. The majority of these were inner-city and suburban cinemas, and from 1960 reports of cinema closures tended to place greater emphasis on the impact of television. When the West End Picture House closed, a representative stated that it could not 'compete any more with television and the growth of motoring and outside sport ... People's habits are changing, and a night out at the cinema doesn't mean the same as it did. Independent owners haven't a chance today'.[87] In 1960, *Kine Weekly* commented that there was a 'growing demand for more showmanship in Northern Ireland cinemas', adding that exhibitors 'seem still to be hesitant to "go out and get" their patrons'.[88] It believed that with the exception of *Hercules Unchained* (Italy, 1958), Northern Ireland exhibitors had not made the most of television promotion. In 1961, it stated that as sixty per cent of the UTV audience was within Belfast 'a campaign mounted even by a cinema itself could be directly beneficial'.[89] Cinemas did, nonetheless, benefit from UTV programming. *Preview*, its entertainment magazine show, featured clips of newly released films and was one of Northern Ireland's most watched programmes in 1962.[90] In Derry, the delayed arrival of BBC television was one of the reasons cinema attendance remained buoyant in the mid-1950s. Figure 5 shows that recorded admissions rose slightly from 2.03 million in 1953 to 2.16 million in 1957. Following test transmissions from the BBC's Sheriff's Mountain transmitter, the *Londonderry Sentinel* reported that 'almost at once, there was a rush for television sets, which one firm sold at a three-figure rate per week'.[91] Television ownership subsequently increased and licences in County Londonderry

Cinema	1953	1957
City	316,920	418,018
St. Columb's Hall	251,295	266,729
Midland	209,749	211,339
Palace	428,142	423,903
Rialto	348,225	359,583
Strand	474,355	484,540
Total	2,028,686	2,164,112

FIGURE 5.
Dutiable admissions at Derry cinemas, years ending March 1953 and 1957. Source: Entertainments Duty weekly returns, Ministry of Finance, FIN/15/6/C/2/85–90, 132–137, Public Record Office of Northern Ireland, Belfast

rose from 2,078 in 1957 to 12,705 in 1960.[92] Large British exhibitors responded to the competition of television by improving and modernising their existing cinemas. In 1960, Associated British Cinemas rebuilt the Rialto as the ABC. *Kine Weekly* commented that, while it was the first cinema built since the introduction of UTV, the lack of signal [in Derry] meant that it was 'unlikely to be affected as much by the growth of television as most other cinemas in the Province'.[93] Cinema manager F. Hyland told the press that:

> we have got to compete with the armchair comfort of television in the home, but it has been found that with the provision of good programmes and a high standard of comfort, the cinema has something that the public will still want to go to the cinema. That is the trend across the water.[94]

By 1960, *Belfast Telegraph* reporter Martin Wallace reported that Ulster cinemas were 'feeling the cold wind of change. Close to a dozen have closed in recent years, and others will follow'. Belfast's suburban cinemas were hardest hit and Wallace stated that while 'a visit to the city centre is still a "night out"—a visit to the local cinema is not. It is the old, uncomfortable, cheaper cinemas which have mostly closed'.[95] Suburban cinemas responded to a lack of new films by diversifying their programmes and introducing stage shows. From 1960 to 1961, Belfast's Troxy cinema hosted 'international wrestling' with 'stars of TV', a talent competition presented by comedian Frank Carson and a Christmas pantomime of *Little Red Riding Hood*. In October 1962, *Kine Weekly* claimed that it was 'instrumental in introducing nudist films to the Ulster public'. It added that, although *West End Jungle* (UK, 1961) was playing at the Troxy, 'the Belfast public is no longer as easily led by an X certificate or by a nudist poster, and some observers say that the demand for sensational films, particularly of the nude variety, is already on the wane'.[96]

There were generational differences in the decline of cinema attendance and Wallace argued that 'cinemas can still count on a young audience, particularly as teenagers have more money in their pockets. But this is not the basis of a large and profitable industry'.[97] Norman Campbell's testimony also shows these generational differences. He stated that television ownership 'didn't affect my personal cinema attendance too much. But on reflection, I think it affected the cinema attendance for mothers and fathers, because it was now possible to sit in at night'.[98] Margaret McDonaugh's testimony also shows the contrast between experiences of television and cinema:

> you went to the cinema to get out and to be with friends or to be with a boyfriend or something. When television came, when we got television first of all it was just BBC. And then, then ITV came, but for a long time it was just two channels and if you'd been in with your parents, there's a lot of people, there might have been six of you in the room watching television.[99]

By the early 1960s, teenagers had more disposable income and there was a greater range of goods and services to spend their money on. When asked by the *Belfast Telegraph* what people of her age did in the evening, eighteen-year-old Pauline McCourt responded that '[t]elevision's only for young children and old people. Jiving's the thing—that's what most of us do around this part of Belfast at night'.[100] While members of this age group stopped going to the cinema as regularly as they had done, exhibitors benefited from the fact that they spent more on individual trips. In March 1962, for instance, youth-oriented Cliff Richard musical *The Young Ones* (UK, 1961) set a new box-office record on the Saturday of its first week at Belfast's upmarket Ritz cinema.[101]

A key characteristic of Northern Ireland's post-war cinema exhibition industry was the Rank Organisation's late arrival in the province. At the end of the Second World War, the company, which operated the Odeon and Gaumont chains, controlled one Belfast cinema, the Classic. In the mid-1950s, Odeon (N.I.) Ltd. purchased the two largest local chains—Curran Theatres and Irish Theatres—and by 1958 operated 23 Northern Ireland cinemas.[102] In April 1958, the Rank Organisation claimed that it was 'determined to fight television locally' and was reconstructing many of its Northern Ireland cinemas to attract larger audiences.[103] From 1959 to 1962, Odeon (N.I.) closed many of its smaller cinemas and completed a programme of 'modernisation, renovation and reorganisation' of its most important cinemas.[104]

In 1959, it renovated Derry's Strand cinema and reopened it as the Odeon. The *Derry Journal* stated that a 'brilliant neon name-sign, that adds colour to the street view, combined with a new canopy and a re-decorated front, provides the immediate outdoor evidence of an attractive large-scale renovation scheme undertaken by the cinema's new owners'.[105] In Belfast, Rank renovated profitable suburban cinemas, such as the Regal, the Stadium and the Astoria and there was greater standardisation in their décor and fittings. In November 1960, it purchased the Grand Opera House and the Royal Hippodrome.[106] The former's seating capacity was reduced to give 'maximum comfort' and a new licensed bar gave it a 'trim sophisticated look'.[107] The Hippodrome underwent significant renovations and reopened as the Odeon. When the Edwardian façade was covered in aluminium cladding, the *Belfast Telegraph* commented that the exterior had received a 'thorough facelift'.[108]

Even with the abolition of Entertainments Duty in 1961, *Kine Weekly* claimed that the 'pattern of cinema holdings in Northern Ireland, despite the rationalization period of the last two years, is not yet steady'[109] In 1962, two Derry cinemas closed: the Midland and St. Columb's Hall. Though it is significant that these closures occurred prior to the opening of UTV's Strabane transmitter in February 1963, their owners were no doubt aware of the impact of commercial television on cinema attendance in other areas. Odeon (N.I.) purchased the Midland from Curran Theatres in 1957. When it closed in February 1962, a company spokesman cited the fact that it 'stands in the path of a road widening scheme' as the main reason for closure. He added that it was:

> an old building and would require a lot done to it if it was to be brought up to the high standards of our theatres elsewhere … we feel unable to spend the money to enable us to give the standard of comfort which the public demands.[110]

After the final performance, the *Londonderry Sentinel* commented that regular patrons who 'enjoyed the Midland's friendly atmosphere, will now content themselves with watching television'.[111] This example illustrates Docherty et al's thesis that the decline in cinema audiences cannot be wholly accounted for by the increase in TV licences and the closure of local cinemas had a significant impact on attendance.[112] In May, St. Columb's Hall stopped film exhibition. Committee Secretary P.J. Downey stated that while television had 'adversely affected attendance', the main reason for its closure was 'that there were so few suitable films being made nowadays and that the Hall could not get any suitable first-run productions. This was because of the fact that such films were tied up by the big circuits'.[113]

Conclusion

This article supports the work of cinema historians who downplay a monocausal relationship cinema and television, and who emphasise the place-specific nature of cinema attendance. It provides new evidence of the geographical diversity of cinema's decline in the United Kingdom, the impact of television in Northern Ireland and the response of cinema exhibitors. It emphasises long-term economic and social changes and downplays the impact of events such as the coronation, which did little to alter the social appeal of the cinema for young people. New cinemas were a relative rarity in the 1950s and, even though Northern Ireland exhibitors were more responsive to population shifts than their UK counterparts, the construction of new cinemas did not prevent long-term declines in cinema attendance. While increased television ownership clearly impacted cinema-going, it is difficult to disentangle the myriad range of factors that exhibitors cited for cinema closures, such as rising overheads, high rates of taxations, population shifts and new forms of entertainment. Though the rise in consumer culture, increased affluence and a shift towards home-centred activities affected leisure habits, high unemployment rates and low average wages delayed their impact in Northern Ireland

The use of a broad range of quantitative and qualitative sources provides evidence of both the nature of cinema's decline and the response of audiences, exhibitors and the press. Television licence figures show the growth of television ownership and cinema attendance data reveals the extent of cinema's decline. These sources, however, tell us little about the nature of people's changing leisure habits. Oral history testimony and newspaper reports reveal the communal nature of television, generational differences in its impact and the reasons why people chose to attend the cinema or stay at home and watch television. It should not be forgotten, furthermore, that these two leisure activities were not always in direct competition and the range of leisure activities available to young people expanded greatly in the post-war period.

This evidence also reveals geographical variations within Northern Ireland. This is a theme ripe for exploration and further research on small towns and rural locations in Northern Ireland would complement recent studies on this subject.[114] While cinema closures were most widespread in Belfast, Derry cinemas closed despite the absence of commercial television. Outside of these cities, there was greater confidence in cinema exhibition. The Whitehead Cinema, County Antrim, closed in October 1961 and re-opened as the Strand in November 1962. *Kine Weekly* claimed that this provided an 'indication of the new found health of the cinema industry in Northern Ireland'.[115] Meanwhile, greater access to television meant that cinema attendance declined earlier than in the Republic of Ireland and this had a clear impact on the built environment. In 1963, the *Irish Independent* stated that in contrast to Dublin, 'Belfast City centre is "dead" at night. It all began with television ... London property men have virtually torn the heart out of Belfast's cinema and theatreland and left behind a great emptiness ... A city cannot lose its places of entertainment without losing much of its character as well'.[116] There were further cinema closures in the mid-1960s and the onset of the Troubles exacerbated cinema closures with the Lido, the Tivoli and the Alpha all closing in the 1970s. The new Comber cinema closed in 1984 and the Iveagh was the only 1950s cinema to survive the multiplex era, shutting its doors in 2001.

Acknowledgements

I wish to thank Sean O'Connell, Stuart Hanson, Mark Benson and Conor Campbell for their comments and suggestions on drafts of this article. I am very grateful to Lorraine Barry, who generously created the map of Northern Ireland included in this work.

Disclosure Statement

No potential conflict of interest was reported by the author.

Notes

1. Dyja, ed. *Film and Television Handbook*, 39.
2. Ibid., 39.
3. Moran, *Armchair Nation*, 115.
4. Spraos, *Decline of the Cinema*.
5. For instance, see Docherty et al., *The Last Picture Show?* and Hanson, *Cinema Exhibition in Britain*.
6. Doyle, "The Geography of Cinemagoing," 59–71.
7. For instance, see Griffith, *The Cinema and Cinema-Going in Scotland*, Jancovich et al., *The Place of the Audience* and Miskell, *A Social History of the Cinema in Wales*.
8. Rockett, *Film Exhibition and Distribution*.
9. *Kinematograph Year Book 1958*, 409–14; *Kinematograph and Television Year Book 1963*, 353–56.
10. Joe Moran claims that, following the introduction of UTV in 1959, there were 90,000 television sets in the Irish Republic and a 'feature of the skyline in Irish towns was the multitude of especially tall aerials erected to pick up the distant signals of British transmitters'. Moran, *Armchair Nation*, 129.
11. Rockett, *Film Exhibition and Distribution*, 461.
12. Cathcart, *BBC in Northern Ireland and Savage, Television and Irish Society*, 318–82.
13. Manning, "Post-War Cinema-Going," 539–55.
14. Excise Duty Branch, Records of Entertainments Duty, Ministry of Finance, FIN/15/6/A-D, Public Record Office of Northern Ireland, Belfast.
15. The oral history testimony is drawn from the author's interviews with twenty residents of Northern Ireland born between 1925 and 1950. All participants were required to sign consent forms and ethical approval was received from Queen's University Belfast's Research Ethics Committee. These thematic, semi-structured interviews focused on the social background of the participants, cinema-going practices, film preferences, leisure habits and the wider social history of post-war Northern Ireland. For further information

on the use of ethnographic research in cinema history, see Kuhn, Biltereyst and Meers, "Memories of Cinemagoing and Film Experience," 3–16.

16. Biltereyst, Lotze and Meers, "Triangulation in historical audience research," 690–715.
17. Dyja, ed. *Film and Television Handbook*, 39.
18. Reduction in rate of Entertainments Duty, 9 June 1958, Ministry of Finance, FIN/15/6/A/12, Public Record Office of Northern Ireland, Belfast.
19. Moran, *Armchair Nation*, 74–75.
20. *BBC Handbook 1955*, 159.
21. *Digest of Statistics Northern Ireland 1961*, 61.
22. *BBC Handbook 1955*, 61.
23. Field and Neill, *New Housing Estates in Belfast*, 43.
24. *Belfast Newsletter*, June 3, 1953.
25. McVeigh, Jean. Interview by author. Belfast, April 2, 2014.
26. McIlwaine, David. Interview by author. Cultra, County Down, July 9, 2015.
27. *Belfast Telegraph*, May 29, 1953.
28. Minutes of the General Purposes and Finance Committee, Belfast Corporation, March 18, 1953, McClay Library, Queen's University Belfast.
29. *Belfast Telegraph*, June 4, 1953.
30. James Chapman, "*A Queen is Crowned*," 82.
31. *Belfast Telegraph*, July 8, 1959.
32. *Belfast Telegraph*, June 6, 1953.
33. *Belfast Telegraph*, June 15, 1953.
34. *Northern Whig*, June 26, 1953.
35. *Belfast Telegraph*, July 17, 1953.
36. *Northern Whig*, June 9, 1953.
37. *The ABC News*, August 1953.
38. *Cork Examiner*, June 11, 1953.
39. *Belfast Telegraph*, June 10, 1953.
40. *Belfast Telegraph*, June 3, 1953; *Kinematograph Weekly*, June 11, 1953.
41. *Sunday Independent,* June 14, 1953.
42. Reduction in rate of Entertainments Duty, 9 June 1958, Ministry of Finance, FIN/15/6/A/12, Public Record Office of Northern Ireland, Belfast.
43. Savage, *Television and Irish Society*, 325. For information on the small number of programmes produced for BBC Northern Ireland, see Hill, *Cinema and Northern Ireland*, 52–60.
44. *Belfast Telegraph*, October 27, 1952.
45. Spraos, *Decline of the Cinema*.
46. For further details on wartime restrictions, see Farmer, *Cinemagoing in Wartime Britain*.
47. *Kinematograph Year Book 1958*, 509; *Kinematograph & Television Year Book 1963*, 445.
48. Docherty et al, *The Last Picture Show?*, 28.
49. Dyja, ed. *Film and Television Handbook*, 39.
50. Reduction in rate of Entertainments Duty, 9 June 1958, Ministry of Finance, FIN/15/6/A/12, Public Record Office of Northern Ireland, Belfast.
51. *Belfast Telegraph*, December 3, 1956.
52. Rockett, *Film Exhibition and Distribution*. 139.
53. *Belfast Telegraph*, January 28 1959; April 17 1959.

54. Government of Northern Ireland, *Census of Population*, xxvii.
55. *Belfast News-Letter*, March 28, 1955.
56. *Banbridge Chronicle*, December 14, 1955.
57. Ibid.
58. Entertainments Duty weekly returns, Ministry of Finance, FIN/15/6/C/2/65, 122, Public Record Office of Northern Ireland, Belfast.
59. Entertainments Duty weekly returns, Ministry of Finance, FIN/15/6/C/2/113, Public Record Office of Northern Ireland, Belfast.
60. *Kinematograph Weekly*, September 27, 1956.
61. *Belfast Telegraph*, August 31, 1956.
62. *Kinematograph Weekly*, September 6, 1956.
63. *Belfast Telegraph*, April 21, 1961.
64. *Belfast Telegraph*, December 5, 1955.
65. *Kinematograph Weekly*, April 4, 1957.
66. *Belfast Telegraph*, October 2, 1959.
67. *Kinematograph Weekly*, December 26, 1957.
68. Spence, Noel. Interview by author. Comber, County Down, March 26, 2014.
69. *Kinematograph Weekly*, December 26, 1957.
70. Hanson, *Cinema Exhibition in Britain*, 94–99.
71. *Kinematograph Weekly*, July 10, 1958.
72. *Belfast Telegraph*, December 17, 1958.
73. *Belfast Telegraph*, June 4, 1956; June 11, 1956.
74. *Kinematograph Weekly*, July 5, 1956.
75. For changes in rates of Entertainments Duty, see Rockett, *Film Exhibition and Distribution*, 125–40. In Northern Ireland, receipts from Entertainments Duty paid by cinemas fell from £640,246 in 1956–57 to £140,988 in 1960–61. Payments ceased after 27 May 1961. *Digest of Statistics Northern Ireland 1961*, 74.
76. *BBC Handbook* 1957, 200; BBC *Handbook 1961*, 172.
77. *Kinematograph Year Book 1950*, 465–70; *Kinematograph Year Book 1958*, 409–14.
78. Spraos, *Decline of the Cinema*, p. 34.
79. *Irish Independent*, June 1, 1957.
80. *Kinematograph Weekly*, January 2, 1958.
81. *Belfast Telegraph*, February 14, 1958.
82. *Belfast Telegraph*, October 31, 1959.
83. *Belfast Telegraph*, October 5, 1960; *Digest of Statistics Northern Ireland 1961*, 74.
84. Savage, *Television and Irish Society*, 335–6.
85. *Belfast Telegraph*, December 12, 1961.
86. *ITV 1963: A Comprehensive Guide to Independent Television*, 135.
87. *Belfast Telegraph*, May 16, 1960.
88. Kinematograph Weekly, October 20, 1960.
89. *Kinematograph Weekly*, June 15 1961.
90. *Kinematograph Weekly*, October 11, 1962; December 13, 1962.
91. *Londonerry Sentinel*, December 12, 1957.
92. *BBC Handbook 1958*, 214; *BBC Handbook 1961*, 172.
93. *Kinematograph Weekly*, June 9, 1960.

94. *Londonderry Sentinel*, August 26, 1959.
95. *Belfast Telegraph*, October 5, 1960.
96. *Kinematograph Weekly*, October 18, 1961.
97. *Belfast Telegraph*, October 5, 1960.
98. Campbell, Norman. Interview by author, Belfast, June 4, 2014.
99. McDonaugh, Margaret. Belfast, May 18, 2015.
100. *Belfast Telegraph*, September 14, 1960.
101. *Kinematograph Weekly*, March 1 1962.
102. *Kinematograph Year Book 1958*, 212.
103. *Belfast Telegraph*, April 12, 1958.
104. *Ideal Kinema*, February 8, 1962.
105. *Derry Journal*, May 1, 1959.
106. *Belfast Telegraph*, November 18, 1960.
107. *Ideal Kinema*, February 8, 1962.
108. *Belfast Telegraph*, September 28, 1961.
109. *Kinematograph Weekly*, October 12, 1961.
110. *Derry Journal*, February 2, 1962.
111. *Londonderry Sentinel*, February 21, 1962.
112. Docherty et al, *The Last Picture Show*, 23–29.
113. *Derry Journal*, February 23, 1962.
114. For instance, see Thissen and Zimmermans, eds. *Cinema Beyond the City*.
115. *Kinematograph Weekly*, November 11, 1962.
116. *Irish Independent*, August 5, 1963.

Bibliography

Kinematograph Year Book 1958. London: Odham's Press, 1958.

Bfiltereyst, Daniel, Kathleen Lotze, and Philippe Meers. "Triangulation in Historical Audience Research: Reflections and Experiences from a Multi-methodological Research Project on Cinema Audiences in Flanders." *Participations: Journal of Audience and Reception Studies* 9, no. 2 (2012): 690–715.

British Broadcasting Corporation. *BBC Handbook*. London: BBC, 1955–61.

Cathcart, Rex. *The Most Contrary Region: The BBC in Northern Ireland*. Belfast: Blackstaff, 1984.

Chapman, James. "Cinema, Monarch and the Making of Heritage: *A Queen is Crowned (1953)*." In *British Historical Cinema*, edited by Claire Monk and Amy Sergeant, 82–91. London: Routledge, 2002.

Docherty, David, David Morrison, and Michael Tracey. *The Last Picture Show? Britain's Changing Film Audiences*. London: British Film Institute, 1987.

Doyle, Barry. "The Geography of Cinemagoing in Great Britain, 1934–1994: A Comment." *Historical Journal of Film, Radio and Television* 23, no. 1 (2003): 59–71.

Dyja, Eddie, ed. *BFI Film and Television Handbook*. London: British Film Institute, 2003.

Farmer, Richard. *Cinemas and Cinemagoing in Wartime Britain, 1939–45: The Utility Dream Palace*. Manchester: Manchester University Press, 2016.

Field, D. E., and D.G. Neill. *A Survey of New Housing Estates in Belfast: A Social and Economic Study of the Estates Built by the Northern Ireland Housing Trust in the Belfast Area 1945–1954*. Belfast: Queen's University of Belfast, Department of Social Studies, 1957.

Government of Northern Ireland. *Census of Population of Northern Ireland 1961: General Report*. Belfast: Her Majesty's Stationery Office, 1965.

Griffiths, Trevor. *The Cinema and Cinema-going in Scotland, 1896–1950*. Edinburgh: Edinburgh University Press, 2012.

Hanson, Stuart. *From Silent Screen to Multi-screen: A History of Cinema Exhibition Since 1896*. Manchester: Manchester University Press, 2007.

Hill, John. *Cinema and Northern Ireland: Film, Culture and Politics*. London: British Film Institute, 2006.

Independent Television Authority. *ITV 1963: A Comprehensive Guide to Independent Television*. London: Independent Television Authority, 1963.

Jancovich, Mark, Lucy Faire, and Sarah Stubbings. *The Place of the Audience: Cultural Geographies of Film Consumption*. London: British Film Insitute, 2003.

Kinematograph and Television Year Book 1963. London: Odham's Press, 1963.

Kuhn, Annette, Daniel Biltereyst, and Philippe Meers. "Memories of Cinemagoing and Film Experience: An Introduction." *Memory Studies* 10, no. 1 (2017): 3–16.

Manning, Sam. "Post-war Cinema-going and Working-class Communities: A Case Study of the Holyland, 1945–62." *Cultural and Social History* 13, no. 4 (2016): 539–555.

Miskell, Peter. *A Social History of the Cinema in Wales 1918–1951: Pulpits, Coal Pits and Fleapits*. Cardiff: University of Wales Press, 2006.

Moran, Joe. *Armchair Nation: An Intimate History of Britain in Front of the TV*. London: Profile, 2013.

Northern Ireland Ministry of Finance. *Digest of Statistics Northern Ireland No. 16*. Belfast: H.M.S.O., 1961.

Rockett, Kevin with Emer Rockett. *Film Exhibition and Distribution in Ireland: 1909–2011*. Dublin: Four Courts Press, 2011.

Savage, Robert. *A Loss of Innocence? Television and Irish Society 1960–72*. Manchester: Manchester University Press, 2010.

Spraos, John. *The Decline of the Cinema: An Economist's Report*. London: Allen & Unwin, 1962.

Thissen, Judith, and Clemens Zimmerman, eds. *Cinema Beyond the City: Small-town and Rural Film Culture in Europe*. London: British Film Institute, 2017.

MEMORIES OF TELEVISION IN IRELAND
Separating media history from nation state

Edward Brennan

This article emerges from a broader project that explores the history of television in Ireland using audience life story interviews. It argues that a dominant narrative persists in the history of television in the Republic of Ireland. Based in institutional sources this narrative is ideologically narrow although it tells a story of cultural liberation. A key example of its ideological limitation lies in the way that Irish people's experience of British television transmissions has been forgotten. The reason for this lies in historical methods rather than conscious bias. Nevertheless, historical methods themselves can promote limited visons of reality that promote the interests of nation states and national broadcasters. This work argues that a turn to audience memories, as a non-institutional source, can help to disrupt an unannounced alliance between media history scholarship and the nation state.

The claim that television arrived in Ireland on 31 December 1961 is commonplace.[1] However, such claims only make sense when the word 'television' is interpreted to refer solely to television broadcasting rather than viewing, and when 'Ireland' refers only to the Republic of Ireland. This interpretation, more concerned with the Irish State's ability to broadcast than people's ability to watch, is typical of historical approaches. Indeed, the history of television in Ireland is, essentially, just a history of the public service broadcaster Radió Telefís Éireann (RTÉ). The establishment of television broadcasting in Northern Ireland in 1955,[2] for example, and the presence of British broadcasts in homes south of the border pre-RTÉ are remembered as a spur to the creation the state broadcaster. However, they are forgotten as part of social life. Moreover, the history of RTÉ as 'television' has been told within a pervasive dominant narrative, which subsumes the medium into a clash between tradition and modernity. This article emerges from a broader attempt to access audience memories using life story interviews to create a complementary history of television in Ireland. It argues that, through their dependence on institutional sources, orthodox media histories contribute to a view of the relationship between media and society that is bounded by state borders. The use of audience memories provides an alternative perspective. It also disrupts a form of methodological nationalism that creates an unannounced alliance between media history scholarship and the nation state.

Telefís Éireann was launched on New Year's Eve, 1961. The gala celebration was broadcast live from the Gresham hotel in the centre of Dublin.[3] Many academic accounts portray the opening night as a pivotal event in modern Irish history. It was part of the emergence of a 'New Ireland'. The new channel was to serve as a catalyst for Ireland's cultural transformation. That night, it would seem, complex processes of social change obligingly presented themselves before the cameras. Ireland was about to move from a regime that stifled individual freedom to a cosmopolitan society that was open to foreign investment, ideas and culture. Academic representations of this night offer clear-cut characters and an easy-to-follow plot. They present a polarised vision of the ailing forces of tradition and their modern, confident and open-minded successors. A worried clergyman, Cardinal D'Alton, and an anxious elderly politician, President Eamon de Valera, strike a jarring contrast to the glamour and excitement of the evening. They appear defensive; helpless in the glare of a technological future that they can neither control nor understand.

Cardinal D'Alton, the Archbishop of Armagh, 'appeared on the screen to welcome the new service and to warn parents not to allow their children to become television addicts, no matter how meritorious the programme' (*The Irish Times*, January 1, 1962).[4] Horgan remarked on the 'gloomy attitude of the former Taoiseach,[5] Eamon de Valera, who warned his audience about the dangers of the new medium even as he inaugurated its first broadcast'.[6] Academics have ritually cited the following passage from de Valera's inaugural speech.

> I must admit that sometimes when I think of television and radio and their immense power I feel somewhat afraid. Like atomic energy it can be used for incalculable good but it can also do irreparable harm. Never before was there in the hands of men an instrument so powerful to influence the thoughts and actions of the multitude. The persistent policy pursued over radio and television, apart from imparting knowledge, can build up the character of the whole people, inducing a sturdiness and vigour and confidence. On the other hand, it can lead through demoralisation and decadence to disillusion (*The Irish Times*, January 1, 1962).[7]

Morash emphasises how 'later in the evening, the elderly Eamon de Valera peered myopically into the camera, and amid all the champagne and marching bands, introduced a sombre note of warning in words resonant with the tones of Vigilanti Cura'.[8] For Robert Savage, de Valera's warning 'quite dramatically illustrates a turning point in the modern history of the nation'. Ireland was 'emerging from the social and economic torpor that had paralysed the state since its founding' and there was little that the 'venerable President' could do about it.[9] Cormack claims that 'de Valera was right to liken television in Ireland to an atomic blast [sic]' because the 'Ireland that met television had been very much a traditional and closed society'.[10]

De Valera's counterpart, offering hope of escape from cultural and economic stagnation, was the new Taoiseach Sean Lemass. For Horgan he was 'symbolic of the departure of the political old guard'.[11] Lemass defended the mainly imported content of the new broadcaster, opining that 'the reasonable needs of the Irish people ... would not be satisfied by programmes restricted to local origins' (*The Irish Times, January* 1, 1962).[12] This contrasts with the ideals of national self-sufficiency attributed to de Valera. Academic accounts have used de Valera and Lemass as literary devices. De Valera embodies the spent force of Catholic, protectionist conservatism while Lemass represents modernisation and openness. That night, 'Old Ireland', defensive, myopic and out of touch, began to decline as its successor quickened with the introduction of television as a natural ally. Morash describes the television station's launch, and the contrast between de Valera and Lemass, as a moment when social change, normally slow, complex and difficult to discern, somehow became manifest.

> In this moment we see in a split screen, as it were, showing two Irelands. In one, we might see a modernising, new Ireland relishing its porous boundaries; in the other, an older, conservative Ireland of fixed and knowable values, bounded and preserved within the island of Ireland. However, it might be more accurate to say that what was on display that night were two forms of Irish modernity, one established and one just coming into being; either way, it was clear that the medium through which these differences were being staged clearly belonged to the new.[13]

Accounts of the opening night present a dichotomous vision of a complex reality. This is not to say that they are false. They reflect important aspects of the relationship between television and the culture and politics of the Republic of Ireland. However, they also leave much that goes unmentioned and unquestioned. In this they typify the dominant narrative that frames the history of television in Ireland. This dominant narrative does not imply a homogeneity among historical accounts but it does identify a common direction of travel across them. There is, apart from radical accounts that see media acting in the service of power, a story of progress.[14] The dominant narrative describes a common ground that underlies various histories. It does not imply that these histories are without their points of difference or opposition.

Prevalent in history, sociology, media studies and press commentary the dominant narrative is bound up with the modernisation of Irish society and the decline of the former hegemony of tradition, Catholicism, and introverted nationalism. Concerns with the social consequences of television as a medium are lost as they are subsumed into the politics of Irish modernisation. Thus, many questions about how Irish people's social practices changed alongside the new medium are ignored. In its failure to countenance certain facts, and to ask certain questions, the dominant narrative is ideologically conservative. This claim may appear wrongheaded because the story of Irish television, as it is told, is the story of an escape from repression to freedom; from silence to the ability to speak and be heard. Before asking why this narrative dominates we need to take a moment to understand the story it tells.

Breaking the Silence

The Lemass government is commonly seen to have initiated Ireland's economic modernisation. Often at odds with this government, RTÉ is credited with spearheading a parallel process of cultural emancipation. The channel's cultural significance can only be understood in the context of the longstanding censorious activities of the Irish Catholic Church, lay organisations and the Irish State. From the mid-nineteenth century, the Catholic Church had imposed a culture of silence upon the discussion of sexuality. This served, in part, as an ideological support to an agrarian economy. Inglis describes how 'beyond the confessional there was a silence' which, 'imposed in homes, schools, the media and other institutions', 'created and maintained the practices of postponed marriages and permanent celibacy' essential to the preservation of an agricultural economy where only the first-born son could inherit the family farm.[15] After Irish independence, state censorship of publications and films was imposed through a confluence of Catholicism, class-based anxiety about social order, and cultural and economic nationalism.[16] In the 1960s, Ireland began to look outward to foreign markets and investors. Deference to authority, and the silence and shame around sexuality began, at a glacial pace, to recede. RTÉ challenged Ireland's system of moral censorship through programmes that pushed back the limits of what could be publicly discussed.

Woodman, Inglis, Savage and others have argued that television opened Ireland up to foreign cultural influences. For Inglis, 'television changed the face of Catholic Ireland because the practice and discourse of imported programmes was at variance with traditional Catholic principles. They portrayed life-styles in which religion had little or no importance. The concentration was on urban individuals rather than on rural family life'.[17] Indigenous programmes are also seen to have played a role here. Over the course of the 1970s Irish drama productions became increasingly forthright in their treatment of sensitive social issues. Initially coy social representations gave way to the discussion of contraception, marital affairs and divorce in serials like *The Riordans* and *Bracken*.[18] For many writers, such serial drama reflected and facilitated social change in Ireland.[19] However, when it comes to television as a force for change in Ireland academic literature has placed the most concerted emphasis on the role of the iconic *Late Late Show*. Of course, this is not to claim that historians have ignored the social importance of other programmes and genres. The *Late Late Show* is discussed here as common topic across histories. It is also a perfect example of the dominant narrative where television, as a new voice, disrupts the silence imposed by entrenched social power.

Hosted by Gay Byrne, the *Late Late Show* was created in 1962. Its format blended the conventions of entertainment and serious discussion. Horgan claimed that the show 'was to have a profound effect on Irish social mores'.[20] For Ferriter the show quickly came to be seen as 'the bane of the upholder of "traditional" values'.[21] It traded in 'the revelation of intimacies in the glare of the studio lights, the disclosure in public of things that had never been disclosed in private'[22] O'Toole argued that the show, and its presenter, were remarkable precisely because of the silence that suffocated private expression and public debate in Ireland. In 1997, he wrote that 'it is the silences that have made Gay Byrne what he is in Ireland'. These silences 'at the breakfast table, the silences around the fireside, the silences on the pillow'. Without them Byrne would merely be a 'superbly professional broadcaster, confident, adaptable, quick thinking and fast talking - and no more'. With these silences, however, Byrne became 'the voice in which the unspoken can be articulated, the man who gives permission for certain subjects to be discussed. His is the voice, calm, seductive and passionless, in which things that would otherwise be unbearable can be listened to'. Byrne's achievement was 'founded on Irish people's inarticulacy, embarrassment and silence … '.[23] Here, O'Toole captures the central thrust of the dominant narrative. The *Late Late Show* marks a new dispensation where RTÉ programmes give voice to what 'Old Ireland' had silenced.

Robert Savage wrote that the show was one of the 'most provocative features' on RTÉ and that it 'deserves all the credit it has received for helping to open up Irish society'.[24] Lance Pettitt set out the range of social issues that the programme is credited with influencing.

According to one study,[25] *The Late Late Show* has not just aired topics but has been influential in changing social and moral attitudes. It has provoked legislative change and shifted the boundaries of taboos in Irish social discourse on a variety of topics, including unmarried mothers, Travellers' rights, infanticide, different kinds of sexuality, marriage and clerical celibacy.[26]

Pettitt argued that the *Late Late Show* 'challenged authority, which public figures had hitherto *assumed* [Italics in original], and tackled the shibboleths of Irish society in a domestic forum that was disarmingly open for its time'. It 'provoked discussion within Irish homes, in the national daily press and Dáil Éireann'.[27] The programme is credited with addressing myriad difficult issues but sexuality takes centre stage in academic literature.

Ferriter reports that 'any discussion of sex was, of course, as mesmerising to the audience as it was uncomfortable'. He quotes novelist Colm Tóibín who maintained that 'there were so many people "who had never heard about sex"'.[28] Four other writers cite Tóibín's descriptions of watching the show with his family as an illustration of its social effect.

> Down in Enniscorthy when I was a lad we all sat glued to it. We were often glued by embarrassment that someone was talking about sex: there were older people in the room who didn't like sex being talked about. If the *Late Late Show* had not existed it is highly possible that many people would have lived their lives in Ireland in the twentieth century without ever having heard anyone talking about sex. If any other programme had mentioned sex, it would have been turned off. Turn that rubbish off. But nobody ever turned the *Late Late Show* off. The show was too unpredictable.[29]

The story of the *Late Late Show*, and by extension that of RTÉ, is one of television prising open Ireland's culture of silence. Television, through entertainment, documentary, news and current affairs, gave individuals the vocabulary and the social licence to discuss issues, public and private, for themselves. John Bowman wrote 'what has been witnessed is the empowerment of the individual, the strengthening of rights based on individual choice rather than the old hierarchical society with answers handed down from those already characterised as "well-nigh infallible in all matters"'.[30] The dominant narrative emphasises RTÉ's catalytic role in Ireland's modernisation and cultural liberalisation. Nevertheless, its vision is narrow. It is preoccupied with institutions and circumscribed by the nation state.

Closed Accounts of Openness

The limitations of taking 'television' to be synonymous with RTÉ are apparent if we consider, as just one example, the case of early adopters of television and the role of British broadcasting in the Republic of Ireland. Television watching in Ireland began with British broadcasts. Histories that point to the reception of British channels in the Republic, often described as 'fallout' signals, do so to describe cultural and political motivations behind the creation of RTÉ. Cormack notes that the British Broadcasting Corporation (BBC) had 'generated much of the concern about the detrimental cultural influences of television'. She describes how it was 'especially galling to cultural nationalists' that the broadcast of Queen Elizabeth II's coronation in 1953 was 'watched eagerly, if guiltily, in the Republic'. Morash cites a short article from the *Irish Times* under the headline *Rush Order of TV Masts*.[31]

> A rush order of 125 television masts left Cardiff Airport for Dublin yesterday in an Aer Lingus plane. The aerials, ordered by Dublin radio dealers, are of a special type designed for use outside the range of normal television broadcasts. Some for use in Dublin, were attuned to the Holme Moss transmitter and the new Belfast booster station. Others, designed for use in Cork and Wexford, were attuned to the Wenvoe (Glamorgan) transmitter. All of them, it is understood, are to be erected in time for the Coronation (*The Irish Times*, May 27, 1953)

Historians mention such broadcasts but they are discussed, in passing, in terms of their relevance to the creation of Irish television.[32]

The Republic of Ireland was not broadcasting its own programmes in the 1950s but television had already found a place in national discussion and debate as mediated by the press. *The Irish Times,* for example, reported that a man had been arrested for using a hatchet to smash a television in a Dublin pub on the day of the Coronation (*The Irish Times*, June 17, 1953). A humorous letter from a reader in Tullamore described how his attempt to mount a television aerial on a public water tower, to watch the ceremony, was treated as a treasonable act by local authorities, described as the 'County Kremlin' (*The Irish Times,* June 22, 1953). By May 1954, the *Irish Times* was publishing BBC television listings. In 1955, there were an estimated 4000 television sets in the Republic of Ireland with 50 new sets being sold every week.[33] By 1958 there were an estimated 20,000 television sets in the country.[34] 1959 saw 102,000 television licence holders in Northern Ireland.[35] Still, television did not arrive in 'Ireland' until 1961. Shortly after RTÉ's launch, in 1963, the number of television households in the Republic had jumped to an estimated 237,000.[36] This might give some justification to saying, hyperbolically, that television arrived with RTÉ. Nevertheless, in the same year, almost half [37] of Irish television households received British channels.[38] This proportion remained consistent for almost two decades. As Chubb wrote:

> In 1979, 45 per cent of televisions in the Republic would receive British (including Northern Ireland) programmes, and ... these programmes had a considerable attraction. Almost six out of ten Dubliners watched at least some British programmes each day, as did four out of ten urban families generally. Rural—that is, mainly farming—people and the people of Munster generally did not because they could not.[39]

It took almost 20 years after the launch of Irish television for 93% of the households in the Republic of Ireland to have a television set.[40] The proportion of television households receiving British channels dropped to almost one-third of the national total as broadcast coverage for RTÉ spread westwards into counties that initially could not pick up any television transmissions. By 1983, however, half the television households in the country had access to British channels once more.[41] With the advent of satellite and cable distribution, this upward trend continued. By 2010, almost 9 in 10 Irish homes had access to British and other international channels.[42] Still, the dominant historical narrative on television in Ireland is quite blind to people in the Republic of Ireland watching broadcasts from Britain, other than as a political impetus to the creation of RTÉ.

British broadcasts are not the focus of the life story interviews conducted to date but they have inevitably arisen as part of people's recollections of television from its earliest days. Radio introduced Irish homes to international broadcasting. Recalling radio, people spoke about Irish and British programmes without any reference to stations. British-made family favourites like *The Archers, Mrs Dale's Diary* and *Listen with Mother* were interspersed through recollections of Irish shows like *The Kennedys of Castleross* and *Dear Frankie*. Many people remembered family media habits that formed around British programmes. Television did not mark a sudden invasion but rather the continued presence of British and other international broadcasts in Irish homes. Like radio, people recalled that watching television programmes, and particularly variety shows and dramas, became a family habit. Sheila Farrell recalled how the first television star she could remember was Alma Cogan who would sing every week on Ulster Television (UTV) backed by the Beverly sisters. Weekly rituals would emerge around *Coronation Street, Emmerdale* and *Crossroads* as much as they did around Irish productions like *Glenroe*.

Early audiences often watched television collectively. People would gather in public houses or in the homes of friends, family or neighbours. British broadcasts provided the occasions that people would use to visit, or to angle to be invited by, a television household. For many Irish people then, beyond those who owned a set, their first encounters with television were with British channels. Their early favourites, and indeed many of their personal examples of exemplary programming, came from Britain. Tom Shiels, for example, mentioned the ITV sci-fi serials *Pathfinders to Venus* and *Pathfinders to Mars* as two of his early favourites. Watching BBC and UTV was part of family and community life for tens of thousands of Irish people before the arrival of Irish television.

If television was consequential in liberalising Irish culture then British channels had some part to play. Writing in *The Furrow* in 1958, Ethna Conway discussed the merits of the BBC's *Lifeline* programme which had openly addressed homosexuality and prostitution.[43] In an interview, Mary Cooper recalled how, in the 1950s, a British programme about venereal disease had made her mother so uneasy that she needed to ask her daughter to leave the room. It is impossible to know how many people in the Republic of Ireland managed to see such programmes. Nevertheless, a year after RTÉ's launch roughly half of Irish viewers had ready access to such broadcasts. While the *Late Late Show* is regularly mentioned by academics for breaking Ireland's culture of silence, the influence of more forthright British channels, apart from their political role as 'fallout' signals, remains unexplored.

The Irish experience of television was decidedly international. Although politicians announced their concerns about the cultural dangers of British programming, people interviewed appeared to have been unphased. Television was a spectacle. Watching British broadcasts was about experiencing an exciting new technology, getting to see more of the world and, quite often, visiting one's neighbours. It, apparently, was not about a zero-sum vision of nationalism. One could feel untroubled in their identity while watching the Coronation, *Z-Cars*, or *Coronation Street*. Matt Fossett thought that early adopters like his own family 'identified with a more Anglocentric world than those who did not watch TV, or those whose TV experience began with [R]TÉ'. Fossett also recalled how, in 1961, his family began to notice a huge tower dominating the landscape beyond their back windows. This was the RTÉ transmission mast. He continued:

> I don't remember my parents being particularly enthused at the prospect of a home-grown television channel, although they had been, and continued to be, listeners of Radio Éireann. They were happy and comfortable with the concept of television being the way it was, a British thing (Matt Fossett).

Most other viewers did not identify with Britain like Fossett's family but television nonetheless provided an unprecedented view of the wider world. Ironically, some people described how they had welcomed RTÉ because of the increased number of US shows it offered. Roddy Flynn's recent exploration of RTÉ schedules from the 1960s addresses the high volume of imported programmes carried by the emerging Irish broadcaster.[44] To date, however, there has been no historical exploration of Irish people's engagement with British channels. The transmissions from the BBC and UTV that Irish people watched and discussed are absent from academic commentary.[45] Ironically, the consensus on how television opened up Irish society is itself somewhat blinkered and introspective. The limitations in these accounts stem, in large part, from a methodology that is, unintentionally but nonetheless effectively, nationalist.

The Institutional Lens Focused on the Nation State

Typical of an international tendency, academic commentaries on television in Ireland have depended on institutions as sources of historical evidence.[46] They have relied on what Bourdon described as sources 'from above', the state and broadcasters, and 'from the side', the press and other media reportage and commentary on broadcasting.[47] Work based in such material can, of course, be invaluable. Detailed archival research, like Savage's, demonstrates the complex political, economic and technological forces, national and international, that shaped RTÉ as a broadcaster. In much other work, there is a focus on the political machinations within and around RTÉ.[48] The methodological difficulties with a dependence on institutional sources begin where they have been used, not as a way of understanding RTÉ, but as a means of divining how Irish people used and understood television and acted in relation to it.

Writers have consistently used institutional, press and even literary sources as indicators of how Irish people experienced, and reflected upon, television as a new medium. There is frequently an assumption that what RTÉ transmitted, and what newspapers printed about those transmissions, can be read as an unproblematic reflection of how Irish people thought about television. Earls provides an example of this in his description and defence of the methods he used in understanding *The Late Late Show*. The study of the programme proved difficult because many archive copies had been deleted. Nevertheless, he argued that 'because the show has been at the top of the TAM [Television Audience Measurement] ratings for 20 years' the public were 'deeply familiar with its format and its presenter'. Lacking alternative means, Earls relied on the national press, which had taken part in and reported upon the controversy that followed certain episodes, to access public debate. He notes that his study is somewhat uneven in that the 'controversies of the 1960s received more attention because the public debates which followed were far more extensive than any which occurred in the seventies'.[49]

Although he did not describe them explicitly, Earls recognised 'the limits of this methodology'.[50] The 'public' are described as a monolith whose familiarity with the presenter and the show's format is taken for granted. More importantly, however, the press is accepted as a direct reflection of how the public experienced and discussed television and its controversies. Earls does not mention the possibility that controversies from the 1960s may have simply received more newspaper coverage when RTÉ was still relatively new and newsworthy. Many commentaries have had similar shortcomings but have been less ready to admit to them. Researchers typically cite newspapers as if they flawlessly channelled the perceptions and opinions of Irish people. The role of news values and other journalistic processes of selection and framing are ignored.

One could attempt to explain the omission of British programming from the history of television in Ireland in terms of a conscious nationalist or pro-RTÉ bias. However, a simpler explanation is that British programmes left relatively few traces in sources 'from above' and 'from the side'. People were unlikely to write to the *Irish Independent* to complain about UTV. The belly aching of rural politicians was unlikely to be directed towards, or heard by, the Director General of the BBC. There was little political capital to be gained from condemning British broadcasters in the Dáil.[51] British broadcasts were inside Irish homes but lay largely outside the game of Irish politics. They have been overlooked because academic commentaries have viewed television through the lens of the Republic of Ireland's parliamentary and cultural politics as recorded by the State, RTÉ and Irish newspapers. Practices lying outside this game, and its official records, have gone unseen and unreported. As a result, academic literature has consecrated certain ideas about television and Irish society as common sense. It has silenced others.

While they may not be motivated by nationalism, social histories built on institutional and media sources reproduce outlooks on the relationship between television and society that are fused with the nation state. In the Irish case, they are also nationalist in the sense that they tend to frame the state as the subject of its own history and deny its existence as the object of external influence. The 'New Ireland' that began to emerge in the 1960s depended on the wholesale embrace of international culture, technology and capital, which came chiefly from American transnational corporations.[52] The dominant narrative describes Irish politics but it also plays a political role by perpetuating a simplified vision of social change. RTÉ is cast as a modernising force in an increasingly open and outward-looking nation. Here, the work of media historians is compatible with the interests of the Irish State and the national broadcaster. It amplifies memories of broadcasts from within the state and mutes those from outside. By reproducing the mythological binary of 'old' and 'new' it offers the State's, and RTÉ's, preferred visions of itself. By only looking inward, the dominant narrative transmutes Ireland's dependent modernisation into a willed, autonomous national project. Alexander Dhoest argued 'any historical account of media which excludes its audiences is incomplete'.[53] The methodological nationalism of the dominant narrative is rooted in the fact that is has remembered institutions but forgotten viewers.

Accessing memory creates unique methodological frustrations. The interviews for this research have all taken place in a single city, Dublin, which, as the Irish capital, contains one-third of the national population. The city has a history of immigration that accelerated dramatically during Ireland's industrialisation in the 1960s. Thus, it provides access to recollections from across the island of Ireland. The interviews are long, semi-structured life story interviews where television is a feature in, but not the exclusive focus of, the conversation.[54] Here, recollection is a co-creative activity that implicates the researcher, it is not simply data retrieval. People do not simply access the past. They create a narrative that makes sense of their past in light of their present. Thus, what is recalled may tell us as much about the social identity of the narrator today as they do about television in the past. Memory is at its weakest where chronology is concerned. Multiple incidents may be conflated into a single event. As historical sources, memory accounts must be triangulated with sources 'from above' and 'from the side'.[55]

Despite these weaknesses, audience memories present rich opportunities. Interviews can tell us about how viewers related to television at different stages in their lives. People often remember television programmes that institutional histories forget. Recollections can lend depth and texture to exising knowledge. Indeed, they also demonstrate that television had varied uses and meanings for different social groups. Audience memories can reveal a diversity of audience experiences that may be homogenised by national, institutional histories. Life story accounts are not just about television. They are about the connections between the medium and everyday social practice.[56] They tell us about what it felt like to experience television and the new forms of connection and separation that it brought to families and society at large. In all these ways, memory work offers an outlook on the nation, its global context and processes of social change that are very different to those discussed in orthodox histories. Arguably, this shift in historical sourcing can offer a look beyond the blinkers of the nation state. However, to date, while research on audience memories has been carried out across Europe, there are no national or supranational initiatives for the collection, archiving or analysis of audience memories.

There are political stakes in the way that media, and their historical role, are imagined and represented. Histories of television in Ireland are limited by, and to, a nation state perspective. In the absence of alternative accounts, they have become the background common sense on television and Irish society. In 1984, McLoone and MacMahon noted that 'most worthwhile writing on television in Ireland has tended to concentrate on the institutional structures of RTÉ and on the relationship between RTÉ and the State'.[57] Little has changed in the intervening 30 years where commentators have continued to divine historical changes in public culture related to television by using political, academic and journalistic reactions to RTÉ and its programmes. In the Irish context, turning to the audience as a historical source can contribute to an 'entangled' media history that challenges the homogenous, hermetically sealed and autonomous visions of the nation state presented by more orthodox accounts.[58] A by-product of the use of sources from below then is that it may promote a rupture in the unannounced connection between media history scholarship and state nationalism.

Disclosure Statement

No potential conflict of interest was reported by the authors.

Notes

1. Tovey and Share, for example, write that 'television arrived in Ireland at 7pm on New Year's Eve 1961 though for a short period prior to that, some enthusiasts on the east coast were able to pick up British TV signals', 376.

2. The Irish Independent. 'North's new'.
3. The service was initially called Telefís Éireann. It was later combined with radio under the name Radió Telefís Éireann.
4. Also cited in Gibbons, "From Kitchen Sink," 21; Savage, *Irish Television*, 1; Morash, *A history*, 172–73.
5. Irish Prime Minister.
6. De Valera also alluded to the positive qualities of television and expressed his hope that the audience would demand beneficial programming over damaging content. Horgan, *Irish Media*, 84.
7. Also cited in Savage, *Irish Television*, xi; by Savage 1996: xi, Morash, *A history*, 172; Cormack, "Angelus, bells, television," 274; Horgan, *Irish Media*, 84, Wylie, "Streaming history," 237; Gibbons, "From Kitchen Sink," 21; Pettitt, *Screening Ireland*, 147.
8. This was a Papal Encyclical on the dangers of motion pictures from 1936. This informed Irish legislation on the censorship of films in 1939. Morash, *A History*, 172.
9. Savage, *Irish Television*, xii.
10. Cormack, "Angelus, Bells, Television," 274.
11. Horgan, *Irish Media*, 83–84.
12. Also cited in Morash, *A History*, 171.
13. Ibid.,173.
14. Kelly and Rolston, "Broadcasting in Ireland", Kelly, "The Poor Aren't News", Curtis, *Ireland Propaganda War*.
15. See Inglis, *Lessons in Irish Sexuality*, 36.
16. Woodman, *Media Control in Ireland*; Morash, *A History*, 138–47; Horgan, *Irish Media*, 12.
17. Inglis, *Moral Monopoly*, 92.
18. Gibbons, "From Kitchen Sink"; Sheehan, *Irish Television Drama*; O'Connor, "The Presentation of Women".
19. Gibbons, "From Kitchen Sink"; Silj, *East of Dallas*; Sheehan, *Irish Television Drama*; O'Donnell, *Good Times, Bad Times*.
20. Horgan, *Irish Media*, 89.
21. Ferriter, *Occasions of Sin*, 374.
22. O'Toole, *Lie of the Land*, 145.
23. Ibid., 146–7.
24. Savage, "Loss of Innocence," 207.
25. This study is not described beyond a reference to Collins, "Late Late".
26. Pettitt, *Screening Ireland*, 169–70; *also cited in* Savage, *Loss of Innocence?*, 207.
27. Pettitt, *Screening Ireland*, 169.
28. Ferriter, *Occasions of Sin*, 376; also cited in Bowman, *Window and Mirror*, 221.
29. Tóibín, "Gay Byrne," 66; also quoted in Sweeney, "RTÉ Public Service Broadcaster," 78; Morash, *A history*, 180; Horgan, *Irish Media*, 89; Pettitt, *Screening Ireland*, 169.
30. Bowman, *Window and Mirror*, 232.
31. See Morash, *A History*, 168.
32. See Savage, *Irish Television*, 18; Cormack, "Angelus, Bells, Television," 273; Horgan, *Irish Media*," 79.
33. See Morash, *A History*, 168.
34. Central Statistics Office (CSO), *That Was Then*, 57.

35. *The Cork Examiner.* "Commercial T.V".
36. McLoone and MacMahon, *Television and Irish Society*, 150.
37. 48% of television households could receive British channels in 1963. See McLoone and MacMahon, *Television and Irish Society*, 150.
38. Ibid., 150.
39. Chubb, *The Government*, 73.
40. Ibid., 73.
41. McLoone and MacMahon, *Television and Irish Society*, 150.
42. Comreg, *Irish Communication Market*, 71.
43. Conway, "Ireland and Television," 33.
44. Flynn, "It is Against".
45. Morash does acknowledge that Irish people were watching television from the early 1950s. However, his subsequent discussion concentrates on the institutional creation of RTÉ rather than on the activity of Irish television audiences, 168–69. Pettitt also acknowledges multi-channel viewing and comments that after 1976 the availability of British programmes undermined Irish attempts at censorship of paramilitary groups, 149–50.
46. See Schudson, "Historical Approaches," 188–89; Curran, "Narratives of Media History," 1; O'Sullivan, *Television Memories and Cultures*; Dhoest, "Audience Retrospection," 66; Penati, "Remembering Our First," 7–8.
47. Bourdon, "Detextualizing," 12–16; Dhoest, "Audience Retrospection," 66.
48. See Horgan, *Irish Media*; Doolan, Dowling, and Quinn, *Sit down*; Bowman, *Window and Mirror*.
49. Earls, "The Late Late Show," 107–8.
50. Ibid., 108.
51. The Irish parliament.
52. Bell and Meehan, "International Telecommunications Deregulation," 77.
53. Dhoest, "Audience Retrospection," 65.
54. See Bourdon and Kligler-Vilenchik, "Together, Nevertheless"; Dhoest, "Audience Retrospection"; Penati, "Remembering Our First"; O'Sullivan, *Television Memories and Cultures*.
55. Dhoest, "Audience Retrospection," 65.
56. Bourdon and Kligler-Vilenchik." Together, Nevertheless," 35.
57. McLoone and MacMahon, *Television and Irish Society*, 8.
58. Cronqvist and Hilgert, "Entagled Media Histories".

References

Bell, Desmond, and Niall Meehan. "International Telecommunications Deregulation and Ireland's Domestic Communications Policy." *Journal of Communication* 38, no. 1 (1988): 70–84.

Bourdon, Jérôme. "Detextualizing: How to Write a History of Audiences." *European Journal of Communication* 30, no. 1 (2015): 7–21.

Bourdon, Jérôme, and Neta Kligler-Vilenchi. "Together, Nevertheless? Television Memories in Mainstream Jewish Israel." *European Journal of Communication* 26, no. 1 (2011): 33–47.

Bowman, John. 2011. *Window and Mirror: RTÉ Television-1961-2011*. Cork: Collins.

Chubb, Basil. *The Government and Politics of Ireland*. London: Longman, 1987.

Çinar, Alev. "Globalism as the Product of Nationalism: Founding Ideology and the Erasure of the Local in Turkey." *Theory, Culture & Society* 27, no. 4 (2010): 90–118.

Collins, L. ""Late Late" dying soul of the nation." *The Sunday Independent*, August 9, 1998.

Comreg. *Irish Communication Market: Quarterly Key Data Report*. Commission for Communications Regulation, 2010. [Online http://www.comreg.ie/_fileupload/publications/Comreg1019.pdf].

Conway, Ethna. "Ireland and Television." *The Furrow* 9, no. 1 (1958): 33–38.

The Cork Examiner. "Commerical T.V. for Six Counties." March 10, 1959.

Cormack, Patricia. "Angels, Bells, Television and Ireland: The Place of the Angelus Broadcast in the Republic." *Media, Culture & Society* 27, no. 2 (2005): 271–287.

Cronqvist, Marie, and Christoph Hilgert. 2016. "Entangled Media Histories: The Value of Transnational and Transmedial Approaches in Media Historiography." *Media History* 23 (1): 1–12.

CSO (Central Statistics Office). *That was Then This is Now: Change in Ireland, 1949-1999. A Publication to Mark the 50th Anniversary of the Central Statistics Office*. Dublin: Central Statistics Office, 2000.

Curtis, Liz. 1984. *Ireland—The Propaganda War*. London: Pluto Press.

Dhoest, Alexander. "Audience Retrospection as a Source of Historiography: Oral History Interviews on Early Television Experiences." *European Journal of Communication* 30, no. 1 (2015): 64–78.

Doolan, Lelia, Jack Dowling, and Bob Quinn. 1969. *Sit Down and be Counted: The Cultural Evolution of a Television Station*. Dublin: Wellington Publishers.

Earls, Maurice. 1984. "The Late Late Show, Controversy and Context." In *Television and Irish Society, 21 Years of Irish Television*, edited by Martin McLoone and John MacMahon. Dublin: RTÉ/IFI.

Ferriter, Diarmaid. 2010. *Occasions of Sin: Sex and Society in Modern Ireland*. London: Profile books.

Flynn, Roddy. "" It Is Against the Basic Concepts of Good Government to Subject Our People to Rosemary Clooney at the Public Expense": Imported Programming on Early Irish Television." *Éire-Ireland* 50, no. 1 (2015): 66–94.

Horgan, John. 2001. *Irish Media: A Critical History Since 1922*. London: Routledge.

Inglis, Tom. 1998. *Lessons in Irish Sexuality*. Dublin: University College Dublin Press.

Inglis, Tom. 1998. *Moral Monopoly: The Rise and Fall of the Catholic Church in Modern Ireland*. Dublin: University College Dublin Press.

The Irish Independent. "North's New Television Station." July 22, 1955.

Kelly, M. "The Poor Aren't News: An Ian Hart Memorial Lecture." In *The Poor Aren't News: Ian Hart Memorial Lectures*, edited by Simon Community, 6–11. Dublin: Simon Community, 1984.

Kelly, M., and B. Rolston. "Broadcasting in Ireland: Issues of National Identity and Censorship." In *Irish Society: Sociological Perspectives*, edited by P. Clancy, S. Drudy, K. Lynch, and L. O'Dowd, 563–592. Dublin: Institute of Public Administration, 1995.

McLoone, Martin, and John MacMahon. 1984. *Television and Irish Society: 21 Years of Irish Television*. Dublin: RTÉ/IFI.

Morash, Chris. *A History of the Media in Ireland*. Cambridge: Cambridge University Press, 2010.

O'Connor, Barbara. "The Presentation of Women in Irish Television Drama." *Television and Irish Society* 21 (1984): 123–133.

O'Donnell, Hugh. 1999. *Good Times, Bad Times: Soap Operas and Society in Western Europe*. London: Leicester University Press.

O'Sullivan, Tim. 1991. "Television Memories and Cultures of Viewing, 1950-65." In *Popular Television in Britain: Studies in Cultural History*, edited by John Corner, 159–181. London: BFI.

O'Toole, Fintan. 1997. *The Lie of the Land: Irish Identities*. London: Verso.

Penati, Cecilia. "'Remembering Our First TV Set'. Personal Memories as a Source for Television Audience History." *VIEW Journal of European Television History and Culture* 2, no. 3 (2013): 4–12.

Pettitt, Lance. 2000. *Screening Ireland: Film and Television representation*. Manchester: Manchester University Press.

Savage, Robert J. 1996. *Irish Television: The Political and Social Origins*. Cork: Cork University Press.

Savage, Robert J. *A Loss of Innocence?: Television and Irish Society, 1960-72*. Manchester: Manchester University Press, 2010.

Schudson, Michael. 1991. "Historical Approaches to Communication Studies." In *Qualitative Methodologies for Mass Communication Research*, edited by Klaus Bruhn Jensen and Nicholas Jankowski, 175–190. London: Routledge.

Sheehan, Helena. 2004. *Irish Television Drama: A Society and its Stories*. Dublin: Radio Telefís Éireann.

Sweeney, William. "RTÉ Public Service Broadcaster? An Examination Using an Analysis of Broadcasting Schedules and Conten and the Perceptions of Staff." Doctoral dissertation., Liverpool John Moores University (unpublished), 2007.

Tóibín, Colm. "Gay Byrne: Irish Life as Cabaret." *The Crane Bag* 8, no. 2 (1984): 65–69.

Wylie, Liam. "Streaming History Increasing Access to Audiovisual Archives." *Journal of Media Practice* 7, no. 3 (2007): 237–248.

SEAMUS O'FAWKES AND OTHER CHARACTERS
The British tabloid cartoon coverage of the IRA campaign in England

Roseanna Doughty

On 8 March 1973, the violence of Belfast spread to the streets of London as the IRA launched their bombing campaign in England. This article examines the cartoon coverage of IRA bomb attacks on English cities published in the British press during the early 1970s. By investigating political cartoons from leading national newspapers, this article sheds new light on reactions to the violence and explores how this affected the lived experiences of the Irish in Britain. It highlights how newspapers used symbols of Britishness and WWII iconography to (re)construct an imagined British community in the face of the IRA threat. The cartoons also indicate a more ambiguous image of the Irish in Britain, one of both harbourers and victims of terrorists. This focus on pictorial representations reveals the complexity of press attitudes towards IRA bombings as the humour inherent in cartoons enables them to allude to ideas journalists could not.

The early 1970s saw the violence of Belfast spread to the streets of English cities. On 8 March 1973, two IRA bombs exploded outside the Old Bailey and the London Central Army Recruiting Office, killing one person and injuring a further 265. This was the start of a campaign of violence in England, which would last twenty-five years, causing the death of 115 people and injuring countless others.[1] The day after the Old Bailey bombings, *The Sun*'s editorial cartoonist Paul Rigby published a cartoon featuring Lady Justice, the statue situated on the top of the Old Bailey, with a severed left hand holding the scales of justice (Figure 1). The cartoon focused on the physical impact of the bombing, suggesting that the attack had threatened core British values. Lady Justice's intact sword arm indicated that Britain and justice would prevail and promised swift retribution in the face of IRA savagery.

Scholars have long used political cartoons to shed light on the complex relationship between Ireland and Britain. In 1971, historian, L. Perry Curtis was the first to use cartoons to explore Victorian attitudes towards Ireland and the Irish people. Focusing on the comic art of satirical magazines *Punch* and *Judy*, Curtis controversially argued that nineteenth-century caricatures reflected the increasingly popular view in Britain of the Irish as racially inferior.[2] As Curtis observed, cartoons are 'multilayered graphic texts filled with values and beliefs of political import' and as a result, they offer unique insights into contemporary

"Murder may pass unpunish'd For a time, But tardy Justice will o'ertake the crime . . ."

FIGURE 1
Paul Rigby, 'Murder may pass unpunish'd For a time, But tardy Justice will o'ertake the crime', The Sun, 9 March 1973, News UK, 'British Cartoon Archive, University of Kent'.

debates and opinions.[3] The humour inherent in cartoons enables them to address ideas not easily expressed in written reportage, making them a valuable source for establishing attitudes towards contemporary events.[4]

Following Curtis' example, historians have drawn on cartoons to illuminate a wide range of topics relating to Ireland, particularly the 'Troubles'. John Kirkaldy, Liz Curtis, John Darby, and Roy Douglas *et al.*, have all analysed pictorial representations of the Northern Ireland conflict in the British press.[5] Little attention, however, is given to the cartoon coverage of IRA attacks on English cities during this period, in marked contrast with contemporary media coverage. Throughout the 'Troubles', IRA bomb attacks in England dominated headlines, leading one IRA spokesperson to observe that 'in publicity terms one bomb in Oxford Street [was] worth ten in Belfast'.[6] Accordingly, an examination of the cartoon coverage of IRA violence in England is important if we are to obtain a comprehensive picture of how the British media represented the conflict.

This article undertakes a systematic investigation of how the IRA bombing campaign in English cities during the early 1970s was portrayed in cartoons of the British tabloid press.Whilst the cartoons that appeared in broadsheets during this period mainly covered political developments in Northern Ireland, the tabloid papers provided more detailed cartoon coverage of the bombing campaign in England. The tabloid press also provides a unique window onto popular culture, allowing us to explore how representations of the conflict were developed and disseminated through society.[7] In particular, this article will explore how cartoons in two of the most popular titles, the *Daily Mirror* and *The Sun* represented the bombings. These papers have been selected because they offer contrasting political orientations: the *Daily Mirror* being left-of-centre, whilst *The Sun* has traditionally aligned itself with the right. By investigating the cartoon coverage of the bombing campaign this article will highlight how the tabloid press drew on British motifs and Second World War iconography to (re)construct an imagined British community in the face of the IRA threat. The cartoons also indicate a more ambiguous image of the Irish in Britain, simultaneously portraying them as both harbourers and victims of terrorists.

The attitude of the *Daily Mirror* and *The Sun* towards the IRA are best illustrated in the way they drew comparison to the British population. Throughout the bombing campaign both papers consistently employed the trope of the 'British', itself an amorphous grouping, as a stoic people facing down the IRA threat. In doing so, they reinforced an idea of Britishness, cultivated by both papers in order to create, and maintain, an imagined national community of readers.[8] The invocation of 'Britishness' to make news stories relevant to all potential readers is a traditional tool used by the press to market itself at a national level.[9] National identity, however, is not a fixed notion and is continuously being renegotiated, with the press playing a leading role.[10] In the latter half of the twentieth century, the decline of Britain as a world power and high levels of immigration brought into question what it now meant to be British. As Chris Waters argues, migrants played an influential role in the post-war reconfiguration of notions of national belonging.[11] Black migrants in particular were constructed as the 'dark strangers' and contrasted with the white British population, redefining the boundaries of national belonging. During the 1970s, the characteristics of the IRA were contrasted with those of their victims in order to bolster what it meant to be British. The IRA's association with the Irish living in Britain, however, meant that they too were cast once more as an internal 'other'.

One technique used by the *Daily Mirror* to (re)construct a sense of Britishness was through reference to a shared history.[12] Since 1945, the Second World War has become a 'routine trope of audience-identification' and as a result, almost all national crises have been viewed through the prism of Second World War imagery.[13] During the IRA's bombing campaign Second World War memories, particularly those of the Blitz, were mobilised by the *Mirror* to invoke in readers a similar stoicism to that associated with the response to German aggression in the 1940s. For example, in an editorial published after the Old Bailey bombings the *Daily Mirror* remarked that 'The London, that took the blitz, and made cups of tea and joked, is not going to have its nerve shattered by bombs'.[14] Similarly, following a spate of bomb attacks in September 1973, the paper remarked: 'The terrorists will not break the nerve- or even start to break the nerve- of a nation that stood up to the weight of Hitler's bombs'.[15] Filtering the Old Bailey bombings and other IRA attacks through images of the Blitz, the paper harnessed the concept of a united British community fighting a common enemy. In doing so, it strove to both minimise the perceived IRA threat and reassure readers by reminding them of a period when Britain had been victorious against a far greater enemy.[16]

By drawing on Second World War imagery, the *Daily Mirror* equated the IRA with the Nazis. Hitler was a common feature in cartoons referring to the IRA attacks in England. On 21 November 1974, two bombs exploded in the 'Tavern in the Town' and 'Mulberry Bush' pubs in Birmingham, killing 21 and injuring 183 people.[17] In response to the bombings, the *Daily Mirror's* cartoonist Keith Waite drew Hitler telling the IRA that 'Bombing doesn't work around here'. Waite evokes the memory of the Blitz, resurrecting associated stereotypes of the British as resilient in the face of adversity. It is worth noting, however, that drawing analogies to the Nazis was common currency during the 'Troubles', and used in reverse by the republican movement. In his account of life in Long Kesh, for example, Gerry Adams describes the prison as 'Britain's concentration camp'.[18]

The reasoning behind the Nazi comparison was to reinforce the fact that the bombers were nothing more than brutal murderers. As Mark Connelly points out, after the Second World War Hitler became a touchstone by which to measure evil.[19] In the aftermath of the Birmingham pub bombings, *The Sun*'s cartoonist Stanley Franklin took the analogy further. His cartoon showed Hitler making room for the IRA as Stalin, Emperor Nero, Genghis Khan and Attila the Hun stepped down from a podium labelled 'The Most Odious Murderers in History'.[20] The cartoon not only drew parallels to Hitler, but a long history of brutality, implying that the IRA had surpassed all five in cruelty.

In contrast with the *Daily Mirror*, *The Sun* largely avoided referencing the Second World War in its coverage of the IRA's campaign in England. Instead, the paper sought

FIGURE 2
Keith Waite, 'Bombing doesn't work around here- I've tried it', Daily Mirror, 27 November 1974, Keith Waite, British Cartoon Archive, University of Kent.

to create a sense of Britishness through other national motifs. Following a bomb attack on Westminster Hall on 17 June 1974, Franklin's predecessor at *The Sun*, Paul Rigby, produced a cartoon depicting a monstrous creature, labelled violence, about to destroy two of the central pillars of British society, law and democracy (Figure 3). In the background, used detonators stand beside fragmented pillars, and this, alongside the crumbling nature of the pillars, suggested that the IRA had already succeeded in destabilising the foundation of British society. The two remaining pillars, civilisation and decency have yet to be primed: Rigby warns that if the IRA are allowed to continue these will soon be next. The cartoon suggested that the IRA had threatened the British way of life by attacking the Houses of Parliament, a symbol of the rule of law and other British values. On the horizon, however, Big Ben rises from the smoke in defiance of the IRA's attack.[21] Rigby uses the image of the clock tower not only to signify the bomb's location, but to symbolise British resilience and courage. He draws Big Ben undamaged and operational indicating that despite the IRA's efforts, the British government and the values it represented would endure.

In its coverage of the Westminster bombing, the British press used the image of Big Ben extensively, to signify British fortitude.[22] Pictorial representations have traditionally played a significant role in the establishment of a national community. In order for cartoons to be effective, the reader must be able to interpret the message or joke being conveyed, therefore cartoonists rely on easily recognised motifs and preconceptions.[23] The reader's ability to interpret these images helped reinforce notions of a shared identity; in much the same way emphasising a shared history can promote common affiliations.

In the wake of the Tower of London bombing on 18 July 1973, *The Sun* drew on another trope of Britishness, the Beefeater. This attack caused particular outrage as it

FIGURE 3
Paul Rigby, '... Five, four, three, two, one', The Sun, 18 June 1974, News UK, 'British Cartoon Archive, University of Kent'.

FIGURE 4
Paul Rigby, 'Satisfied?', The Sun, 19 July 1974, News UK, 'British Cartoon Archive, University of Kent'.

was seen to have deliberately targeted children visiting the site on the first day of the school holidays. In his cartoon, Rigby emphasised the pointlessness and brutality of the bombing. Figure 4 shows a Beefeater, drawn to resemble a Marvel comic superhero, carrying the inert body of a young woman simply captioned 'Satisfied?'. The Beefeater, whose history can be traced back to the Norman Conquest, was intended to represent what Paul Ward has described as 'a sense of "national" permanence'.[24] Rigby depicts the Beefeater as a powerful figure, somewhat at odds with the retired non-commissioned officers of the Tower of London guard, to symbolise the perceived heroism of the British people.

The woman pictured in Rigby's cartoon represented forty-seven-year-old Dorothy Household who died in the bombing. Throughout the early 1970s, both the *Daily Mirror* and *The Sun* frequently focused on the plight of women and children caught up in the bombings to emphasise the horror of the Northern Ireland conflict and elicit a more powerful reaction from readers. The mutilation or death of women and children, characterised as 'innocent' victims, is seen as especially horrifying and the perpetrators of such violence beyond contempt.[25] The tabloid press regularly employed the association between child- and female-victims and innocence to spotlight the contemptuousness of the IRA bombers. Both papers presented the IRA's female-victims as young, beautiful and by implication innocent, regardless of age or physical attributes, for example Rigby's depiction of Household as a significantly younger looking damsel in distress.

In comparison, female republicans were portrayed as hideous and animal-like. In the early 1970s, Bernadette Devlin, the MP for Mid-Ulster, frequently featured in cartoons on Northern Ireland portrayed in a negative light. Young and outspoken she had initially been popular with the British press, but with the outbreak of violence in Northern

Ireland, she was increasingly depicted as a petulant child.[26] The 'Irish child' has long been an established figure in cartoons commenting on Ireland and reflects the enduring stereotype that the Irish were politically immature and in need of guidance from Britain.[27] British tabloid papers often rationalised the 'Troubles' as evidence of this lack of political maturity in order to justify the British presence in Northern Ireland. Devlin and other female republicans were also presented as monstrous harpies.[28] Commenting on a meeting, hijacked by female supporters of the Provisional IRA in April 1972, the *Daily Express* cartoonist Michael Cummings depicted the women as vampires confronting the Northern Ireland Secretary, William Whitelaw. A thought bubble coming from Whitelaw reads 'Maybe they should be given a sex-test to check if they really ARE women'.[29] The cartoon presents these women as unfeminine and therefore, not belonging to the standard narrative that women were expected to fit. By distinguishing them from 'real' women, Cummings suggests that they were irrational, and subsequently their support for the IRA irrational.[30] Irish republicans depicted as vampires and other monsters were also a common trope of earlier cartoons.

In cartoons depicting IRA violence in England during the 1970s, the *Daily Mirror* and *The Sun* drew on a range of long-established symbols of Ireland and the Irish. The simian or monstrous Irishmen in particular, were resurrected by both papers in their coverage of IRA bomb attacks on English cities. The *Daily Mirror*'s cartoon (Figure 2) commenting on the Birmingham pub bombings for example, showed a simianised IRA man, recognisable by his black beret, sunglasses and monkey's tail. By portraying the bomber as ape-like, cartoonist Keith Waite sought to highlight the inhumanity of the IRA's actions. In a similar way, following the Westminster bombing *The Sun*'s cartoonist, Paul Rigby, depicted the IRA as a hunched-back Frankenstein-esq monster primed to blow up the British establishment (Figure 3). The simian Irish terrorist was a recurrent theme throughout the British tabloid press's cartoon coverage of the 'Troubles'. Michael Cummings and the *Evening Standard*'s cartoonist Jak in particular, specialised in drawing the Irish as ape-like, violent figures that bore a strong resemblance to the bestial 'Paddy' of Victorian cartoons.[31]

The tradition of drawing the 'enemy' as ape- or animal-like dates back to the late eighteenth century and continues to the present day.[32] In the latter half of the nineteenth century, however, the simianised caricature was closely associated with the Irish. The Fenian movement especially, popularised the image of the Irish as subhuman and violent, as cartoonists sought to emphasis the danger of the Fenians by depicting them as ape-like monsters.[33] What these cartoons reveal about the nature of nineteenth-century British attitudes towards the Irish, however, has been the subject of much debate. As indicated, L. Perry Curtis' argument that the simian 'Paddy' reflected an increasingly racialised view of the Irish has received significant criticism, most notably from Sheridan Gilley and Roy Foster.[34] Gilley refuted Curtis' claims that British stereotypes of the Irish were racial, asserting that the Irish 'Paddy' was as much an Irish as a British creation. He argues that nineteenth-century British attitudes towards the Irish were inconsistent and social commentators equally as likely to be pro-Irish.[35] Foster concurred, arguing that the bestial Paddy was one of a variety of ways in which cartoonists drew the Irish.[36] Both Gilley and Foster suggested that religion, class and political violence played a more significant role in shaping British prejudices towards the Irish than ideas of race. More recently, Michael de Nie has argued that in the nineteenth century race was used 'as a vehicle for expressing multiple anxieties and preconceptions, among them class concerns and sectarian prejudices'.[37]

Curtis' thesis, however, continues to be applied without question by scholars examining British attitudes towards the Irish since the nineteenth century. John Kirkaldy, for example, has argued that the resurrection of the simianised 'Paddy' in coverage of the Northern Ireland conflict during the late twentieth century demonstrated 'the very depths of English anti-Irish feeling'.[38] It is worth noting that Rigby and Waite were from Australia and New Zealand respectively; accordingly, they were more removed from British stereotypes of the Irish. That said, both cartoonists would produce several drafts from which their editor would select the next day's cartoon. Waite acknowledged that his cartoons were often rejected 'because they did not conform with the newspaper's point of view'.[39] The published work of both cartoonists therefore, represent their respective newspaper's editorial strategies as much as their own opinions and prejudices.

The correlation between the ape-like, monstrous IRA featured in the cartoons of the early 1970s and those of the Fenians shows that some anti-Irish stereotypes persisted into the late twentieth century. As de Nie has argued, however, in the nineteenth century simianised representations of the Irish were in the minority as many other characters were used to represent Ireland and the Irish people, including 'Erin', 'the Irish pig' and various Irish politicians.[40] The *Daily Mirror* and *The Sun*'s cartoon coverage of the late twentieth-century bombing campaign in England include a similarly diverse range of characters. Not only do these cartoons feature the ape-like 'Paddy' referred to by Kirkaldy, but they also employed other motifs common to Victorian cartoons.

In Figure 4, for example, the image of Household being carried from the Tower of London is reminiscent of nineteenth-century depictions of Erin. The female personification of Ireland, Erin was one of the most common symbols in nineteenth-century cartoons commenting on the Irish Question.[41] She was typically portrayed as a young maiden in need of saving from the violent 'Paddy', usually by Britannia or St George, both potent symbols of British- and Englishness respectively.[42]

Keith Waite's cartoon in the *Daily Mirror* the day after the Westminster bombing referenced Guy Fawkes.[43] Throughout the nineteenth century, Fawkes was widely used as a satirical device and there are several Irish cartoons of this period that allude to the Gunpowder Plot, notably John Tenniel's 'The Fenian Guy Fawkes'.[44] In his cartoon, Waite pictures children collecting pennies for a Guy dressed in IRA uniform from the Prime Minister Harold Wilson (Figure 5). By drawing parallels to the Gunpowder Plot Waite underlined the destabilising effect of the IRA on the British state. In focusing on the custom of burning the Guy he reminds his readers that Fawkes had failed in his attempts to blow up Parliament; Waite asserts that the IRA too had failed to bring down the state.

The racial diversity of the children featured in the cartoon, proposes an inclusive image of Britain at odds with the apparent construction of black and Asian ethnic minorities as un-British during the post-war period.[45] This disparity highlights the complexities of national identity and ideas of Britishness during the late twentieth century. Waite's cartoon suggests that all these different people could buy into the concept of Britishness based on their opposition to the IRA. By constructing the IRA as an internal threat potentially affecting everyone, he reinforced the notion of a shared Britishness. As Eric

FIGURE 5
Keith Waite, Daily Mirror, June 18, 1974, Keith Waite, British Cartoon Archive, University of Kent.

Hobsbawm argued, 'There is no more effective way of bonding together the disparate sections of restless people than to unite them against outsiders'.[46] By generating 'a sharpened awareness of "us" as against "them"', this perceived IRA threat fostered a sense of unity, which reinforced notions of British defiance in the face of a common enemy.[47]

The British press repeatedly drew on the theme of Guy Fawkes and the Gunpowder Plot in its coverage of the bombing campaign. William Jones' (Jon) cartoon in the *Daily Mail* responding to the Westminster bombing depicted a policeman questioning a construction worker who identifies himself as 'Seamus O'Fawkes, sorr'.[48] Similarly, after the Birmingham pub bombings the *Sunday Telegraph* reproduced Tenniel's cartoon 'The Fenian Guy Fawkes' superimposed onto a photograph of an inert body lying in the rubble caused by the bombing with the caption 'A century of progress!'.[49] By replicating the actual nineteenth-century caricature, this image drew attention to the long history of republican aggression and in doing so reinforced the traditional stereotype that the Irish were inherently violent.

The Guy Fawkes cartoons also tap into well-established anti-Catholic prejudices. Historically, Catholicism had been regarded as an internal threat to a British identity centred on Protestant values.[50] The foiling of the Gunpowder Plot was representative of British resistance to a Catholic peril. During the latter half of the nineteenth century acts of perceived papal aggression led to a resurgence of anti-Catholicism in Britain.[51] Popular opinions on Catholicism in turn reinforced anti-Irish attitudes in Britain and explain the popularity of the Guy Fawkes motif in satirical cartoons.[52] Some historians have argued that the growth of secularism in the twentieth century meant that anti-Catholicism played a lesser role in hostility towards the Irish than in previous centuries.[53] The Guy Fawkes in cartoons relating to the IRA's bombing campaign in the early 1970s, indicate that such prejudices continued to inform British attitudes to Ireland and the Irish people. de Nie argues that during the nineteenth century ethnic, religious and class prejudices, informed British conceptions of Irish identities.[54] The revival of traditional anti-Catholic prejudices in cartoons of the early 1970s would indicate that religious stereotypes, as well as the racial stereotypes emphasised by Kirkaldy, played an important role in shaping late twentieth-century British attitudes towards the Irish.

The debate over the extent to which racial prejudices have influenced British attitudes towards the Irish, in turn raises questions as to the extent to which Irish migrants assimilated into British society throughout the nineteenth and twentieth centuries. Many historians have argued that by the early twentieth century the Irish had fully assimilated into British society, evidenced by high rates of social mobility and inter-marriage, amongst other factors.[55] Since the 1980s, this 'assimilationist' model has come under attack. Sociologist Mary Hickman in particular, argues that the Irish residing in Britain during the late twentieth century continued to be subject to discrimination.[56] She argues that these experiences have been rendered invisible, however, due to the incorporation of the Irish into a homogenous white British race in response to increased immigration from the Caribbean, Africa and South Asia.[57] Although there is evidence of greater integration by the late twentieth century, especially amongst the Irish middle-class, the position of Irish people in Britain remained precarious.[58] The IRA's campaign in the early 1970s brought about a surge of hostility rooted in a longer history of prejudiced behaviour directed towards the Irish.

The presence of a supposedly integrated Irish population exacerbated fears that the IRA had infiltrated Britain.[59] Two days after the Westminster bombing Rigby published a cartoon showing three men in IRA uniform scaling Big Ben as the police struggled to reach them.[60] Rigby criticised the security services for allowing themselves to be hoodwinked by the IRA, who it was believed gained access to Westminster Palace disguised as construction workers. This criticism reflected a wider fear over the relative ease with which the attack had been carried out. The fact that the IRA were pictured climbing all over Big Ben, a symbol of the British state, pandered to fears that the bombers were operating from within Britain.

The IRA were repeatedly associated with the Irish living in Britain during the 1970s.[61] Following the funeral of James McDade, killed attempting to plant explosives at the Coventry telephone exchange on 14 November 1974, the *Daily Mirror* noted that 'hundreds of Irish sympathisers in Britain are planning to give a "martyr's farewell" to McDade'.[62] By linking the term 'sympathisers' with a reference to the Irish the paper suggested that hundreds of Irish people living in Britain were involved in some way with the violence. The paper reinforced this notion of complicity by using the same term but prefixed with IRA in a follow-up article, reporting that 'IRA sympathisers were ... warn[ed] against wearing para-military uniforms in Britain'.[63]

Similarly, following the bombing of the National Defence College (12 February 1974) the paper observed that the IRA were using safe houses 'owned by IRA sympathisers who take in lodgers, including Irish labourers- and terrorists'. By equating Irish labourers with terrorists, the article implies that they were the same.[64] As sociologist Paddy Hillyard noted, by sustaining this idea that the IRA were infiltrating Britain through the Irish population, the press 'perpetuate[d] the impression that the whole of the Irish community ... [was] suspect'.[65] Accordingly, both papers re-imagined long-established Irish residents as a potential threat.

Many Irish people suffered from social ostracism, verbal and even physical abuse because of the bombings. Following the Birmingham pub bombings, Irish businesses were attacked, while thirty factories in Birmingham were forced to close in order to guarantee the safety of Irish workers.[66] In addition, the Irish faced discrimination and harassment from the authorities. The Prevention of Terrorism Act (PTA), introduced in November 1974, gave the police the power to examine, detain and arrest without grounds for due suspicion. Many Irish people were wrongfully arrested, indeed of the 7052 people detained in connection with Northern Ireland between 1974 and 1991, 86% were released without any further action being taken.[67] The press was complicit in encouraging the authorities' policing of the Irish, calling for people to report any suspicious activities. For example, following attacks on Euston and King's Cross in September 1973, the *Daily Mirror* reminded readers:

> The police need every scrap of help and information that the public can give. Someone, somewhere, must have a suspicion- however tiny- that might give the police a lead. It should be passed on quickly.[68]

Faced with this level of hostility many Irish people living in Britain adopted a low profile.[69] An Irish accent was often enough to attract abuse and suspicion, subsequently many members of the Irish community sought to modify or hide their accents.[70] One woman, interviewed in the late 1980s, confessed that 'When a bombing or anything like that happens I say, "Thank God for supermarkets", because you don't have to speak, you don't have to ask for a loaf of bread'.[71] It was also common for Irish people to refrain from participating in political activities for fear of being identified as sympathetic to the IRA.[72]

Both the *Daily Mirror* and *The Sun*, however, recognised that not all Irish people were IRA supporters and the Irish were victims of the bombs themselves. The tabloid press gave

Irish victims particular attention, as they allowed them to advance the idea that the IRA's campaign was internecine. Paradoxically, both papers presented the Irish population as harbourers of terrorists while also highlighting the fact that the wider Irish community in Britain did not endorse the attacks. In the wake of four bomb attacks on 18 December 1973, the *Daily Mirror* spotlighted Rosina Harrington who had suffered severe shrapnel wounds. Emphasising the fact that she was second generation Irish Catholic, the paper highlighted the heinous nature of the IRA who were willing to sacrifice their own compatriots. In a follow-up article, the paper printed well wishes sent anonymously to Rosina by an Irish couple, condemning the attacks: 'Try not to hate the Irish. We will never forgive the animals who did this'.[73] By demonstrating to its' readers that the IRA did not have the support of the majority of the Irish population, the newspaper conferred a sense of illegitimacy onto the group.

Similarly, *The Sun* called attention to the Irish roots of brothers Desmond and Eugene Reilly who died in the Birmingham pub bombings, quoting their mother: 'we are all from Donegal, but both my sons were born in Birmingham. They were youngsters. They didn't want to know about fighting and killing in Northern Ireland'.[74] Mrs Reilly presented her sons as apolitical and innocent, emphasising their age and ignorance. References to the 'innocent' Irish, however, by definition implied that there were also 'guilty' Irish, reinforcing the notion that the Irish population were harbouring terrorists.[75] The ambiguity over which elements of the Irish population in Britain supported the IRA meant that perceived blame was potentially spread to any Irish person. Even those Irish deemed 'innocent' were imagined in some way as complicit in the IRA's activities by not being seen to be pro-active in condemning the bombings. As Alessandro Portelli argues, this dynamic emerges from 'the purely negative definition given of innocence', that suggests a sense of 'harmlessness': 'having done nothing wrong is one thing, but having done nothing against wrong is another'.[76] Seán Sorohan observes that pressure was exerted on the Irish in Britain to publicly disassociate themselves from the IRA.[77]

The IRA's campaign in England was viewed as a serious threat to the British way of life. Not only had conflict spilt onto British soil for the first time since the Second World War, the enemy was difficult to distinguish from the large number of Irish people living in Britain. The British press responded to the IRA threat by re-emphasising conceptions of Britishness. The IRA were enlisted to help foster a sense of togetherness during a period of change resulting from heightened immigration, providing a common enemy against which the nation could unite. In both their written reportage and political cartoons, the *Daily Mirror* and *The Sun* evoked the stereotypes of the British as a stoic people facing down adversity by using memories of the Second World War and mainstream national motifs to symbolise British resilience and courage. It is worth noting, however, that the manner in which the IRA were presented was as much guided by commercial interests as patriotism. By fostering the concept of a national community united against the IRA threat, newspaper editors sought to increase their appeal to a wider audience.

Anger at the bombers was transferred onto the Irish living in Britain, serving to reinforce perceptions of them as an internal other, whilst both papers stoked feelings of suspicion by depicting the Irish in Britain as harbourers of terrorists. In their presentation of the IRA, the British tabloids also drew on a wide range of long-established stereotypes of the Irish. Kirkaldy has rightly observed, in the early 1970s cartoonists resurrected the simian Paddy of nineteenth-century caricatures. Yet, this article demonstrates that the *Daily Mirror* and *The Sun*'s cartoon coverage of the late twentieth-century bombing campaign in England re-employed a variety of motifs common in Victorian cartoons. This highlights the complex range of well-established and enduring racial and religious stereotypes, which re-emerged during the early-1970s in light of the terrorist threat, shaping British attitudes towards the Irish.

The IRA bombing campaign in England was a transitional moment in the Northern Ireland conflict, determining how the 'Troubles' came to be interpreted in Britain. Cartoonists were instrumental in this process: by building on existing national tropes of resistance, the cartoons of the early 1970s offer an insight into the construction of Britishness as well as the other. Following the recent terrorist attacks in London and Manchester, the British media have again employed such methods. Not only have they reverted to seeing the crisis through the prism of Second World War images and other national motifs, but they also evoked memories of the IRA attacks in order to exult notions of British fortitude. It would seem that the IRA bombing campaign in England has itself become part of the range of stock motifs drawn upon in response to violent threats and used to emphasise national identity at times of uncertainty. Then as now, cartoons are central to shaping our understanding of national crises and issues of identity.

Acknowledgements

I would like to thank Renee Waite, News UK and the British Cartoon Archive, University of Kent for kindly providing me with the following cartoons and the British Association for Irish Studies for their generous support, without which this article would not be possible.

Disclosure Statement

No potential conflict of interest was reported by the author.

Funding

This work was supported by British Association for Irish Studies (Postgraduate Bursary).

Notes

1. McGladdery, *The Provisional IRA in England*, 3; 63.
2. Curtis, *Apes and Angels*, xxxi.
3. Ibid., 147.
4. de Nie, *The External Paddy*, 34.
5. Kirkaldy, "English Cartoonists"; Curtis, *Nothing but the Same Old Story*, 82–6; Darby, *Dressed to Kill*; Douglas et al., *Drawing Conclusions*.
6. Walker, 1975, "If the New Convention Breaks Down- how Close will Ulster be to the Brink?" *The Times*, 7 May.
7. Bingham, "Reading Newspapers," 142.
8. Conboy, *Tabloid Britain*, 14.

9. Conboy, "Introduction," 514.
10. There is a considerable wealth of scholarship on the formation of Britishness for example see Colley, "Britishness and Otherness," 309–29; Weight, *Patriots*; Mandler, *The English National Character*; Kumar, "Negotiating English Identity," 469–87.
11. Waters, ""Dark Strangers" in our Midst," 208.
12. Conboy, *Tabloid Britain*, 69.
13. Conboy, "Introduction," 511.
14. "The Answer to Bloody Terror," 1973, *Daily Mirror*, 9 March.
15. "The Terror that must Fail," 1973, *Daily Mirror*, 11 September.
16. Connelly, *We can Take it!*, 268.
17. McGladdery, *The Provisional IRA in England*, 90.
18. English, *Armed Struggle*, 190.
19. Connelly, *We Can Take It!*, 270.
20. Franklin, 1974, "It's all Yours," *The Sun*, 23 November.
21. This image is particularly reminiscent of the iconic photograph 'St Paul's Survives'.
22. See *The Sun*, 18 June 1974; *Daily Mirror*, 18 June 1974.
23. de Nie, *The External Paddy*, 34.
24. Ward, "Beefeaters, British History and the Empire," 241–2.
25. Newby, "Victims, Participants or Peacemakers?," 17–19; Brocklehurst, *Who's Afraid of Children?*, 14–18.
26. Douglas et al., *Drawing Conclusions*, 284–5.
27. de Nie, "Pigs, Paddies, Prams and Petticoats," 46; de Nie, *The Eternal Paddy*, 222–3.
28. It is worth noting that although Devlin was a staunch republican and socialist she was not affiliated with the Republican movement.
29. Cummings, 1972, *Daily Express*, 7 April; Curtis, *Apes and Angels*, 175.
30. Sjoberg and Gentry, *Mothers, Monsters and Whores*, 50.
31. The cartoons of both these artists provoked protests especially from Irish people in Britain. In 1982, the Greater London Council withdrew advertising from the *Evening Standard* following the publication of a Jak cartoon depicting a cinema poster advertising a film called 'The Irish: The Ultimate in Psychopathic Horror', arguing that it cast aspersions on the Irish people generally. (Kirkaldy, "English Cartoonists," 27; 34; Curtis, *Nothing but the Same Old Story*, 82–3.
32. For examples of eighteenth-century simianised caricature see James Gillray's 'Promised Horrors of the French Invasion' (20 October 1796) and 'The Consequences of a Successful French Invasion' (1 March 1798).
33. Curtis, *Apes and Angels*, 37.
34. Ibid., xxxi.
35. Gilley, "English Attitudes to the Irish Minority in England," 85–7.
36. Foster, *Paddy and Mr Punch*, 174; 191–4.
37. de Nie, *The Eternal Paddy*, 5.
38. Kirkaldy, "English Cartoonists," 30.
39. "Keith Waite: Biography"; "Paul Rigby: Biography".
40. de Nie, "Pigs, Paddies, Prams and Petticoats," 43.
41. Ibid., 46.
42. Curtis, *Apes and Angels*, 37.

43. In 1605 Guy Fawkes along with eleven other men were implicated in a failed assassination attempt on James VI/I. Known as the Gunpowder Plot, the plan had been to blow up the House of Lords as the prelude to a popular revolt which would see James's daughter installed on the throne as a Catholic monarch.

44. Bryant, "Remember, Remember … ," 55.

45. Waters, ""Dark Strangers" in our Midst," 208.

46. Hobsbawn, *Nations and Nationalism since 1780*, 91.

47. Colley, "Britishness and Otherness," 322.

48. Jon, 1974, "Seamus O'Fawkes, Sorr," *Daily Mail*, 18 June.

49. Jensen, 1974, "A century of progress!," *Sunday Telegraph*, 24 November.

50. Colley, "Britishness and Otherness," 320.

51. de Nie, *The External Paddy*, 15.

52. Gilley, "English Attitudes to the Irish in England," 93.

53. Holmes, *A Tolerant Country?*, 50; Kirkaldy, "English Cartoonists," 42.

54. de Nie, *The Eternal Paddy*, 5.

55. Ryan, "Assimilation of Irish Immigrants in Britain". For an example of the assimilationist argument, see Hornsby-Smith and Dale, "The Assimilation of Irish Immigrants in England".

56. See Hickman, "Alternative Historiographies of the Irish in Britain," 236–53.

57. Hickman, "Reconstructing Deconstructing 'Race'," 298.

58. William Ryan observes that in the late 1960s/early 1970s 45% of non-manual Irish workers were highly assimilated into Britain compared to 23% of manual labourers. (Ryan, "Assimilation of Irish Immigrants in Britain," 47–8; 91; Delaney, *The Irish in Postwar Britain*, 2.

59. At the start of the campaign in 1973, the number of Irish people in Britain was approximately 950,000, plus an estimated 1.3 million second generation Irish. (Walter, "The Irish Community in Britain"; Hickman and Walter, *Discrimination and the Irish Community in Britain*, 19.

60. Rigby, 1974, "'Shure an' we're Just Good Honest Destruction Workers, or Somet'ing loike dat.'" *The Sun*, June 19.

61. Hickman et al., "Suspect Communities?," 16.

62. Thompson and Daniels, 1974, 'That IRA funeral', *Daily Mirror*, 20 November.

63. "Black Beret Mob Warned," 1974, *Daily Mirror*, 21 November.

64. Tullet and Laxton, 1974, "Ten Hurt as Bomb Rips College," 13 February.

65. Hillyard, *Suspect Communities*, 146.

66. "'Revenge' Fire Bomb Hits a Pub", 1974, *Daily Mirror*, 23 November; Daniels et al., "Backlash Fury at the Factories," 1974, *Daily Mirror*, 23 November.

67. Home Office Statistical Bulletins 1974–91, cited in Hillyard, *Suspect Community*, 5.

68. "The Terror that Must Fail", 1973, *Daily Mirror*, 11 September; For further investigation into the media's role in policing the Irish in Britain see Hillyard, *Suspect Communities*, 130–1; 259.

69. Hickman and Walter, *Discrimination and the Irish Community in Britain*, 216–19.

70. Walter, "Shamrocks Growing out of their Mouths," 64.

71. Lennon et al., *Across the Water*, 175.

72. Further historical analysis on the effect of the IRA campaign in England on the lived experiences of the Irish in Britain is available in my Ph.D. thesis.

73. Gordon, 1973, "Why Me? The Whispered Words of a Young Mother Caught in the Blast," *Daily Mirror*, 19 December; Gordon, 1973, "Thank You, Kind Hearts," *Daily Mirror*, 24 December.
74. Connew, 1974, "Bombs City Weeps for its Victims," *Daily Mirror*, 4 December.
75. Hickman et al., "Suspect Communities?", 17.
76. Portelli, *The Battle of Valle Giulia*, 150.
77. The majority of the Irish in Britain did seek to disassociate themselves with the IRA and Irish community leaders in Britain would often publicly condemn the violence; Sorohan, *Irish London During the Troubles*, 88.

Bibliography

Bingham, Adrian. "Reading Newspapers: Cultural Histories of the Popular Press in Modern Britain." *History Compass* 10, no. 2 (2012): 140–150.

Brocklehurst, Helen. *Who's Afraid of Children? Children, Conflict and International Relations*. Aldershot: Ashgate Publishing Limited, 2006.

Bryant, Mark. "Remember, Remember … ." *History Today* 59, no. 11 (2009): 53–55.

Colley, Linda. "Britishness and Otherness: An Argument." *Journal of British Studies* 31, no. 4 (1992): 309–329.

Conboy, Martin. *Tabloid Britain: Constructing a Community Through Language*. London: Routledge, 2006.

Conboy, Martin. "Introduction: How Journalism Uses History." *Journalism Practice* 5, no. 5 (2011): 506–519.

Connelly, Mark. *We Can Take It! Britain and the Memory of the Second World War*. Harlow: Pearson Educated Limited, 2004.

Curtis, Liz. *Nothing but the Same Old Story: The Roots of Anti-Irish Racism*. London: Information on Ireland, 1991.

Curtis, L. P. *Apes and Angles: The Irishman in Victorian Caricature*. Washington: Smithsonian Books, 1997.

Darby, John. *Dressed to Kill: Cartoonist and the Northern Ireland Conflict*. Belfast: The Appletree Press, 1983.

Delaney, Enda. *The Irish in Postwar Britain*. Oxford: Oxford University Press, 2007.

de Nie, Michael. *The External Paddy: Irish Identity and the British Press, 1798-1882*. Madison: University of Wisconsin, 2004.

de Nie, Michael. "Pigs, Paddies, Prams and Petticoats: Irish Home Rule and the British Comic Press, 1886-93." *History Ireland* 13, no. 1 (2005): 42–47.

Douglas, Roy, Liam Harte, and Jim O'Hara. *Drawing Conclusions: A Cartoon History of Anglo-Irish Relations 1798-1998*. Belfast: The Blackstaff Press, 1998.

English, Richard. *Armed Struggle: The History of the IRA*. London: Pan Books, 2012.

Foster, Roy. *Paddy and Mr Punch: Connections in Irish and English History*. London: Penguin Group, 1995.

Gilley, Sheridan. "English Attitudes to the Irish Minority in England, 1789–1900." In *Immigrants and Minorities in British Society*, edited by Colin Holmes, 81–110. London: Allen & Unwin, 1978.

Hickman, Mary J. "Reconstructing Deconstructing 'Race': British Political Discourse about the Irish in Britain." *Ethnic and Racial Studies* 21, no. 2 (1998): 288–307.

Hickman, Mary J. "Alternative Historiographies of the Irish in Britain." In *The Irish in Victorian Britain: The Local Dimension*, edited by Roger Swift, and Sheridan Gilley, 236–253. Dublin: Four Courts Press, 1999.

Hickman, Mary J., Henri Nickels, and Sara Silvestri. "'Suspect Communities?' Counter-Terrorism Policy, the Press, and the Impact on the Irish and Muslim Communities in Britain," 2011. Accessed May 11, 2015. http://www.city.ac.uk/__data/assets/pdf_file/0005/96287/suspect-communities-report-july2011.pdf.

Hickman, Mary, and Bronwen Walter. *Discrimination and the Irish Community in Britain: A Report of Research Undertaken for the Commission for Racial Equality*. London: Commission for Racial Equality, 1997.

Hillyard, Paddy. *Suspect Communities People's Experience of the Prevention of Terrorism Acts in Britain*. London: Pluto Press, 1993.

Hobsbawn, Eric. *Nations and Nationalism since 1780: Programme, Myth, Reality*. Cambridge: Cambridge University Press, 2012.

Holmes, Colin. *A Tolerant Country?: Immigrants, Refugees and Minorities in Britain*. London: Routledge, 2015.

Hornsby-Smith, M. P., and A. Dale. "The Assimilation of Irish Immigrants in England." *British Journal of Sociology* 39, no. 4 (1988): 519–544.

"Keith Waite: Biography". *British Cartoon Archive*, University of Kent. Accessed January 25, 2016. www.cartoons.ac.uk/artists/keithwaite/biography.

Kirkaldy, John. "English Cartoonists; Ulster Realities." *Eire-Ireland* 16, no. 3 (1981): 27–42.

Kumar, Krishan. "Negotiating English Identity: Englishness, Britishness and the Future of the United Kingdom." *Nations and Nationalism* 16, no. 3 (2010): 469–487.

Lennon, Mary, Marie McAdam, and Joanne O'Brien. *Across the Water: Irish Women's Lives in Britain*. London: Virago Press, 1988.

Mandler, Peter. *The English National Character: The History of an Idea From Edmund Burke to Tony Blair*. New Haven: Yale University Press, 2006.

McGladdery, Gary. *The Provisional IRA in England: The Bombing Campaign 1973-1997*. Dublin: Irish Academic Press, 2006.

Morgan, Sarah. "The Contemporary Racialization of the Irish in Britain: An Investigation into Media Representations and the Everyday of being Irish in Britain." *PhD diss.*, University of Northern London, 1997.

Newby, Lucy. "Victims, Participants or Peacemakers? Representations of Children and Young People in Memorialisation of the Northern Irish 'Troubles'." *MSc diss.*, University of Edinburgh, 2014.

"Paul Rigby: Biography". *The British Cartoon Archive*, University of Kent. Accessed January 23, 2016. www.cartoons.ac.uk/artists/paulrigby/biography.

Portelli, Alessandro. *The Battle of Valle Giulia: Oral History and the Art of Dialogue*. Madison: The University of Wisconsin Press, 1997.

Ryan, Rev William. "Assimilation of Irish Immigrants in Britain." *PhD diss.*, Saint Louis University, 1973.

Sjoberg, Laura, and Caron E. Gentry. *Mothers, Monsters and Whores: Women's Violence in Global Politics*. New York: Zed Books, 2007.

Sorohan, Seán. *Irish London During the Troubles*. Dublin: Irish Academic Press, 2012.

Walter, Bronwen. "The Irish Community in Britain- Diversity, Disadvantage and Discrimination." *Runnymede Trust*. Accessed May 26, 2015. www.runnymedetrust.org/bgIrishCommunity.html.

Walter, Bronwen. "Shamrocks Growing out of their Mouths": Language and the Racialisation of the Irish in Britain." In *Language, Labour and Migration*, edited by Anne J. Kershen, 57–73. Aldershot: Ashgate, 2000.

Ward, Paul. "Beefeaters, British History and the Empire in Asia and Australasia." *Britain and the World* 5, no. 2 (2012): 240–258.

Waters, Chris. ""Dark Strangers" in our Midst: Discourse of Race and Nation in Britain, 1947-1963." *Journal of British Studies* 36, no. 2 (1997): 207–238.

Weight, Richard. *Patriots: National Identity in Britain, 1940-2000*. London: Pan Books, 2003.

'MORE DIFFICULT FROM DUBLIN THAN FROM DIEPPE'
Ireland and Britain in a European network of communication

Yann Ciarán Ryan

Recent Early Modern news histories have tended to emphasise the international scope of the networks on which news travelled. New techniques, falling under the umbrella term 'digital humanities', allow for the examination of news as a complete network, and this article will explore the ways in which, using these techniques, the connections between Ireland and Britain can be thought of as not only local, peripheral and bilateral but also within a larger, European news system. Using network science, originally developed for the analysis of the World Wide Web, this article shows that the European system has universal network properties: it is scale-free, divided into clusters and exhibits the 'small world' phenomenon, explaining its resilience to interruption and the relative efficiency of early modern information transfer.

In a story from the *Moderate Intelligencer,* a London newsbook, datelined Hamburg, July 21, 1649, the author writes thus of the war between the Polish and the Cossacks:

> ..that as of old in the War of Alexander and the Romans, so lately in Ireland, and in this, it appears, that it's not the multitude that overcomes, but the wisdom and valour of men, of a very numerous Army, a few usually turns the Scale[1]

How could a writer of news, based in Hamburg, writing about war in Poland, know about the wars in Ireland? It is an unlikely phenomenon: two events, very much unrelated to each other and separated by well over a thousand miles, are connected through a largely unplanned system of communication. Recent research has emphasised the pan-European nature of the flow of news. This article attempts to show some concrete ways in which we can understand Britain and Ireland's place within this complex and organic system. How can a system be both local and international? How can it work with such efficiency despite no central planning? What does it mean to be 'central' to the news network, and how does that fit in to our ideas of centre and periphery? The article analyses data collected from London newsbooks in two key ways to suggest answers to these questions, using both mapping software and network analysis. These methods allow for the production of maps which show Britain and Ireland's position in the overall geography of news, network diagrams which examine the flow of information, and produce network centrality scores which highlight structurally important nodes.

London's first real newspapers, the 'newsbooks' of the 1640s contain a great deal of content from Ireland; a quick scan of a handful of titles would make this immediately clear. Only a few European cities could boast as much coverage as Ireland in London newsbooks.[2] Regular periodical news is dependent on a regular periodical post, and the rise of the newsbook was contingent on the development of the postal service, and its Irish news dependent on a good postal route to and from its shores. By the end of the Stuart reign this had been achieved to some degree: by the 1640s there were two packet boats to Ireland, usually on the routes from Chester to Dublin and Milford Haven to Waterford.[3] News from Ireland could arrive in England from one or the other, and often both.[4] Crucially, news could also easily get from London to these packet boats: there was a post route as far as Holyhead, for royal use but permitted to carry private mail.[5] Mark Brayshay's recent work on the Tudor and Stuart postal system has shown it to have a depth of sophistication and reliability, and contributed to a realm that was becoming 'significantly more joined-up'.[6] It was reasonably priced and relatively quick: The post from London to Chester took an average of about forty hours.[7] This was connected, through Dover, to a European postal network that was going through a 'communications revolution', one in which the space-to-time ratio was steadily shrinking.[8]

There is textual evidence for interest in Irish news. In June 1649, as rumour began to overtake official reports of events in Ireland, *The Kingdomes Weekly Intelligencer* began with the following:

> The general Demand of the people is, What is your Newes from Ireland? The sellers of the weekly sheets make answer, aloud in the streets, Newes hot from Ireland.[9]

Most of 1649 had been the same: With the death of Charles I at the end of January, the interest of news was shifting from strictly domestic politics to other topics and Irish news, operating within a 'paradigm of barbarity', partially satiated this appetite.[10]

News-writers were concerned with capitalising on this interest in Irish news: Richard Collings, the editor of the *Kingdom's Weekly Intelligencer* wrote in June 1649:

> There is a Report of a Battell fought betwixt the Lord *Inchequine*, and *Owen Roe* in which it is sayd, that the *Lord Inchequine* had the better, I have been diligent in the Inquirie, and can find nothing but a Report to confirm it.[11]

Using traditional methodology and textual evidence based on close reading, the historian of the English newspaper has long known that Irish news had an importance. But news has further properties which do not reveal themselves with these methods.

History has in recent years undergone a 'spatial turn', although this is not the first time: Braudel and the Annales were the first to link geography and history.[12] The difference here is data and computation: data can now be harvested from increasingly enormous databases and can be displayed and mathematically analysed using easily-available computing power. Projects like Cameron Blevin's 'Mapping the Production of Space' have taken the idea of people 'producing' space, outlined by Henri Lefebvre, and using data models and text mining have put forward ideas and visualised how this actually worked in practise, using nineteenth century American newspapers.[13] 'Mapping the Republic of Letters', a project undertaken by the Stanford Spatial History group, has created interactive maps tracing the dissemination of information throughout Europe and America.[14]

Perhaps in the historiography of news it would be more apt to think of a 'networked' rather than spatial turn. Going beyond the idea of simply mapping and visualising geographic connections between places, a networked approach considers information as a system of dynamic flow. *News Networks in Early Modern Europe* published in 2016 and edited by Joad Raymond and Noah Moxham is the most significant study in this regard, pushing the scholarship in a new direction: looking both at the overall picture whilst filling in the individual component parts of the system, drawing together several sources and work from many distinct national news databases. Raymond pushes for the utilisation of techniques from other disciplines, in this case STEM subjects, in order to fully understand the system of news in Europe.[15] The volume uses the science of network analysis to show that the European news system can be understood using the same universal science behind the understanding of many other networks: biological, neurological, social and purely mathematical.[16] Raymond's chapter in that volume is not a case study, although there are others in the text dealing with specifics: Renate Pieper's chapter is particularly relevant, as it deals with geographic information flow rather than content.[17] This builds on other work analysing the geographic distribution of datelines, including that of Paul Arblaster, looking at news in Antwerp, and Nicholas Schobesberger, whose work on the manuscript newsletters of the Fugger family has shown how mapping places of dispatch can create a geography of the movement of news throughout Europe. Several articles in *News Networks in Early Modern Europe* use network theory for part or all of their research. This article develops these ideas to form a concrete analysis of British and Irish information exchange in the civil war period.

Network theory developed from the mathematics of graph theory and social network analysis pioneered by Mark Granovatter and others in the nineteen seventies, and was further developed in the late nineteen-nineties by Alberto Barabasí. It is a system for dealing with complex networks using computational data and physics.[18] Originally developed with the purpose of putting structure to the incomprehensibly vast map of the internet, studies have shown that the same underlying network structure can be found in connected systems of all types, both natural and man-made. Many of these are 'scale-free' (the degree distribution follows a power law, meaning that the vast number of connections go to a small number of nodes), and that a 'small-world phenomenon' can usually be observed, which means that despite the sparseness of a network, every part of it can be reached in a small number of 'hops' thanks to its structure as a series of densely connected individual clusters.[19] Small-world networks display properties of both random and ordered graphs: this means that they are both highly clustered, like a lattice, and have small path lengths, like a random graph.[20] Networks of this type allow for the quick movement of information through them. For example, small-world networks allow infectious diseases to spread more easily than other network types.[21] The network of news found through the collection of data described here fits this universal pattern, confirming the theory put forward by Raymond et al: that news was a self-organised network which displayed small-world properties.[22]

To determine the properties of the news network, metadata from news stories printed in London has been collected. As a project concerned with information flow through cities rather than tracing text reuse through titles, two sample databases were chosen, designed to be complementary. The first is the entire run of the *Moderate*

Intelligencer, a title published by John Dillingham which contained both domestic news and probably the best foreign news coverage in London, a total of two hundred and thirty nine issues in twenty two titles, printed between 1645 and 1649. The second dataset is a cross-sectional one, three hundred and forty two titles, of every newsbook printed in 1649 until the licensing act in October forced the closure of all existing publications, and includes long-running titles such as *Perfect Diurnall, Perfect Occurrences* and *Kingdomes Weekly Intelligencer*, as well as a number of ephemeral or short-lived publications. Royalist and Republican polemical titles, such as the various *Aulicus* and *Elencticus*, are not possible to parse into structured data, and have been omitted.

News in the seventeenth century is broken into individual chunks: paragraphs which are translated, transformed, inserted and removed at will by editors.[23] Much of the foreign news printed during the first era of newsbooks followed a similar 'macrosyntactic' organisation: a date-line and location, but no headline, consistent with older manuscript newsletters and *avvisi*.[24] These units, rather than full titles, move through space and time. Will Slauter, writing about the eighteenth century, calls them 'paragraphs'.[25] They have also been referred to as 'snippets' and Brendan Dooley uses the term 'periods' in a recent article, a term used to describe a circulating composition of words, and implies 'segmentation as opposed to continuousness'.[26] Newsbooks, then, can be thought of as a common protocol for the spread of individual, discreet units of information (much like a neutral system for doing the same on the internet like TCP/IP). It is these units which form the basis of the following analysis. For each paragraph, information has been collected about where it has been dispatched from, further places of dispatch, when it was sent, received and published, and information about the category of news. The *Moderate Intelligencer* gives an overview of Ireland's position in a title concerned with foreign news and is just about long enough to show trends over time, and the January to October 1649 material gives an overall 'snapshot' of everything printed from London, albeit with a restricted time-frame.

To start with a straight-forward quantitative question: How much news from Ireland was being reported in London sheets, and what was it about? Of the 170,000 lines of text counted, from both datasets, 3384 come from Dublin, 1282 the more general 'Ireland', and another 680 from Cork: 5346 lines in total, or 3.14%. Looking at individual cities, news from Dublin is dedicated the fifth-largest number of lines, after Paris, Venice, Naples and Rome. Table 1 shows that there is also a strong correlation between number of lines and a city's population. Much of the Irish news was related, unsurprisingly, to the military campaigns of the New Model Army, but also the political intrigues of the main players: Owen Roe, the Earl of Ormond, and various generals with responsibility for Irish affairs. Domestic Irish issues, either political or otherwise, are almost non-existent. Figures 1 and 2 show the geographical distribution of news reported in London newsbooks.

At the heart of this distribution is a postal network. Mapping the origin of news shows that source cities follow a rough outline of the various postal routes of central Europe, and in the case of England, the main 'spokes' of the postal system can be determined by looking at the pattern of towns with a high volume of news stories. Both in England and continental Europe, the system is based more on the postal network than on other variables such as population. Political and economic properties affect news volume. Key cities are underrepresented in London news, particularly Catholic rivals such

TABLE 1
Key statistical and network measures, all newsbook data 1645–1649

Place of despatch	Lines	Population in 1650*	Average time	Weighted degree	Betweenness centrality**
London	57,093	400,000	NA	NA	0.024958
Paris	8064.5	430,000	12.27	112	0.070613
Venice	5517	176,000	26.48	253	0.02503
Naples	5357	176,000	33.81	68	0.010004
Rome	3384	124,000	29.25	46	0.026264
Dublin	**3344**	**17,000**	**12.50**	**142**	**0.020939**
The Hague	2975	18,000	8.28	78	0.059728
Newcastle	2821	13,000	7.55	31	0.002676
Berwick	2786	Unknown	8.03	62	0.001703
Edinburgh	2679	35,000	10.33	89	0.004584
Oxford	1827	9000	NA	8	0.001016
Chester	1766	Unknown	7.24	87	0.001319
Milan	1362	100,000	24.46	25	0.009773
Turin	1302.5	37,000	18.59	14	0.003634
Ireland	**1282**	**NA**	**NA**	**35**	**0.000115**
Genoa	1055	90,000	23.12	70	0.008298
Lisbon	942	130,000	39.63	25	0.005307
Hamburg	861	75,000	26.52	77	0.007388
Munster	849	8000	16.83	35	0.015702
Danzig	831	70,000	NA	41	0.002973
Bristol	791	20,000	NA	18	0.000339
Pontefract	748	Unknown	NA	2	0
Prague	692.5	20,000	18.58	45	0.020254
Cork	**680**	**2000**	**NA**	**13**	**0**
Newark	665	Unknown	NA	2	0.000041
Vienna	623	60,000	23.42	49	0.014067
Frankfurt	611	17,000	21.05	28	0.008986

*Figures from Jan de Vries, *European Urbanisation: 1500–1800.*
**Rank of times node used in shortest paths between each pair of nodes, normalised between [0,1], calculated using Gephi.

as Madrid, and others are overrepresented, usually information and trading hubs like Venice. In the case of the cross-sectional data, it is clear that in terms of foreign news, Paris holds a particular importance to London news. The foreign specialist *Moderate Intelligencer* data shows a larger spread of locations, including more stories from Italy and the Netherlands. Good foreign news coverage needed a larger geographic coverage, as well as greater overall volume.

Looking specifically at Britain and Ireland: what can be said about the flow, or connectivity of this news—that is, where is Irish news travelling from and through? Looking at the news which has Dublin as its first source—that is, news arriving in London *from* Dublin, gives an idea of the secondary places in Ireland news was coming from. News from further afield than Dublin, on the rare occasions we are given secondary points of contact, usually comes from nearby counties: Kilkenny, Kildare, Carlow and more rarely from other parts of Ireland (Table 2).

Each entry in the database contains the date the story was sent, along with the date of its publication. This means we can also estimate the length of time news from Ireland

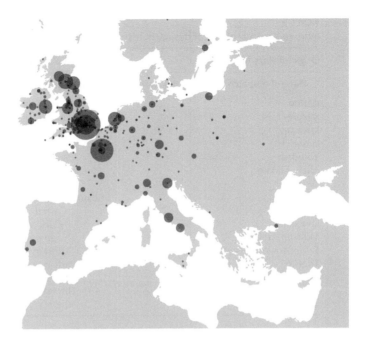

FIGURE 1
Geographical Distribution of Jan-Jun 1649 news paragraphs

FIGURE 2
Geographical Distribution of The Moderate Intelligencer news paragraphs, 1645–1649

TABLE 2
Story origins and places of despatch, Irish news printed in London

Origin of story in Ireland:		Last place of despatch before London:	
Place of despatch	Total stories	Place of despatch	Number of stories
Carlow	6	Chester	42
Kildare	5	Bristol	10
Kilkenny	5	Edinburgh	4
Limerick	2	Anglesey	3
Youghall	2	Berwick	3
Allen, Kildare	1	Houses of Parliament	3
Derry	1	Liverpool	2
Drogheda	1	Beaumorris (Anglesey)	1
Dundalk	1	Cashel	1
Enniskillen	1	Cork	1
Munster, Ireland	1	Drogheda	1
Talbotstown, Wicklow	1	London	1
Thurles	1	Parliament	1
Trim, Ireland	1	Patrick Port	1
		The Hague	1
		The Navy	1

took to reach London streets, and therefore get a more 'real-world' picture than possible with postmarks (stamps on letter packets which record when they were received at various posts). Dublin and Cork are the only two places in Ireland for which enough data is available to make a meaningful conclusion. For the first ten months of 1649, there is an average of 12.5 days between the news being sent from Dublin and its publication in London; for Cork just over fifteen. Temporally then, Dublin is similar to Antwerp (11.5 days), Paris (12.3), Amsterdam (12.8), and news from Cork compares to the German cities of Cologne (15.6) and Munster (16.8). Full figures are in Table 1 above. Counting datelines in this way shows us valuable information on the routes news from Ireland took, and the length of time it took to travel, but it is possible to go beyond this statistics-based approach and understand the system of news through its networked properties.

Understanding the underlying network structure of the news system can help to fully understand the geography of news in Europe. The network has been analysed visually and also using several key measurements: degree, betweenness centrality and eigenvector centrality. A network is emphatically not a map, though because news is based on the postal system and the geography of movement, it can often appear as one. A line through several nodes does not necessarily imply movement, or a knowledge of each node of any others except its immediate neighbour. Network diagrams work, rather, on pairs of connections.

Visualising all nodes in their relationship to the network as a whole we can get an overall picture of how Britain and Ireland fit in. For this the algorithm 'Force Atlas 2' was used, part of the *Gephi* network analysis package. This is a force-directed layout, which simulates a physical system to visually represent an abstract network.[27] This visualisation method places highly connected nodes close to each other, based on the movement of information between them, and it puts places with high connectivity overall towards the centre of the diagram. The network diagrams below show a network with Britain and

Ireland extremely close to each other—contrasting with, for example, important outliers like Venice and its connections to the Adriatic. The network drawn here follows roughly the contours of the postal network, with some key exceptions, discussed below.

Figure 3 is a network of the data from the Moderate Intelligencer, published between 1645 and 1649. Nodes with one connection or less have been removed for visibility but are included in the data modelling. This map shows a central core of highly-connected German states, with clusters based in Italy, Central/East Europe, and Britain and Ireland. The

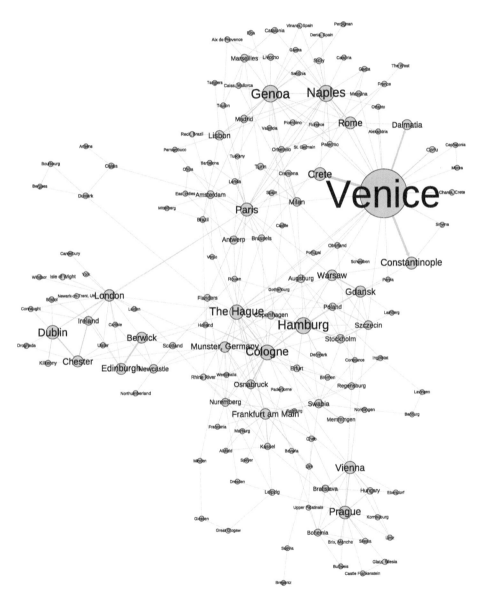

FIGURE 3
Force-directed network diagram, Moderate Intelligencer 1645–1649

Moderate Intelligencer contains very regular news from Venice, usually with news from the Adriatic and the Eastern Mediterranean, explaining its disproportionate size. To an extent the network map follows postal routes, but interesting anomalies are visible: Edinburgh and Northern England are placed closer to continental Europe because of direct connections to the Netherlands and Scandinavia, for example.

Figure 4 is a close-up of Britain and Ireland, taken from the *Moderate Intelligencer* data. This shows the nodes of Chester and Dublin as very close pairs. The news network between Britain and Ireland is reliant (but not entirely dependent) on key connecting nodes on English border or port towns. Edinburgh and Berwick show similar properties.

Figure 5 contains all the metadata from the January—October dataset, and shows a slightly different map of Europe to that seen in the *Moderate Intelligencer* data. Structural and generic differences between news systems are apparent in the topology of the network. There is a clear divide between Italian cities and Northern Europe, a division which can be seen elsewhere in the news system—Italian news still based largely on handwritten avvisi versus the printed news of Northern Europe. Some alternative routes of the network are clear here: there is a line running from Cork, to Scilly, to Jersey, to Paris. Routes like this are particularly important when usual channels of information are blocked, whether due to censorship, war or weather. Figure 6 is the January—October 1649 data, focused on Britain and Ireland. This diagram shows the importance of the middle cities: Bristol, Drogheda, Liverpool, Derry and Chester all act as points through which news passes on its way from Ireland to London.

Scale-free network topology describes a network that is a series of highly-connected individual clusters, with relatively few (and therefore very important) connections to the wider network.[28] These clusters are determined using an algorithm that checks every node against every other node to find the optimum 'neighbourhood' for each one.[29] The network analysis here shows three clusters in Britain and Ireland: one based around London and England, another based around Dublin-Chester and a third around Newcastle, Berwick and Edinburgh, which are highly connected, but their connecting parts, Dublin in one case, and The Hague going to continental Europe, mean that even with very few outgoing links, a strong and consistent connection can be made with the entire European network. These wider connections are reliant on nodes within the network which have particularly high *centrality measures*.

Network analysis allows us several different ways to measure the importance, or centrality, of individual nodes. The first of these, *degree*, simply counts the incoming and outgoing connections. Nodes with many connections are called hubs and are important for the facilitation of information transmission. A degree score gives a measure of the importance of parts of the network based on the overall volume of information travelling through the points. Dublin scores highly here: Sixth-highest after Venice, Paris, the Houses of Parliament in London, The Hague and Genoa. A weighted measure—counting the volume as well as the quantity—puts Dublin first. The traffic of information between London and Dublin is more frequent than anywhere else on the network.

There are alternative methods to determine centrality, and these can expand our understanding of how a networked system works. *Betweenness centrality* looks at the likelihood of a node being used as a 'path' from each node in the network to every other node.[30] The measure is determined by calculating the shortest path between every pair

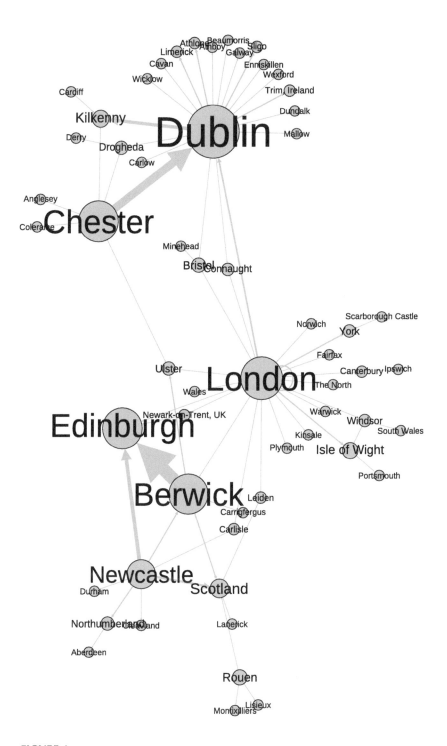

FIGURE 4
Force directed network diagram of British and Irish links, Moderate Intelligencer, 1645–1649

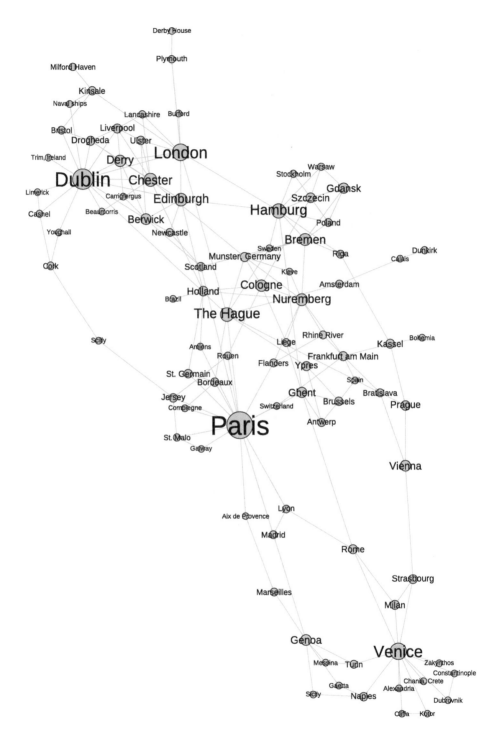

FIGURE 5
Force directed network diagram, all titles, January—October 1649

FIGURE 6
Force directed network diagram of British and Irish links, all titles, January - October 1649

of nodes in the network and ranking each node by how many of these paths pass through it.[31] This measurement can be used to determine a node's structural importance, and therefore influence as a facilitator of information flow through a network, and has been used, for example, to discover previously unknown but important influencers in the secret Protestant letter network during the reign of Mary I.[32] In the case of the news network, well-known communications hubs such as The Hague, Venice, Regensburg, Augsburg and Venice stand out; within the British–Irish system, Dublin, as the hub of news from Ireland, scores highly here. Dublin receives news from all over Ireland and sends it outward to London. These are the nodes which allow for the 'small-world' phenomenon described above, ensuring easy propagation of information through the network.

Another measure of importance or centrality is *eigenvector centrality*: this measures the importance of nodes based on its connections to other *important* nodes. This is similar to the PageRank method for determining the authority of search results, developed by Google. This measure tends to find places which produce authoritative and trustworthy information. Cities such Vienna, Munster, Augsburg and Frankfurt score highly here, forming a central core of authoritative hubs in Central Europe, as well as a number of coastal towns on the Mediterranean. Britain and Ireland score lower than their continental counterparts: most cities in these regions are only connected to other non-important nodes. This suggests a certain degree of exceptionalism for Britain and Ireland in the European news system. Britain and Ireland are part of the overall network, but very much on the periphery, and although re-routing happens, there are less possible paths across the network than for cities in Continental Europe. In the case of Ireland, most nodes have low eigenvector scores. Irish cities are not directly connected to the central parts of the network but rather travel through secondary nodes such as Dublin and Chester.

Networks are resilient. Non-hierarchical, scale-free networks, that is, networks with important hubs, but also multiple potential paths between nodes, are highly efficient ways of moving information through a complex but somewhat anonymous system. Ant colonies, for example, rely on a scale-free network design in order to create food gathering systems and allow for wide scale re-routing in cases of obstruction, even though each individual organism is not aware of the whole. European news also operates within this structure. Looking specifically at Irish news shows how a decentralised, hub-based system works in practise. Chester, Bristol, Milford Haven and Liverpool are by far the most likely relay points between Britain and Ireland in both datasets, but more are available. News also often travels on a route from Dundalk, to Derry, to Edinburgh and finally to London. News can reach London first having travelled from Paris, Flanders, or the Hague. In a similar vein, news from the continent can occasionally bypass the ports of South East England and travel directly to Edinburgh from Antwerp, potentially reaching London along this route. The network is not entirely decentralised but rather relies on *multiple* hubs for efficiency and resilience. News also moves on informal channels when more formal or trustworthy sources are not available.

There are several reasons why network analysis is of interest to the study of news. Firstly, it allows us to approach the history of Irish–British connections in a different way. We can see that rather than being unimportant parts, these clusters are integral to the network as a whole; when taking a full overview, a network is the sum of its individual clusters rather than simply a dichotomy of centre vs periphery. Secondly, discovering formal network structures within this system of news allows the possibility of more detailed analysis using universal network mathematics, opening up the possibility of further research: for example, very recent published work on the 'resilience' of networks could, with enough data, shed light on reasons for lower communication at certain times, and suggest the likelihood of interruptions in communication being because of failures in the network or censorship at the end point.[33] It can potentially predict the effect of interrupting events on the overall flow of news. Network analysis works alongside maps and postal itineraries, suggesting other measures of centrality that are not solely based on either geography or volume, showing cities which otherwise may have their role downplayed. Additional data, whether from printed or manuscript sources, private letters or public news, is needed in cases like this to flesh out the skeleton of the network topology. With data from enough cities, a much clearer picture of the spread of news should be possible.

The existing English language newsbook corpora: the *Zurich English Newspaper Corpus*, the *Florence Early English Newspaper Corpus* and the *Lancaster Newsbooks Corpus* allow for the study of news flow insofar as patterns of text reuse can be ascertained and traced through different titles. An addition to this would be to treat each news-unit as an individual object in a database, and record evidence of connections between cities. Existing newsbook databases could be reconfigured with different purposes in mind, incorporating a structured database which allows for the creation of entries for each story, which alongside semantic tagging would allow for the large-scale analysis of the circulation of news in a way not possible with a standard XML document. This database could be made easily transnational: network analysis alongside the identification of text reuse using plagiarism software allows for easy tracing over multiple titles and through multiple languages.

Such a database should allow for the recording of several important pieces of information: where a story has come from, where it has been sent to, and the topic of the story itself. This information should be linked, in a relational database schema, with geolocation data about each node, information about the publisher and printer of the title, and where possible, information about the creator of the paragraph. Doing this would allow for very quick and sophisticated analysis: one could quickly call up every paragraph from Dublin printed by Robert Wood, across multiple titles, to see how they compare, for example.

Machine learning and neural networks allow us to programme a computer to 'learn' and develop its own algorithms by providing it with examples, and this has had success figuring out semantics and Natural Language Processing (NLP), as well as vastly improving Google's translation engine.[34] Machine learning may allow us to finally perform accurate Optical Character Recognition (OCR) on early modern print, and there are now tools available to transcribe manuscript sources.[35] Using NLP it should be possible to extract network metadata from the results. Existing projects to extract temporal data from modern news texts may eventually be reconfigured to do the same for early modern text. This would greatly improve the ability to understand the flow of information over the period—automatically populating a database as described above. As more material gets digitised, either manually or by sophisticated computer programs—pamphlets, private letters, newsbooks, whether by hand or through digital means, in both Ireland and Britain, to get the full value, it may be necessary to rethink the way in which they are collected: not only content but time and place metadata adds greatly to our knowledge of the communications system and our understanding of shared cultural transfer.

Official news from Ireland may have been frequent but was often delayed or failed to arrive at all. It was heavily dependent on weather: both stormy conditions and unfavourable winds could interrupt the packet boats. In November 1646 Dillingham, the publisher of the *Moderate Intelligencer*, seems to have lost his patience with the lack of news—his annoyance coming out on the page:

> 'No newes was come this day that our forces are got into Dublin, nor what is become of them', he writes, "More constant newes from Rome, Venice, from Turky, yea, almost from Jerusalem. Sure its not more difficult to hear from Dublin then from Deep?"[36]

Perhaps this frustration was justified, and there is evidence of the difficulty and sporadic nature of news from Ireland to be found elsewhere in the London newsbooks. Writing, perhaps drily, in March 1649, Dillingham commented that 'There is no news from Ireland, except that the packet boat that should bring it is taken'.[37] A month later, *The Moderate Intelligencer* once again reports no news from Ireland: 'We have no Letters from *Dublin* this week', writes Dillingham, although he notes that 'the winde would have afforded

Letters', implying there must be some other reason for the delay.[38] But news continued to arrive in London, and continued to be printed in London newsbooks, week after week, and through the resilience of the network, arrived on informal and alternative channels when the main routes were blocked.

The same summer, the second issue of a shortly lived seventeenth century newsbook, *A Moderate Intelligence*—not to be confused with the *Moderate Intelligencer*—contained a letter sent from Chester. Amongst some news about changing attitudes towards Parliament because of changing fortunes in the Irish wars, there's a marked tone of disapproval: 'We wonder at your news in London', writes the author of the letter, 'In the last weeks Moderate Intelligencer of a sheet and a half it was said that London Derry was taken, which to us is very false'.[39]Evidence of the reading of periodical news like this is relatively scarce. We do have a handful of diaries, and there is some manuscript and evidence in private correspondence, but every direct mention of a particular newsbook has historical significance.[40] A news unit like this tells us, in a line or two, about the type of content and its importance, but also something about the *flow* of news. News here is being sent from Derry, in Ireland, across to Chester, on both formal and informal channels. It's then being sent (in letters like the above) to London to be printed in its news-sheets.

This also tells us that readers in Chester had access to London news, that it is being sent back towards Chester on the same route. It's likely that the news gets passed on and crosses back over the Irish sea, either in its original form in texts such as the *Moderate Intelligencer*, or at the very least as part of the informal passage of information, as it gets read and disseminated, talked about in marketplaces and taverns, and brought across the sea as part of the cultural porousness between the two places.

News is critically evaluated. The *Moderate Intelligencer* might have had four years of authority, but the Chester reader knew to evaluate based on their superior place on this particular part of the network. The story may have been invented by the author, perhaps to discredit the *Moderate Intelligencer*, but the sentiment remained the same. Local knowledge produced a series of bilateral connections. Mini news-networks, with local hubs and structures, feed into a macroscopic, pan-European system. Local knowledge feeds back to the overall system, critically commenting on news stories and allowing for sources to be evaluated. The regularity and periodicity of newsbooks meant that they could be held somewhat accountable: at the very least they had to suffer the loss of reputation if they printed 'fake news'.

By looking at other sources we can infer further parts of the network: the quote from *The Moderate Intelligencer* from the correspondent in Hamburg at the beginning of this article is in some ways proof of the circulation of knowledge in two directions: a rather vast line of information stretching from the battlefields of Ireland to the news-writers of Hamburg—not direct in the sense that information from Dublin was being deliberately sent straight to Hamburg, but indirectly, through several channels and probably over a long period. Posts, letters and newsbooks all facilitated this flow of information, but they do not fully explain it. The Hamburg writer doesn't know the Chester writer, but in an indirect way may have got his news from him, and vice-versa.

The news system, then, is both local and global in scope. Where does this place Britain and Ireland? The media connections between the two regions in the latter half of the 1640s were unique but also part of a wider system. Dublin served as a hub for news throughout the rest of Ireland, and Chester and Bristol served as chief relay points for news from Dublin itself. We can also say that the network of these two places can be described as part of a wider entity: an overall European system that can be said to have properties of a universal network along the lines of the Barabási–Albert model: it is scale-free, has a concentrated degree distribution, and relies on the 'strength of weak links' to allow for easy passage between its constituent parts. It is both international in scope and heavily reliant on local connections. The network is efficient, resilient to random failures, easily re-routable, and does not rely on each node having an awareness of any other node except its nearest neighbours. This helps to explain how the system of news can be both local and international. There is much work to be done: connecting individual databases can increase our knowledge of the system as a whole as well as its local strengths, weak points and eccentricities. Although this method currently needs manual input, much of the work can be done with datelines and locations, rather than full transcription, with the advantage that a picture of European news flow can be built up relatively quickly.

Reading news creates identity, but also contributes to a sense of place. Figuring out what the news is about and where it has come from contributes to that sense. Viewing the network of news allows us to think about the connection between Britain and Ireland as something uniquely bilateral but also as part of a wider European system. Media connections create identity: that Ireland and Britain share these connections points to a shared history, but also points to a shared history with Europe, one in which both Britain and Ireland were and still are prominent actors rather than peripheral or secondary partners, a sense of identity that is shared but also individual, and a view of space that is both local and at the same time expansive. A network is not a map: it is important to break through geographical boundaries to really establish the flow of information.[41] A map draws our eyes to those well-worn lines of land and sea borders, places the two regions firmly at the corner of Europe rather than its centre, and makes it hard not to see Ireland and Britain as peripheral but somehow uniquely connected: a network diagram gives a true picture of that connectivity. 'More difficult from Dublin than from Dieppe' may not have been literally true, but illustrates the inherent entanglement of Ireland, Britain, and the rest of Europe.

Acknowledgements

I would like to thank Professor Joad Raymond (QMUL) for general PhD supervision and guidance, and Dr. Mark O'Brien (DCU) for organising the 2016 conference where I presented the first draft of this paper. I would also like to extend my gratitude to both reviewers for their extremely helpful and extensive suggestions. My understanding of network analysis, on which much of the article is based, is mostly thanks to participation in EMDA2017 institute at the Folger Library in Washington D.C., and I would lastly like to thank the organisers and visiting faculty for the programme, including Drs Jonathan Hope and Ruth Ahnert.

Disclosure Statement

No potential conflict of interest was reported by the author.

Notes

1. *The Moderate Intelligencer* 231, 16–23 August 1649, 2220.
2. See Table 2 below.
3. Brayshay, *Land Travel and Communications*, 300.
4. *The Moderate Intelligencer* 231, 16–23 August 1649, 2215.
5. Arblaster et al., "European Postal Networks," 51.
6. Brayshay, *Land Travel and Communications*, 1.
7. Ibid., 287.
8. Behringer, "Communications Revolution," 339.
9. *The Kingdomes Weekly Intelligencer 315*, 19–26 June 1649, 1401.
10. O' Hara, *English Newsbooks and Irish Rebellion*, 17.
11. *The Kingdomes Weekly Intelligencer* 313, 29 May–5 June 1649, 1384.
12. Braudel, *The Mediterranean*, 12.
13. Blevin, "Space, Nation and the Triumph of Region," 124.
14. Ceserani, "Interactive Visualizations for British Architects on the Grand Tour."
15. Raymond, "News Networks in Early Modern Europe," 5.
16. Raymond, "News Networks: Putting the 'News' and 'Networks' Back in," 115.
17. Pieper, "News from the New World," 498.
18. Barabasí, "Scale-free Networks," 52.
19. Barabasí, *Linked*, 67; for 'small world' discussion see 49.
20. Watts, "The 'New' Science of Networks," 244.
21. Watts and Strogatz, "Collective Dynamics of 'Small-world' Networks," 442.
22. Raymond, "Putting the 'News' and 'Networks' back in," 115.
23. Raymond, *Invention of the Newspaper*, 266.
24. Brownlees, "Narrating Contemporaneity: Text and Structure in English News," 233.
25. Slauter, "The Paragraph as Information Technology," 253.
26. Dooley, "International News Flows in the Seventeenth Century," 175.
27. Jacomy et al., "ForceAtlas2, a Continuous Graph Layout."
28. Barabasí, "Scale-free Networks," 53.
29. Van Dongen, "Graph Clustering by Flow Simulation," 1.
30. Freeman, "Measures of Centrality," 35; Brandes, "A Faster Algorithm for Betweenness Centrality," 2.
31. Ibid.
32. Ahnert, "Maps versus Networks," 144.
33. Gao, Barzel, and Barabasi, "Universal Resilience Patterns in Complex Networks," 307.
34. Johnson et al., "Google's Multilingual Neural Machine Translation System," 1.
35. Mühlberger, Colutto, and Kahle, (forthcoming) 'Hand- written Text Recognition (HTR) of Historical Documents as a Shared Task for Archivists, Computer Scientists and Humanities Scholars. The Model of a Transcription & Recognition Platform (TRP)' (pre-print)
36. *The Moderate Intelligencer* 91, 26 November–3 December 1646, 773.
37. *The Moderate Intelligencer* 209, 15–22 March 1649, 1654.
38. *The Moderate Intelligencer* 1, 29–5 May 1649, 8 (one week using new numeration).
39. *A Moderate Intelligence* 2, 24–31 May 1649, 16.

40. For example, see discussion of the diaries of Nehemiah Wallington in Raymond, "International News," 239.
41. Ahnert, "Maps versus Networks," 131.

Bibliography

Ahnert, Ruth. "Maps vs Networks." In *News Networks in Early Modern Europe*, edited by Noel Moxham, and Joad Raymond, 130–157. Leiden: Brill, 2016.

Arblaster, Paul. "Posts, Newsletters, Newspapers: England in a European System of Communications." In *News Networks in Seventeenth Century Britain and Europe*, edited by Joad Raymond, 19–34. London: Routledge, 2006.

Barabasi, Albert-Laszlo. 2003. *Linked: How Everything is Connected to Everything Else and What it Means for Business and Everyday Life*. Reissue ed. New York: Plume Books.

Behringer, Wolfgang. "Communcations Revolutions: A Historiographical Concept." *Germany History* 24, no. 3 (2006): 333–374.

Blevins, Cameron. "Space, Nation and the Triumph of Region: A View of the World from Houston." *Journal of American History* 101 (June 2014): 122–147.

Braudel, Fernand. *The Mediterranean and the Mediterranean World in the Age of Philip II*. Translated by Sian Reynolds. London: The Folio Society, 2000.

Brayshay, Mark. *Land Travel and Communications in Tudor and Stuart England: Achieving a Joined-up Realm*. Liverpool: Liverpool UP, 2014.

Brownlees, Nicholas. "Narrating Contemporaneity: Text and Structure in English News." In *The Dissemination of News and the Emergence of Contemporaneity in Early Modern Europe*, edited by Brendan Dooley, 225–250. Aldershot: Ashgate, 2010.

Ceserani, Giovanna. "Interactive Visualizations for British Architects on the Grand Tour in Eighteenth-century Italy." [Palladio Components, HTML, CSS, Javascript, JSON, and Markdown files]. Stanford Digital Repository, 2015. http://purl.stanford.edu/ct765rs0222.

Dooley, Brendan. "From Literary Criticism to Systems Theory in Early Modern Journalism History." *Journal of the History of Ideas* 51, no. 3 (1990): 461–486.

Dooley, Brendan. "International News Flows in the Seventeenth Century: Problems and Prospects." In *News Networks in Early Modern Europe*, edited by Noel Moxham, and Joad Raymond, 495–511. Leiden: Brill, 2016.

Freeman, Linton C. "A Set of Measures of Centrality Based on Betweenness." *Sociometry* 40, no. 1 (1977): 35–41.

Gao, J., A. Barzel, and A. Barabasí. "Universal Resilience Patterns in Complex Networks." *Nature* 530 (2016): 307–312.

Gibbs, Owens. "The Hermeneutics of Data and Historical Writing." doi:10.3998/dh.12230987.0001.001.

Infelise, Mario. "News Networks between Italy and Europe." In *The Dissemination of News and the Emergence of Contemporaneity in Early Modern Europe*, edited by Brendan Dooley, 51–67. Aldershot: Ashgate, 2010.

Jacomy, M., T. Venturini, S. Heymann, and M. Bastian. "ForceAtlas2, a Continuous Graph Layout Algorithm for Handy Network Visualization Designed for the Gephi Software." *PLoS ONE* 9, no. 6 (June 2014). Accessed September 4, 2015. http://journals.plos.org/plosone/article?id = 10.1371/journal.pone.0098679.

Johnson, Melvin, et al. 2017. "Google's Multilingual Neural Machine Translation System." https://arxiv.org/abs/1611.04558.

Kadushin, Charles. *Understanding Social Networks: Theories, Concepts and Findings*. New York: Oxford UP, 2012.

Munter, Robert. *The History of the Irish Newspaper, 1685–1760*. Cambridge: Cambridge UP, 1967.

O'Hara, David A. *English Newsbooks and Irish Rebellion, 1641–1649*. Dublin: Four Courts Press, 2006.

Pieper, Renate. "News from the New World: Spain's Monopoly in the European Network of Handwritten Newsletters during the Sixteenth Century." In *News Networks in Early Modern Europe*, edited by Noel Moxham, and Joad Raymond, 495–511. Leiden: Brill, 2016.

Raymond, Joad. "Introduction: Networks, Communication, Practice." In *News Networks in Seventeenth Century Britain and Europe*, edited by Joad Raymond, 1–17. London: Routledge, 2006.

Raymond, Joad. 2013. "International News and the Seventeenth-century English Newspaper." In *Not Dead Things. The Dissemination of Popular Print in England and Wales, Italy and the Low Countries, 1500–1820*, edited by Joad Raymond. Leiden: Brill.

Raymond, Joad. "News Networks: Putting the 'News' and 'Networks' Back In." In *News Networks in Early Modern Europe*, edited by Noel Moxham, and Joad Raymond, 102–129. Leiden: Brill, 2016.

Slauter, Will. "The Paragraph as Information Technology: How News Traveled in the Eighteenth Century World." *Annales. Histoire, Sciences Sociales* 67, no. 2 (2012): 253–278.

Van Dongen, Stijn. "Graph Clustering by Flow Simulation." *Unpublished PhD thesis*, University of Utrecht, 2000. Accessed September 4, 2015. http://dspace.library.uu.nl/bitstream/handle/1874/848/full.pdf?sequence = 1.

Newsbooks

A Moderate Intelligence 2, 24–31 May 1649.

A Modest Narrative of Intelligence 5, 28 April–5 May 1649.

A Perfect Diurnall 295, 19–26 March 1649.

The Irish Mercury 1, 25 January–25 February 1649.

The Kingdomes Faithfull and Impartiall Scout 14, 26 April–4 May 1649.

The Kingdomes Faithfull and Impartiall Scout 8, 16–23 March.

The Kingdomes Weekly Intelligencer 313, 29 May–5 June 1649.

The Kingdomes Weekly Intelligencer 315, 19–26 June 1649.

The Moderate Intelligencer 209, 15–22 March 1649.

The Moderate Intelligencer 231, 16-23 August 1649.

The Moderate Intelligencer 91, 26 November–3rd December 1646.

Index

Adams, Gerry 153
advertising 31, 51–52
agony aunt 109
Anglo-Irish conflict 69, 83–84
Anglo-Irish Press 4, 6
Anglo-Irish relationship 89
Anglo-Irish Treaty 54, 70, 74–75, 85
anxieties 30–31, 35–36, 41
artistic training 6
audience memories 136, 145

Balfour, Arthur 12
BBC Radio Network 105–106, 110–113
Beaverbrook 89–99
Beaverbrook-Healy friendship 89
Beaverbrook-Healy nexus 92, 98, 100
Belfast Corporation 120
Belfast Telegraph 120–121, 123–124, 128–129
Bennett, James O'Donnell 47
Blue-books 11
Blunt, Wilfrid 12
Blythe, Ernest 63
Borden, Robert 95
Boyd, David 63
British Broadcasting Corporation (BBC) 140
Britishness 152, 154, 157, 161–162
British newspapers 89
British tabloid cartoon coverage 150
Butt, Isaac 16
Byrne, Frankie 109–110
Byrne, Gay 139

Campbell, Howth Margaret 17
Cathcart, Rex 119
censored material 75, 79–81, 84
censorship 41, 45–46, 48–49, 68, 74–75, 77, 79–80, 84–85, 98, 176, 180
Chalmers, Sandra 114
cinema 41, 53, 118–131; closures 118, 126–127, 130
Cole, Alan Summerly 4–5, 7

Coleman, J.A. 34
Collins, Michael 65, 83
Collins, Norman 108
communication 74–75, 94, 168, 180
confiscations 40
convict Kirwan 16
Cooper, Bryan 78
Cork Exhibition 5, 8
coronation 119–121, 130, 140–142
Cummings, Michael 156
Curran, John Philpot 51
Curtis, L. Perry 150, 156

Daily Mirror 151–153, 155–157, 160–162
D'Alton, Cardinal 137
Daly, G. H. 97
De-Anglicisation speech 42
Decies 77–82, 84–85
Defence of the Realm Act (DORA) 77
Dillingham, John 171
domestication 106, 108
Dublin Catholic Vigilance Association 41
Dublin press 19–21, 24

easter rising 60, 74, 77, 82
Edwardian Ireland 33
Edwardian picture postcard 30
Éire Ireland 46–47
England 6, 8, 11, 17–20, 40, 49–51, 54, 80–81, 150–153, 156–157, 161–162, 169, 171
European Network 168, 176

'A Fascinating Book' 4–8
female employees 105
Finnerty, Peter 51

Gaelic League 36, 38, 40, 64, 69–70
George, Lloyd 76
Granovatter, Mark 170
graph theory 170
Griffith, Arthur 45–54, 65, 67, 69, 78, 108

INDEX

Griffiths, Joan 108
guerrilla war 75

Healy, John Edward 77
Healy, Tim 89
Healy-Beaverbrook nexus 90
Helland, Janice 9
Herald, Fermanagh 36, 76
Hickman, Mary 159
historical items 50
historical metanarrative 40
Hitler 152–153

imagery 23, 31–32, 36
image wars 30, 36, 38
international broadcasting 142
IRA bombing campaign 150–151, 162
Ireland 3–12, 17–25, 30–42, 45–54, 60–69,
    74–85, 90–100, 105–115, 119–121, 125,
    128–131, 136–145, 150–153, 156–157,
    159–161, 168–172, 174–176, 179–183
Irish Caricatures 36
Irish Catholic Church 138
Irish Civil War 74
Irish diaspora 12
Irish entrepreneurs 33
Irish Identity 30, 36, 41, 159
Irish Journalist's Association (IJA) 61–62,
    65, 67–70
Irish Justice on Trial 20
Irish lacemaking 6
Irish murder trial 16
Irish needlework 6, 10
Irish politics 11, 105, 144
Irish Press 8, 18, 22–25, 69–70, 76–78
Irish Provincial Press 74, 76–77
Irish Republican Army (IRA) 75
Irish television 119, 138, 141–142

journalists 12, 18, 24, 45–46, 60–63, 65, 67–70,
    77, 93, 105, 108, 110–111

Kenneally, Ian 77
Kirkaldy, John 157

Lefebvre, Henri 169
Legg, Marie-Louise 76
Lemass government 138
Lester, Seán 62–63
London 3, 5–10, 35, 47, 49–51, 91–92, 119, 121,
    169–172, 174, 176, 179–180, 182
London Evening Standard 16, 19, 21
Ludwig, Emil 97

machine learning 181
McMahon, Richard 18

magistrates 39–40
Marquis, Alice Goldfarb 76
Martin, Hugh 84
Maxwell, Sir John 77
media sources 144
memories 21, 112, 120, 144–145, 152, 161
Minic, Danica 115
moderate intelligencer 168, 171, 175–176,
    181–182
modernisation 129, 137–138
moral censorship 139
Moxham, Noah 170
Murphy, William Lombard 92
Murray, Jenni 114

nationalism 3, 10, 41, 61, 74, 136, 138–139, 142,
    144–145
nationality 54, 67, 78, 99
nation state 136, 140, 143–145
needlework 4–5, 8, 11
networks 3, 7, 92, 170, 174–176, 179–180,
    182–183; analysis 168, 170, 176, 180–181;
    theory 170
neural networks 181
new cinemas 119, 122–125, 130
non-censored Material 79
Northern Ireland 63, 95, 118–127, 129–130, 136,
    141, 151, 155–157, 160–162
North-Roscommon by-election 78

obscene postcards 39
O'Higgins, Kevin 81, 84
O'Kelly, Seán T. 63

Pettitt, Lance 140
philanthropy 8, 10
picture postcards 30–33, 35–36, 38, 40–42;
    in Edwardian Ireland 33; imagery 36;
    phenomenon 30–31, 33
postcard senders 35
press censor 77–83, 85
press censorship 67, 77–79
provincial newspapers 75, 82–85

Queen Elizabeth II 119, 140

radicalism 61–62, 69
Radió Éireann 105–108
radio programmes 108–110
Raymond, Joad 170
Republic of Ireland 110, 121, 130, 136, 138,
    140–142
Restoration of Order in Ireland Act (ROIA) 77
revivalism 5, 8
revolutionary movements 60, 62–63, 69
revolver 52

INDEX

rifles 52, 65
Rigby, Paul 154
Rokeby Venus 39
Rosehill, Ernest 39

Salome dance 38
Savage, Robert 119, 121, 137, 139
Second World War 108, 118, 122, 129, 152–153, 161–162
self-determination 10
sexuality 138–140
sexual politics 114
Shelley, Percy Bysshe 51
Sinn Féin 45–46, 48–49, 52, 65, 69, 75, 77–85, 121
social histories 144
social identity 145
social network analysis 170
Stack, Austin 65
stereotypes 30, 37–39, 152, 156–157, 159, 161–162
suppression 45, 49, 52–53, 68, 74–75, 82–85

tabloid press 151–152, 155, 160
television 111, 114, 118–122, 124–130, 136–145; ownership 118–120, 122, 126–128, 130

Ulster Television's (UTV) Strabane transmitter 119
Ulster Volunteer Force 60

Velasquez painting 39
violence 18, 22, 85, 150, 155, 160

Wallace, Martin 128
Ward, Paul 155
wartime censorship regulations 77
Waters, Chris 152
Wilde, Oscar 3–12, 38
Wilson, Sir Henry 91
Wolfe Tone Memorial Committee 53
Woman's Hour 105–115
women 3–4, 8–9, 11, 17, 22, 34, 36, 105–115, 155–156; needlework 5, 8
Women's Liberation Movement 110